POCKET NATURE

INSECTS
AND SPIDERS

GEORGE C. MCGAVIN

DK

DORLING KINDERSLEY

LONDON, NEW YORK, MUNICH,
MELBOURNE, AND DELHI

DK LONDON
Senior Art Editor Ina Stradins
Senior Editor Angeles Gavira
Editors Georgina Garner, Ben Hoare
DTP Designer John Goldsmid
Picture Editor Neil Fletcher
Illustrator Karen Hiscock
Production Controller
Melanie Dowland
Managing Art Editor Phil Ormerod
Publishing Manager Liz Wheeler
Art Director Bryn Walls
Publishing Director Jonathan Metcalf

DK DELHI
Designers Shefali Upadhyay,
Kavita Dutta
DTP Designers Sunil Sharma,
Pankaj Sharma
Editors Dipali Singh, Glenda Fernandes,
Chumki Sen, Rohan Sinha
Managing Art Editor Aparna Sharma

First published in Great Britain in 2005 by
Dorling Kindersley Limited
80 Strand, London WC2R 0RL

A Penguin Company

Copyright © 2004
Dorling Kindersley Limited

ISBN 1-4053-0596-7

Reproduced by Colourscan, Singapore
Printed and bound by South China
Printing Co. Ltd, China

see our complete catalogue at
www.dk.com

CONTENTS

How this book works

This guide covers the most important families of insects, spiders, and their relatives found in northern and western Europe, together with a selection of other arthropods; butterflies and moths are not included, but are described in another title in this series. At the beginning of the book is an introduction, which focuses on the process of species identification in the field. This is followed by four pages describing the key characteristics of the different groups of arthropod. The guide is then divided into three chapters: Insects, Arachnids, and Other Arthropods. Species are arranged by family for ease of comparison.

CHAPTER HEADING

SCIENTIFIC FAMILY NAME

FAMILY NAME

120

Sno

Boreic

These s
in colo
The he
formin
are qui
resemb
scales i

SEEN *in autumn and winter on the surface of snow or among mosses, mainly in cold regions or mountains.*

NOTE

Superbly adapted for life in the cold, these scorpionflies die if held in a warm hand for too long. They walk rapidly across the ground and can also jump.

ovij

bronzy sheen
to body

ORDER *Mecoptera*
FAMILY *Boreidae.*
NUMBER OF SPECIES *30.*
SIZE *3–5mm.*
FEEDING *Larvae and adults: heri (mainly mosses and lichens), scar*
IMPACT *Harmless.*

▽ CHAPTER INTRODUCTIONS
Each of the three chapters opens with an introductory page describing the shared characteristics of species covered by the chapter.

Insects
Insects survive in a huge range of environments throughout Europe, from cold, snowy mountainsides to arid sand dunes. They have amazingly diverse lifestyles: many feed on plant matter, some are parasites or scavengers, while others are fierce predators capable of killing small fish. However, all share the basic structure of a head, thorax, and abdomen. The thorax has three pairs of legs and – in adults – usually one or two pairs of wings. Beetles (such as *Trichodes umbellatarum*, below) account for one-third of all insects; other major groups include grasshoppers and crickets, bugs, bees, wasps, and ants; and flies.

NOTES ___
Describe striking or unique features or behaviours that will aid identification, and may also provide interesting background information.

ANNOTATION ___
Characteristic features of the species pictured are picked out in the annotation.

HABITAT PICTURE ___
Shows an example of the type of habitat in which you may find species from the family.

HABITAT CAPTION ___
Describes the habitat or range of habitats in which you are likely to find species in this family.

FOUND *in low-growing vegetation in shady places such as woods.*

Co

Panorp

The hea
elongat
mouthp

LARVAE

The larvae look like caterpillars, with eight pairs of short abdominal feet and (often) spines.

▶ **PANORI**
COMMUN
*cool, mois
feeds on d
insects. Th
genitalia e
are clearly*

elon
hea

▼ **PANORPA MERIDIONALIS**
is a pale, heavily spotted species from the southern regions of Europe.

pale
yellow
body

LARVAE BOX ___
Artworks show typical larvae or nymphs of species in the family, and are followed by a description of their appearance or life cycle.

PHOTOGRAPHS
Images of representative species show the diversity of groups included in the chapter.

BUGS   ARTHROPOD   DRAGONFLIES   DANCE FLIES

▷ FAMILY ENTRIES
The typical page describes one or two families. Family entries always follow the same easy-to-access structure. All have one main photograph of a species, taken in its natural setting in the wild wherever possible. This is often supported by one or more photographs of other species in the family. Annotations, an artwork of the larva or nymph, and a concise data box add key information and complete the entry.

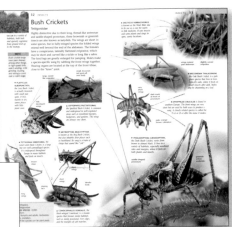

MAIN TEXT
Conveys the main distinguishing features of the family.

rpionflies

re very dark brown or bronze to black
strongly against a snowy background.
orpionflies, is extended downwards,
eak that bears the jaws. The antennae
e wings are very much reduced,
ks in the males or

BOREUS HYEMALIS
belongs to the most
widespread genus
and is seen here on
the surface of snow.

♀

head
elongated
downwards

fairly long
antennae

LARVAE

The larvae hatch
from eggs laid in
moss. They look
like small, curved
caterpillars.

n Scorpionflies

ownish yellow and black insects is
ls to form a beak that carries biting
ngs often have dark markings. Males
pturned abdomen with bulbous
lia; the abdomen of females
ers towards the rear.

spotted wings

♀

pointed abdomen

ORDER Mecoptera.
FAMILY Panorpidae.
NUMBER OF SPECIES 360.
SIZE 0.9–2.5cm.
FEEDING Larvae: scavengers. Adults: liquid-
feeders (nectar, honeydew), scavengers.
IMPACT Harmless.

△ DOUBLE-PAGE ENTRIES
Large families, those with many common or widespread
species, and those of special interest are given two pages.

CAPTION
Provides useful information about the
species pictured, such as its identification,
behaviour, habitat, or lifestyle.

PHOTOGRAPHS
Illustrate some of the most interesting,
important, or easily observable species.

COLOUR BANDS
Bands are colour-coded, with a different
colour for each of the three chapters.

SYMBOLS
For clarity, the following symbols are used to denote males
and females (where these are visually distinct).

Female ♀   Male ♂

SUPPORTING IMAGES
These appear in a blue box overlapping the appropriate
species and illustrate the sex not shown in the main
photograph (if visually different), an immature stage, or
a particular aspect of anatomy or behaviour.

OTHER KEY INFORMATION
These panels provide consistent information on the following points:
ORDER: the order to which the animals belong.
FAMILY: the family to which the animals belong.
NUMBER OF SPECIES: an approximation of the total number of
known species in the family anywhere in the world.
SIZE: unless otherwise stated, provides the body length, ranging
from the smallest to the largest.
FEEDING: lists the typical diet of members of the family, for both
immature and adult stages.
IMPACT: describes the main impact on humans of species in the
family, including as pests, vectors of disease, or beneficial control
agents of harmful pests.

Anatomy

Insects belong to a large group of animals called arthropods. Other arthropods include myriapods (millipedes, centipedes, and relatives), arachnids (spiders and relatives), and crustaceans (land-living woodlice and marine species such as shrimps and crabs). Arthropods have a protective outer skeleton, or cuticle, made of a tough material called chitin and pairs of jointed legs arising from the body segments. The body segments are arranged to form a number of functioning units.

Insects

Unlike other arthropods, insects possess only three pairs of legs and they usually have wings. The word "insect" is derived from the Latin for "cut into", and refers to the separate body sections that make up an insect: the head, thorax, and abdomen. The head carries the mouthparts, antennae, and eyes. The thorax has three segments, with legs and sometimes wings. The abdomen has up to 11 visible segments and may carry terminal "tails" known as cerci. Through the process of evolution, these basic insect body parts have become modified in different species.

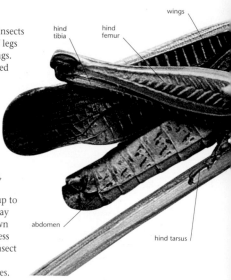

wings
hind tibia
hind femur
abdomen
hind tarsus

Arachnids

The arachnids include spiders, scorpions, ticks, and mites. They differ from insects in that their bodies are divided into two, not three, segments. These are the cephalothorax, formed from the head and thorax fused together, and the abdomen. The cephalothorax bears six pairs of appendages. The first pair (chelicerae) may be pincer- or fang-like and are used mainly for feeding. The second pair (pedipalps) have several functions, including capturing prey and fertilizing the female. The other four pairs are walking legs.

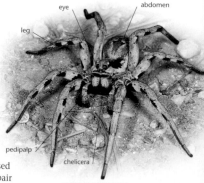

eye
abdomen
leg
pedipalp
chelicera

POISON GLANDS
Most spiders, such as this wolf spider, have eight eyes and poison glands. The chelicerae have a hinged fang at the tip.

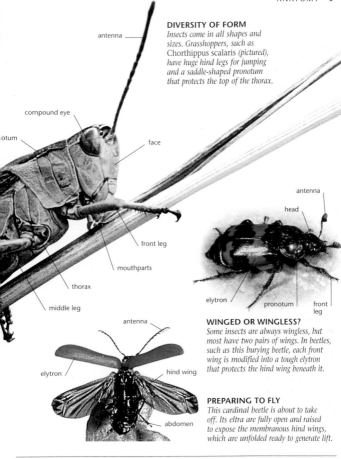

DIVERSITY OF FORM
Insects come in all shapes and sizes. Grasshoppers, such as Chorthippus scalaris (pictured), have huge hind legs for jumping and a saddle-shaped pronotum that protects the top of the thorax.

antenna

compound eye

otum

face

front leg

mouthparts

thorax

middle leg

antenna

head

elytron

pronotum

front leg

WINGED OR WINGLESS?
Some insects are always wingless, but most have two pairs of wings. In beetles, such as this burying beetle, each front wing is modified into a tough elytron that protects the hind wing beneath it.

antenna

elytron

hind wing

abdomen

PREPARING TO FLY
This cardinal beetle is about to take off. Its elytra are fully open and raised to expose the membranous hind wings, which are unfolded ready to generate lift.

Other Arthropods

Hexapods are a group of six-legged arthropods, divided into insects (above) and non-insect hexapods, which are wingless, with their mouthparts enclosed in a pouch under the head; when in use, the mouthparts are pushed out to feed. Crustaceans have a hardened carapace and a second pair of antennae. Myriapods have many legs and a long trunk.

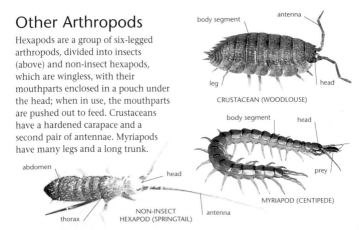

body segment

antenna

leg

head

CRUSTACEAN (WOODLOUSE)

body segment

head

prey

MYRIAPOD (CENTIPEDE)

abdomen

head

NON-INSECT HEXAPOD (SPRINGTAIL)

thorax

antenna

Identification

When you find a land-living arthropod, start by deciding which group it belongs to. In general, if the specimen has eight or more pairs of legs and a long body, it is a myriapod. If it has seven pairs of legs, it is a woodlouse. If it has four pairs, it must be an arachnid, and if it has three it is a hexapod. To narrow it down further, however, you will need to look more carefully and consider the factors outlined on the following pages. You will soon be able to determine which family an individual belongs to and start to identify a number of species.

Insect Life Cycle

All arthropods must shed their protective outer skeleton (see p.8) at intervals to grow, but the development from egg to adult varies between the different groups. Nearly all insects change appearance in some way from the immature to the adult stage. Some groups of insect, such as bugs, grasshoppers, damselflies, and dragonflies, undergo a gradual change and their metamorphosis is described as incomplete. Other insect groups, such as beetles, ants, bees, and wasps, undergo a much more dramatic change, known as complete metamorphosis.

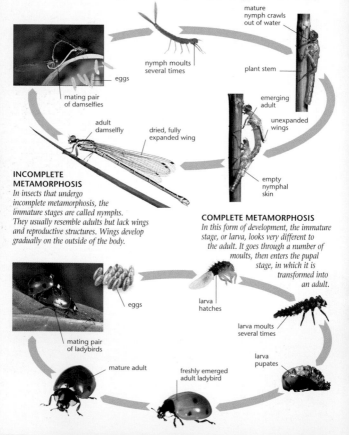

eggs

mating pair of damselflies

nymph moults several times

mature nymph crawls out of water

plant stem

emerging adult

unexpanded wings

adult damselfly

dried, fully expanded wing

empty nymphal skin

INCOMPLETE METAMORPHOSIS
In insects that undergo incomplete metamorphosis, the immature stages are called nymphs. They usually resemble adults but lack wings and reproductive structures. Wings develop gradually on the outside of the body.

COMPLETE METAMORPHOSIS
In this form of development, the immature stage, or larva, looks very different to the adult. It goes through a number of moults, then enters the pupal stage, in which it is transformed into an adult.

eggs

larva hatches

larva moults several times

mating pair of ladybirds

mature adult

freshly emerged adult ladybird

larva pupates

immature

adult

WOODLICE

Other Immatures

Myriapods, arachnids, woodlice, and two groups of insect – bristletails and silverfish – do not change shape as they develop. They continue to moult their exoskeleton throughout their lives in order to grow, and the immature stages look like smaller versions of the adults.

Sex

In many arthropods, the sexes look the same, but in others the male and female differ. Sometimes, as in crab spiders, the sexes are different sizes or colours. In other groups, such as velvet ants, only one sex is winged. Often an appendage is unique to one sex, such as the ovipositor of female horntails or the large jaws of male stag beetles.

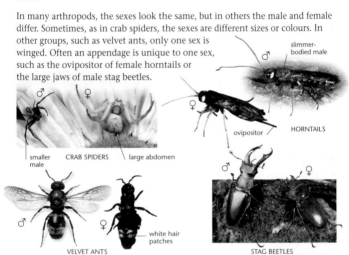

slimmer-bodied male

ovipositor

HORNTAILS

smaller male

CRAB SPIDERS

large abdomen

white hair patches

VELVET ANTS

STAG BEETLES

Camouflage and Warning

Many arthropods have dull or mottled coloration as camouflage or are a similar tone to their habitat. Usually, this is for defence, but sometimes it hides a predator from its prey. Other arthropods have bright warning colours that tell predators of their chemical defences. Some mimic other, more dangerous, species.

white coloration matches petals

CRAB SPIDER

drab colour

green camouflage

BUSH CRICKET

mottled coloration

black-and-red warning coloration

bee-like appearance

RED BUGS

ASSASSIN FLY

WEEVIL

Habitats

Arthropods are found in huge numbers almost everywhere. Their habitats can be grouped into broad types, such as woodland, grassland, heathland, or aquatic, each of which can be further subdivided. For example, woodland can be either deciduous, coniferous, or mixed. Each type of habitat has a different selection of species. Freshwater habitats are home to species such as mayflies, dragonflies, damselflies, and caddisflies; some members of other groups, such as flies, beetles, and bugs, also breed or live in fresh water. Insects such as ants occur in virtually every habitat on land, but many species are specialists found only in association with decaying wood or plant matter, dung, carcasses, or fungi. Some arthropods are parasites that live on or in the bodies of their animal hosts.

FRESH WATER
Freshwater habitats have a unique range of arthropods. Only about five per cent of insect species are aquatic, yet their abundance means they are vital parts of aquatic food chains.

GRASSLAND
Many insects and spiders live in meadows and other grasslands. Flower-rich grassland has most species; if it is heavily grazed or used for cultivation, the invertebrate diversity declines.

WOODLAND
Woods are home to many arthropod groups. Fertile soil, broad-leaved trees, deep leaf litter, and decaying wood all provide ideal conditions for arthropods.

DUNG
Several groups of insect are associated with the dung of mammals. Some, such as scarab beetles, eat only dung. Others, including dung beetles and many flies, use dung to rear their young.

DECAYING WOOD
The soft, rotting wood of dead or dying trees is a food resource for many insects, including both adults and, in particular, the larvae. A few attack only living or recently dead wood.

CARCASSES
Scavenging is a common lifestyle among arthropods and many species are attracted to carrion. Some feed on the flesh, and many lay their eggs on carcasses, which provide food for the young.

FUNGI
Some groups of arthropod are adapted for feeding on fungi, including springtails and the larvae of many flies and beetles. These can often be found inside the tissues of the fungal fruiting body.

SEASHORES
There are a surprising number of opportunities for insects and other arthropods among rocks, sand plants, and decaying seaweed along coasts. Beetles, flies, pill woodlice, and bristletails (pictured) are particularly abundant.

GARDENS
Arthropods thrive in gardens and even the smallest town garden can provide a refuge for a good variety of species. Some species enter greenhouses or buildings or are associated with rubbish.

Signs

Although you often cannot see arthropods, they may leave clear evidence of their activity. Things to look out for include holes and tunnels in wood, blotchy patches on leaves, yellowed or damaged vegetation, galls on leaves, spider webs, and frothy, saliva-like "cuckoo spit".

CUCKOO SPIT
Some immature sap-sucking bugs use their watery excrement to protect themselves from drying out.

TUNNELS IN WOOD
Holes and tunnels in live or dead wood are a sign that arthropods have been at work.

GALLS
Some insects induce abnormal growths called galls on their host plants.

LARVAL MINE
The larvae of some insects eat leaves on the inside, making a mine with a characteristic shape.

SPIDER WEB
The shape and location of a web can help in identifying a spider.

Collecting

It can be a good idea to catch an arthropod to permit closer study and identification, before letting it go unharmed. Equipment for catching arthropods includes butterfly nets, pond nets, and various beating trays. These can often be improvised at little cost.

BUTTERFLY NET
These nets should be made of fine mesh and are used to catch flying insects. Some have an extendible handle.

BEATING TRAY
A white tray placed under a tree is a good way to catch insects: shake the branch to dislodge them.

Handling

It is important to bear in mind that a few arthropods can inflict nasty bites or stings if handled without proper care. Bees and comon wasps, for example, should never be handled. Never put your hand under a stone or into a crevice to see what is there – always look first. Some species can move quickly and may attack in self-defence.

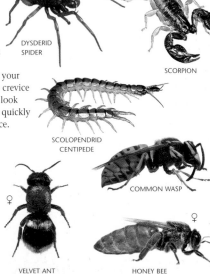

DYSDERID
SPIDER

SCORPION

SCOLOPENDRID
CENTIPEDE

WOOD ANTS

COMMON WASP

♀

VELVET ANT

♀

HONEY BEE

Classification

An order is a group made up of related families and its members all share certain characteristics. For instance, aphids and leafhoppers belong to the order Hemiptera and have distinctive sucking mouthparts. It's not always easy to identify an insect, but with practice and reference to the following section, it should be quite easy to determine the order to which a specimen belongs.

NON-INSECT HEXAPODS   CLASSES PROTURA, COLLEMBOLA, & DIPLURA

ORDERS 3	FAMILIES 31	SPECIES 7,700

PROTURANS   **PROTURA**
4 FAMILIES   400 SPECIES
Very small, sometimes minute; body pale and elongated. Eyes and antennae absent; mouthparts simple and retracted inside head when not in use. Abdomen without cerci.

SPRINGTAILS   **COLLEMBOLA**
18 FAMILIES   6,500 SPECIES
Small; body elongated or globular with hairs or scales. Eyes simple; antennae usually with four segments; mouthparts retracted when not in use. Abdomen has forked springing organ but no cerci.

DIPLURANS   **DIPLURA**
9 FAMILIES   800 SPECIES
Small or very small; body pale and elongated. Eyes absent; antennae long, thread-like, and multi-segmented; mouthparts retracted inside head when not in use. Abdomen has two cerci at the end, which may be either slender or forcep-like.

INSECTS

ORDERS 29	FAMILIES 949	CLASS INSECTA SPECIES 1 MILLION

PRIMITIVE WINGLESS INSECTS

Immature stages look exactly like small adults, but they are not sexually mature. Adults continue to moult throughout their lives.

BRISTLETAILS   **ARCHAEONGNATHA**
2 FAMILIES   350 SPECIES
Small; body elongated and tapering to rear; thorax humped. Antennae long and multi-segmented; eyes large and touching; biting or chewing mouthparts. Abdomen has a pair of cerci and a much longer central filament.

SILVERFISH   **THYSANURA**
4 FAMILIES   370 SPECIES
Small; body elongated and tapering to rear; flattened or slightly convex. Antennae long and multi-segmented; eyes small and separated; biting or chewing mouthparts. Abdomen has three equal terminal filaments.

WINGED INSECTS
THE EXOPTERYGOTA

Immatures, or nymphs, are similar to adults, with the same feeding habits. The wings develop on the outside of the body. The metamorphosis is called simple or incomplete.

MAYFLIES   **EPHEMEROPTERA**
23 FAMILIES   2,500 SPECIES
Medium-sized; body elongated and nearly cylindrical. Antennae short and bristle-like; eyes large; mouthparts vestigial. Front wings large and triangular; hind wings (if present) smaller and rounded. Abdomen has two or three cerci.

**DRAGONFLIES
AND DAMSELFLIES**   **ODONATA**
30 FAMILIES   5,500 SPECIES
Medium- to large-sized; body elongated with large, mobile head. Antennae short and hair-like; eyes very large; biting or chewing mouthparts. Two pairs of similarly sized, richly veined wings.

STONEFLIES **PLECOPTERA**
15 FAMILIES 2,000 SPECIES

Small- to medium-sized; body soft, slender, and slightly flattened. Antennae long, multi-segmented; eyes bulging; mouthparts weakly developed or non-functional. Wings held flat or wrapped closely around body. Front wings narrower than hind wings. Abdomen has a pair of long cerci.

TERMITES **ISOPTERA**
7 FAMILIES 2,750 SPECIES

Small; usually pale, soft-bodied, and wingless. Live socially in colonies with different castes. Antennae have fewer than 32 segments; eyes usually absent in workers and soldiers. Biting or chewing mouthparts.

EARWIGS **DERMAPTERA**
10 FAMILIES 1,900 SPECIES

Small to medium-sized; body elongated, slightly flattened, flexible. Antennae long, multi-segmented; eyes usually present; biting or chewing mouthparts. Front wings short and toughened; hind wings semicircular and folded under front wings at rest. Abdomen has a pair of terminal forceps.

STICK INSECTS **PHASMATODEA**
3 FAMILIES 2,500 SPECIES

Small to large; body slender and stick-like with short prothorax. Antennae slender and multi-segmented; eyes bead-like; biting or chewing mouthparts. Two pairs of wings or none; front wings small, narrow, and toughened; hind wings large and fan-shaped. Males smaller than females.

BARKLICE AND BOOKLICE **PSOCOPTERA**
35 FAMILIES 3,000 SPECIES

Small; soft-bodied with a relatively large head swollen at the front; thorax slightly humped. Antennae long with 10 to 50 segments; eyes bulging; biting or chewing mouthparts. Two pairs of wings held over body at rest. Short-winged or wingless.

BUGS **HEMIPTERA**
134 FAMILIES 82,000 SPECIES

Very small to large; body and antennae both variable; eyes usually conspicuous; mouthparts characteristically take form of an elongated rostrum for piercing and sucking. Typically two pairs of wings; front wings tougher than hind wings.

COCKROACHES **BLATTODEA**
6 FAMILIES 4,000 SPECIES

Medium-sized; body oval and flattened. Head points downwards, largely concealed by pronotum. Antennae long and multi-segmented; eyes well-developed; biting or chewing mouthparts. Front wings toughened and cover the larger membranous hind wings. Females can be short-winged; some species wingless.

MANTIDS **MANTODEA**
8 FAMILIES 2,000 SPECIES

Medium- to large-sized; body slender with triangular head and elongated prothorax. Antennae slender, multi-segmented; eyes large; biting or chewing mouthparts. Front legs enlarged and spiny for feeding. Front wings narrow, toughened; hind wings larger, membranous.

GRASSHOPPERS AND CRICKETS **ORTHOPTERA**
28 FAMILIES 20,000 SPECIES

Medium- to large-sized; body has saddle- or shield-shaped pronotum. Antennae long and multi-segmented; eyes large and well-developed; biting or chewing mouthparts. Front wings narrow; hind wings larger. Large hind legs modified for jumping.

WEB-SPINNERS **EMBIOPTERA**
8 FAMILIES 300 SPECIES

Small; body elongated and cylindrical or slightly flattened. Antennae thread-like with 10 to 35 segments; eyes small, kidney-shaped; biting or chewing mouthparts. Males often have two pairs of wings; females wingless.

PARASITIC LICE **PHTHIRAPTERA**
25 FAMILIES 3,000 SPECIES

Small; soft-bodied with a relatively large head swollen at the front; thorax slightly humped. Antennae long with 10 to 50 segments; eyes bulging; biting or chewing mouthparts. Two pairs of wings held over body at rest. Short-winged or wingless.

THRIPS **THYSANOPTERA**
8 FAMILIES 5,000 SPECIES

Small; slender body. Antennae short with 4 to 9 segments; eyes round or kidney-shaped; mouthparts asymmetrical for sucking or piercing. Two pairs of wings (if present) narrow and hair-fringed.

THE ENDOPTERYGOTA

Immatures, or larvae, look very different to adults and have different feeding habits. The wings develop on the inside of the body. The transformation from larva to adult takes place in the pupal stage and the metamorphosis is complete.

ALDERFLIES AND DOBSONFLIES — MEGALOPTERA
2 FAMILIES — **300 SPECIES**

Medium-sized; head broad and flattened; antennae long and multi-segmented; eyes conspicuous; biting or chewing mouthparts. Two pairs of similarly sized wings held roof-like over body at rest. Hind wings large anal lobes.

LACEWINGS, ANTLIONS, AND RELATIVES — NEUROPTERA
17 FAMILIES — **4,000 SPECIES**

Small to large; body slender. Antennae often long and multi-segmented; eyes large; biting or chewing mouthparts. Two pairs of similarly sized wings held over body at rest; wing venation typically net-like.

STREPSIPTERANS — STREPSIPTERA
8 FAMILIES — **560 SPECIES**

Very small. Grub-like females usually parasitic inside host insects and lack eyes, antennae, mouthparts, legs, and wings. Males winged and free-living, with eyes, antennae, small front wings, and fan-shaped hind wings.

FLEAS — SIPHONAPTERA
18 FAMILIES — **2,000 SPECIES**

Small; body tough, flattened from side to side, with spines and bristles; wingless. Parasitic on mammals and birds. Antennae very short; eyes simple; piercing or sucking mouthparts. Comb-like structures on cheeks and pronotum of many species. Hind legs enlarged for jumping.

CADDISFLIES — TRICHOPTERA
43 FAMILIES — **8,000 SPECIES**

Small to medium-sized; body slender, moth-like, covered with hairs. Antennae slender, multi-segmented; eyes large; mouthparts weakly developed. Two pairs of similarly sized wings held tent-like over body at rest. Larvae aquatic and often live inside a protective case made from small stones or plant materials.

SNAKEFLIES — RAPHIDIOPTERA
2 FAMILIES — **150 SPECIES**

Medium-sized; body slender with head slightly flattened, broad across middle, and tapering to rear; prothorax slender and elongated. Antennae long, multi-segmented; eyes conspicuous; biting or chewing mouthparts. Two pairs of similarly sized wings. Females have a prominent ovipositor.

BEETLES — COLEOPTERA
166 FAMILIES — **370,000 SPECIES**

Very small to large; body typically tough, with large prothorax. Antennae usually have fewer than 11 segments; biting or chewing mouthparts. Front wings toughened as wing cases, covering all or part of abdomen. Hind wings larger and membranous.

SCORPIONFLIES — MECOPTERA
9 FAMILIES — **550 SPECIES**

Small to medium-sized; body elongated; head extended downwards to form a beak. Antennae long with up to 60 segments; eyes large; biting or chewing mouthparts. Two pairs of narrow wings; some species short-winged or wingless.

TWO-WINGED FLIES — DIPTERA
130 FAMILIES — **120,000 SPECIES**

Minute to medium-sized; body variable. Antennae multi-segmented, with bristle at tip; mouthparts for sucking or lapping liquids, sometimes for piercing. Front wings membranous, hind wings reduced to tiny drumstick-like balancing organs (halteres).

MOTHS AND BUTTERFLIES — LEPIDOPTERA
127 FAMILIES — **165,000 SPECIES**

Small to large; body and wings covered with tiny scales. Mouthparts in form of long proboscis for sucking nectar and liquids (can be coiled).

SAWFLIES, WASPS, ANTS, AND BEES — HYMENOPTERA
91 FAMILIES — **198,000 SPECIES**

Minute to large; slender "waist" (except in sawflies). Antennae long, multi-segmented; biting or chewing mouthparts. Two pairs of wings or none. Females often have a conspicuous saw-like or needle-like ovipositor or a sting.

MYRIAPODS

ORDERS 16		**4 CLASSES**
	FAMILIES 144	SPECIES 13,700

PAUROPODS   CLASS PAUROPODA
5 FAMILIES   500 SPECIES

Small; soft-bodied, pale, and elongated. Head has a pair of branched antennae; eyes absent; mouthparts weakly developed. In adults, trunk has 9 to 11 pairs of legs.

SYMPHYLANS   CLASS SYMPHYLA
2 FAMILIES   175 SPECIES

Small; soft-bodied, pale, and elongated. Head has a pair of thread-like, multi-segmented antennae; eyes absent; mouthparts weakly developed. In adults, first 12 segments of trunk have a pair of legs; spinnerets on last segment.

MILLIPEDES   CLASS DIPLOPODA
115 FAMILIES   10,000 SPECIES

Medium to large-sized; tough-bodied and cylindrical. Head has a pair of seven-segmented antennae, a pair of eyes, and biting mouthparts. First four segments of trunk lack legs; the rest have two pairs of legs.

CENTIPEDES   CLASS CHILOPODA
22 FAMILIES   3,000 SPECIES

Medium to large-sized; body elongated and slightly flattened. Head has long, multi-segmented antennae, a pair of eyes, and biting mouthparts. First pair of legs modified as poison claws; rest of trunk segments have a pair of legs.

ARACHNIDS

ORDERS 12		**CLASS ARACNIDA**
	FAMILIES 460	SPECIES 75,000

SCORPIONS   SCORPIONES
9 FAMILIES   1,400 SPECIES

Medium-sized to large. Cephalothorax has four pairs of walking legs and, at the front, a pair of enlarged pedipalps, each with a pincer-like claw. Abdomen has a long, mobile tail bearing a sting.

PSEUDOSCORPIONS PSEUDOSCORPIONES
23 FAMILIES   3,300 SPECIES

Very small, sometimes minute; cephalothorax has a pair of pedipalps, each with a pincer-like claw. Four pairs of walking legs. Abdomen lacks an elongated tail.

HARVESTMEN   OPILIONES
40 FAMILIES   5,000 SPECIES

Small to medium-sized; cephalothorax broadly joined to abdomen; short pedipalps with six segments; four pairs of slender walking legs, which are often long or very long.

SPIDERS   ARANEAE
101 FAMILIES   40,000 SPECIES

Small to large; body variable, but always has distinctive stalk joining cephalothorax and unsegmented abdomen. Pedipalps short; walking legs long, with seven segments; first pair of legs similar size to other pairs. Abdomen has silk-spinning organs (spinnerets) for producing webs, which may often be used to identify families or species.

TICKS AND MITES   ACARI
300 FAMILIES   30,000 SPECIES

Very small; body compact and typically rounded or globular with no obvious divisions or segmentation. Mouthparts often carried on a special extension of head. Pedipalps short; four pairs of walking legs.

CRUSTACEA

ORDERS 14		**6 CLASSES**
	FAMILIES 1,470	SPECIES 76,500

WOODLICE   ISOPODA
32 FAMILIES   3,800 SPECIES

Small to medium-sized; body tough, segmented, oval, and typically flattened, but some species convex in cross-section; seven pairs of legs. Abdominal gills present.

Insects

Insects survive in a huge range of environments throughout Europe, from cold, snowy mountainsides to arid sand dunes. They have amazingly diverse lifestyles: many feed on plant matter, some are parasites or scavengers, while others are fierce predators capable of killing small fish. However, all share the basic structure of a head, thorax, and abdomen. The thorax has three pairs of legs and – in adults – usually one or two pairs of wings. Beetles (such as *Trichodes umbellatarum*, below) account for one-third of all insects; other major groups include grasshoppers and crickets; bugs; bees, wasps, and ants; and flies.

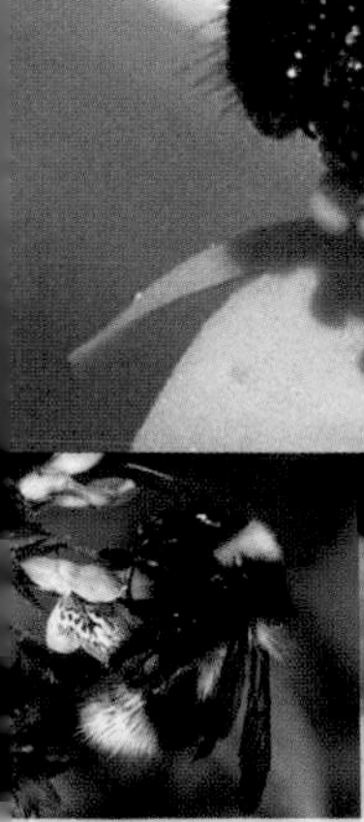

BUMBLE BEES

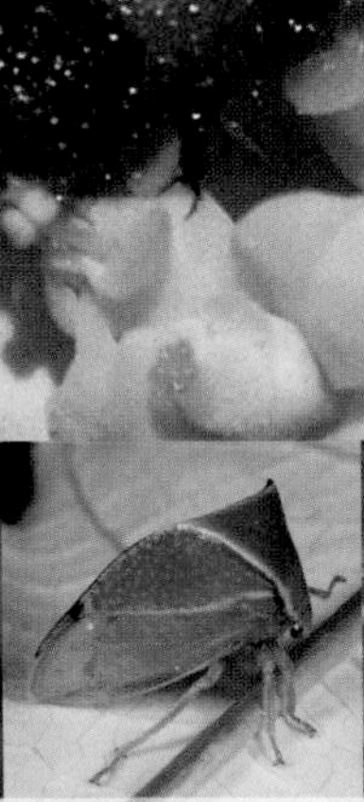

TREEHOPPERS

DRAGONFLIES

DANCE FLIES

Jumping Bristletails

Machilidae

These elongated, cylindrical, wingless insects are usually brownish in colour with a distinctive humped thorax. The body is covered with patterns of scales and the end of the abdomen has three slender "tails", the middle one being longer than the other two. The compound eyes are large and touch each other. Machilids run rapidly and jump when disturbed.

INHABIT *seashores, wooded areas, and grassland, usually under stones or among leaf litter.*

▼ **PETROBIUS MARITIMUS** *is common above the high-tide mark along rocky shores. When disturbed, it runs for a nearby crevice.*

large eyes

humped thorax

central "tail" longest

mottled coloration

▲ **DILTA LITTORALIS** *is one of many similar species found on the ground among low-growing vegetation, leaf litter, and mosses.*

ORDER *Archaeognatha.*
FAMILY *Machilidae.*
NUMBER OF SPECIES *250.*
SIZE *Up to 1.2cm.*
FEEDING *Nymphs and adults: herbivores (algae, mosses, lichens), scavengers.*
IMPACT *Harmless.*

Silverfish and Firebrats

Lepismatidae

These elongated and slightly flattened, wingless insects are brown or tan in colour and usually covered in greyish or silvery scales and hairs. The end of the abdomen has three slender "tails" of a similar length. The compound eyes are small and widely separated. Lepismatids run rapidly, but, unlike jumping bristletails, do not jump.

OCCUR *in a range of habitats such as debris and vegetation, caves, bird nests, and warm places indoors.*

► **LEPISMA SACCHARINA,** *the Silverfish, prefers damp microhabitats in buildings. It is omnivorous.*

separated eyes

body covered in silvery scales

"tails" of similar lengths

▼ **THERMOBIA DOMESTICA,** *the Firebrat, lives near ovens and hot pipes or in heating ducts.*

ORDER *Thysanura.*
FAMILY *Lepismatidae.*
NUMBER OF SPECIES *190.*
SIZE *0.8–2cm.*
FEEDING *Nymphs and adults: scavengers.*
IMPACT *A few species can be pests in homes, bakeries, and commercial kitchens.*

Siphlonurid Mayflies

Siphlonuridae

These mayflies are typically pale reddish brown or yellowish brown in colour. The upper portions of the eyes have larger facets than the lower portions. The front wings are quite narrow rather than triangular and have many veins running crosswise. The abdomen, which may have dark markings above and below, usually has two long tails.

COMMON *in lakes, mountain streams, and newly-created habitats such as drainage ditches.*

SIPHLONURUS LACUSTRIS *is one of several species that have two tails. It is commonest in upland regions.*

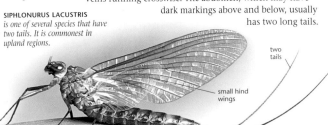

two tails

small hind wings

ORDER *Ephemeroptera.*
FAMILY *Siphlonuridae.*
NUMBER OF SPECIES *30.*
SIZE *6–13mm.*
FEEDING *Nymphs: scavengers, predators. Adults: non-feeding.*
IMPACT *Harmless.*

NOTE

Siphlonurids are important in the aquatic food chain as they form part of the diet of freshwater fish. They also rapidly colonize new habitats.

NYMPHS

The streamlined nymphs have short antennae, and gills on segments one to seven.

Small Mayflies

Baetidae

Small mayflies are pale or dark brown or black with yellowish, grey, or white markings. The front wings are elongated and oval with a reduced number of veins. In some species the hind wings may be small or absent. The males have large eyes, divided into upper and lower portions. The abdomen has two very long, slender tails.

THRIVE *in a wide range of aquatic habitats, such as ditches, pools, lakes, and streams.*

NYMPHS

The small, slender nymphs are active swimmers and climb about on submerged plants.

▼ **BAETIS RHODANI** *breeds in many types of water. The adults have very small hind wings and can be found all year.*

extremely long tails

single pair of front wings

two tails

yellow femora

▲ **CHLOEON DIPTERUM**, *the Pond Olive, breeds in many freshwater habitats, including stagnant pools, water troughs, and rain butts. The adults lack hind wings.*

ORDER *Ephemeroptera.*
FAMILY *Baetidae.*
NUMBER OF SPECIES *900.*
SIZE *4–12mm.*
FEEDING *Nymphs: herbivores (algae). Adults: non-feeding.*
IMPACT *Harmless.*

Stream Mayflies

Heptageniidae

Also known as flat-headed mayflies, these insects usually are dark brown with clear wings, although some are yellow or reddish brown with black, white, or yellow markings. The wings are clear with distinctive (often dark brown) veins. The eyes of males are large but not divided into upper and lower portions. The abdomen has two long tails.

USUALLY found in fast-flowing water such as mountain streams, but also occur in ponds.

two tails

dull colour

SUBIMAGO

NYMPHS

Generally dark in colour, the nymphs are flattened, with antennae and eyes on the upper side.

▶ **ECDYONURUS VENOSUS** *has two long tails; the nymphs are found in rocky streams and rivers.*

small hind wings

◀ **RHITHROGENA SEMICOLORATA**, *pictured here in the typical resting position, lives in gravel-bottomed streams.*

dark eyes

ORDER *Ephemeroptera.*
FAMILY *Heptageniidae.*
NUMBER OF SPECIES *500.*
SIZE *4–15mm.*
FEEDING *Nymphs: herbivores (algae), scavengers, predators. Adults: non-feeding.*
IMPACT *Harmless.*

Burrowing Mayflies

Ephemeridae

The wings of these large mayflies are typically clear or brownish in colour, although they have dark spots in some species. The bodies are often pale yellowish or whitish cream with characteristic dark spots or other markings, especially towards the end of the abdomen, which has two or three very long tails.

FOUND in or near to streams, rivers, lakes, and ponds.

EPHEMERA DANICA *is a large and distinctive species with three long tails. The adult's darkish wings may span up to 4cm.*

dark, mottled wings

three long tails

NYMPHS

Strong front legs enable the nymphs to dig into silt, which is then pushed back by the rear legs.

abdominal gills

NYMPH

ORDER *Ephemeroptera.*
FAMILY *Ephemeridae.*
NUMBER OF SPECIES *150.*
SIZE *1–3.4cm.*
FEEDING *Nymphs: scavengers, predators. Adults: non-feeding.*
IMPACT *Harmless.*

Crawling Mayflies

Ephemerellidae

OCCUR *in a wide variety of running water as well as ponds and margins of lakes.*

The commonest species in this family are pale reddish in colour and often have small dark abdominal markings. The hind wings are relatively large and can be up to one-third as long as the forewings. The end of the abdomen carries two or (usually) three long, slender tails. Females release their eggs in one clump that separates out on the water surface.

NYMPHS

Nymphs crawl on submerged plants. Their legs are usually long and the abdomen has flap-like lateral gills.

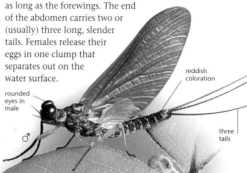

reddish coloration

rounded eyes in male

three tails

♂

ORDER *Ephemeroptera.*
FAMILY *Ephemerellidae.*
NUMBER OF SPECIES *200.*
SIZE *6–10mm.*
FEEDING *Nymphs: scavengers, predators. Adults: non-feeding.*
IMPACT *Harmless.*

EPHEMERELLA IGNITA, *known by anglers as the Blue-winged Olive, is a reddish species with three tails. It is common near fast-flowing streams and rivers. Males have partly rounded eyes.*

Caenid Mayflies

Caenidae

FOUND *in a variety of waterbodies such as large lake margins, ponds, and slow-flowing rivers.*

The front wings of these small, delicate mayflies are very broad with highly distinctive dark longitudinal veins at the front margin and a very rounded hind margin. The hind wings are absent. The eyes in both sexes are small. The thorax is usually a little darker than the abdomen, which can be pale or greyish but always has three very long, slender tails.

short, broad head

CAENIS HORARIA *breeds in muddy lakes, large ponds, and slow-moving rivers. Known as the "angler's curse", it appears in huge numbers.*

pale abdomen with three tails

NYMPHS

The nymphs are slightly flattened with square-shaped gill plates on the second abdominal segment.

ORDER *Ephemeroptera.*
FAMILY *Caenidae.*
NUMBER OF SPECIES *100.*
SIZE *5–12mm.*
FEEDING *Nymphs: scavengers. Adults: non-feeding.*
IMPACT *Harmless.*

Narrow-winged Damselflies

Coenagrionidae

Many of these slender damselflies are beautifully coloured in shades of light blue with dark markings. Others may have blue-green or red-brown coloration, also with dark markings. The adults are generally weak fliers and rest horizontally with their clear wings folded together over the body. Towards the tip at the front margin of both pairs of wings there is a short, diamond-shaped mark called the pterostigma. In most species, the males are more brightly coloured than the females, which tend to be greenish.

MAINLY found along streams and rivers, but also occur around ponds, stagnant pools, and swampy areas.

NYMPHS

The slender-bodied nymphs are variable in colour with three gill filaments arising from the end of the abdomen, the middle filament being the longest.

▶ **PYRRHOSOMA NYMPHULA**, *the Large Red Damselfly, is often one of the first species to be seen flying in spring.*

dark markings

black legs

♂

red eyes

greenish thorax

blue segment

♂

▲ **ERYTHROMMA NAJAS**, *the Red-eyed Damselfly, is an excellent flier. Females have browner eyes and lack the males' blue abdominal tip.*

♂

◀ **ISCHNURA ELEGANS** *is known as the Blue-tailed Damselfly as the male has a blue abdominal segment.*

▼ **COENAGRION PUELLA**, *the Azure Damselfly, has blue and black males and brilliant green and black females.*

diamond-shaped pterostigma

one blue segment

♀

black and green thorax

single black stripe on side of thorax

two blue segments

typical form

♀

♂

▲ **ENALLAGMA CYATHIGERUM**, *the Common Blue Damselfly, resembles Coenagrion males, but has a black club-shaped marking on the second abdominal segment. Females (left) vary from blue to brown.*

ORDER Odonata.
FAMILY Coenagrionidae.
NUMBER OF SPECIES 1,000.
SIZE Most species 2–5cm (wingspan).
FEEDING Nymphs and adults: predators.
IMPACT Harmless.

White-legged Damselflies

FOUND *in pastures and meadows, especially around slow, lowland rivers and canals with plenty of floating and waterside plants. Occasionally found in still waterbodies.*

Platycnemididae

Although hard to see, the feature that distinguishes these medium-sized damselflies from others is the shape of a cell at the wing bases. Known as the quadrilateral, it is roughly rectangular in this family, rather than diamond-shaped. Other features include a narrow head, fairly broad wings, and thickening of the tibiae of the middle and hind legs.

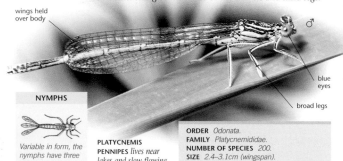

wings held over body

♂

blue eyes

broad legs

NYMPHS

Variable in form, the nymphs have three very long and broad gills at the end of the abdomen.

PLATYCNEMIS PENNIPES *lives near lakes and slow-flowing watercourses with plenty of aquatic vegetation.*

ORDER *Odonata.*
FAMILY *Platycnemididae.*
NUMBER OF SPECIES *200.*
SIZE *2.4–3.1cm (wingspan).*
FEEDING *Nymphs and adults: predators.*
IMPACT *Harmless.*

Broad-winged Damselflies

Calopterygidae

INHABIT *both fast- and slow-flowing streams and rivers, as well as canals; adults also occur in woods far from water.*

Also called demoiselles, these fairly large, metallic-bodied damselflies have wings that narrow gradually towards their bases. The body is metallic green or blue. The male wings have a large dark patch or are entirely dark with a blue or purple sheen; females' wings are tinted green or brown.

♀

brownish wings

▲ **CALOPTERYX VIRGO** *resembles C. splendens, but females have browner wings and males a larger dark wing patch.*

▶ **CALOPTERYX SPLENDENS,** *the Banded Demoiselle, is named for the males' wing patch. Females are greenish.*

NYMPHS

A small head and three flap-like gill filaments are the nymphs' most distinctive features.

♂

slender blue body

ORDER *Odonata.*
FAMILY *Calopterygidae.*
NUMBER OF SPECIES *150.*
SIZE *5–7.5cm (wingspan).*
FEEDING *Nymphs and adults: predators.*
IMPACT *Harmless.*

Stalk-winged Damselflies

Lestidae

Also known as spread-winged or emerald damselflies, these relatively sturdy species are usually metallic green or blue. At rest, they often perch vertically with the wings partly or fully open. The clear wings have narrow, stalk-like bases and a dark, elongated or rectangular pterostigma.

LIVE *around still water, swamps, bogs, drainage ditches, and acidic pools or lakes.*

▼ **LESTES SPONSA**, *the Emerald Damselfly, rests with its wings held out at an angle from the body.*

◄ **SYMPECMA FUSCA** *is a relatively drab species that hibernates as an adult and can be seen very early in the year.*

male has bluish thorax

metallic green abdomen

dull brown coloration

NYMPHS

The slender, long-bodied nymphs are light green to dark brown, with three long abdominal gills.

ORDER *Odonata.*
FAMILY *Lestidae.*
NUMBER OF SPECIES *160.*
SIZE *3.2–6.2cm (wingspan).*
FEEDING *Nymphs and adults: predators.*
IMPACT *Harmless.*

Club-tailed Dragonflies

Gomphidae

These relatively big dragonflies are named for the swelling of the abdomen just before the apex, giving a club-like appearance; this is less noticeable in females and in both sexes of some species. Most species are brightly coloured in black, yellow, or green. The eyes are widely separated.

OCCUR *in or near to rivers, large streams, ponds, and lakes.*

NYMPHS

Either slender or squat, the nymphs have stout legs and rather short, flattened antennae.

black and yellow stripes

ORDER *Odonata.*
FAMILY *Gomphidae.*
NUMBER OF SPECIES *950.*
SIZE *6–8cm (wingspan).*
FEEDING *Nymphs and adults: predators.*
IMPACT *Harmless.*

swollen end of abdomen

GOMPHUS VULGATISSIMUS *has black and yellow females and immature males; mature males are black and green.*

Hawkers

Aeshnidae

USUALLY found near still waters with plenty of aquatic vegetation, but may occur along hedgerows and paths and in urban areas.

Also called darners, this family includes some of the largest and most powerful dragonflies. These robust insects are usually dark green, blue, or brown, with stripes on the thorax and spots or bands on the abdomen. The large eyes touch on top of the head. The wings, which are usually clear, sometimes have an amber or yellowish brown tint. Both pairs of wings have an elongated pterostigma. The end of the abdomen has a pair of claspers and, in males, a smaller appendage in between.

▼ **AESHNA MIXTA**, the Migrant Hawker, is widespread in central and southern Europe. Females are yellow and brown.

clear wings

eyes touch each other

hairy thorax

paired blue spots on abdomen

blue eyes

alternate small white and larger blue marks

▶ **AESHNA CYANEA** has blue eyes and a blue abdominal tip in males; females are yellow and green with brownish eyes.

blue tip to otherwise green-marked abdomen

▲ **BRACHYTRON PRATENSE**, the Hairy Dragonfly, has a thick layer of hairs on the thorax. Females have yellow (not blue) spots.

apple-green thoracic markings

yellow stripes on thorax

▲ **AESHNA GRANDIS**, the Brown Hawker, has brownish wings and distinctive thoracic stripes.

mainly clear wings

black stripe down back

claspers

NYMPHS

The cryptically coloured nymphs have strongly built, cylindrical bodies and large eyes. They live among weeds, crawling on the bottom in search of their prey.

ORDER Odonata.
FAMILY Aeshnidae.
NUMBER OF SPECIES 420.
SIZE 6–14cm (wingspan).
FEEDING Nymphs and adults: predators.
IMPACT Harmless.

▲ **ANAX IMPERATOR**, the Emperor Dragonfly, is very large, with blue males and green females. It breeds in large ponds and even in weedy ditches.

Golden-ringed Dragonflies

Cordulegastridae

These large, sturdy dragonflies are brownish or black with yellow markings and are sometimes called biddies. In both sexes the eyes are large and touch each other at a single point on the top of the head. The wings are transparent, with a long, narrow pterostigma. The abdomen is usually elongated and has numerous distinctive rings.

TYPICALLY *found along streams in upland regions, but also occur near woodland streams at lower levels.*

eyes meet at one point

♀

CORDULEGASTER BOLTONI, *the Golden-ringed Dragonfly, lives in uplands and moorland. The sexes are quite similar in appearance.*

golden yellow rings

NYMPHS

The nymphs are quite elongated and strong, with a noticeably broad head and big eyes.

ORDER *Odonata.*
FAMILY *Cordulegastridae.*
NUMBER OF SPECIES *50.*
SIZE *8–10.5cm (wingspan).*
FEEDING *Nymphs and adults: predators.*
IMPACT *Harmless.*

Green-eyed Skimmers

Corduliidae

These insects – also known as emerald dragonflies – are often quite hairy in appearance, with a distinctive metallic green or bronze coloration. The wings may have a yellow tint, especially at the base. The head and eyes are green in common species; the latter are large and touch each other, and there is a noticeable indentation on their margins.

COMMON *around stagnant water, and sometimes found near streams.*

♂

◀ **SOMATOCHLORA METALLICA,** *the Brilliant Emerald, is scarce and localized in the UK, but fairly common in central and northern Europe.*

metallic green

yellowish tint to wing

NYMPHS

Usually flat with long legs, the nymphs may be either short or stout or elongated.

♂

bronze sheen

▲ **CORDULIA AENEA,** *the Downy Emerald, frequents shaded ponds in wooded areas, flying close to the water surface.*

ORDER *Odonata.*
FAMILY *Corduliidae.*
NUMBER OF SPECIES *400.*
SIZE *5–8cm (wingspan).*
FEEDING *Nymphs and adults: predators.*
IMPACT *Harmless.*

Common Skimmers

Libellulidae

These dragonflies, which represent a large proportion of the order Odonata, are also called darters or chasers due to their fast, unpredictable flight interspersed with short periods of hovering. They are colourful and males often differ from females, their bodies sometimes having a pale blue, powdery appearance. The wingspan is typically longer than the body length and the wings sometimes have dark bands or other markings, especially at their bases. In many species the abdomen is broad and flattened. The large eyes always touch on top of the head.

OCCUR *over still or slow-moving water in a variety of habitats, from mountains and moors to forests.*

NYMPHS

Fiercely predatory and aquatic, the nymphs are short, stocky, and slightly flattened, often with spines projecting from the abdomen. Their facial masks are hollow and large.

NOTE

Adult males are very territorial and command their patch from a perch on an exposed plant stem or twig. They dart away to chase off rival males.

clear wings

blue abdomen

black tip

dark brown band

◀ **ORTHETRUM CANCELLATUM** *is also known as the Black-tailed Skimmer; the female is yellowish with two black stripes along the length of the abdomen.*

brown wing bases

clear wings

▲ **SYMPETRUM PEDEMONTANUM,** *the Banded Darter, has a dark brown mark on the outer part of each wing. The male has a bright red abdomen while the female is yellow with a thin, dark central stripe.*

▶ **LIBELLULA DEPRESSA,** *the Broad-bodied Chaser, breeds in ponds. The abdomen in females is broader than in males and is brown with yellow lateral patches.*

two dark marks on each wing

▶ **LIBELLULA QUADRIMACULATA** *is known as the Four-spotted Chaser on account of the small dark spot in the middle of the front margin of each wing. The sexes are quite similar.*

brown hindwing base

small dark spot

yellow at sides

ORDER *Odonata.*
FAMILY *Libellulidae.*
NUMBER OF SPECIES *1,250.*
SIZE *4–8cm (wingspan).*
FEEDING *Nymphs and adults: predators.*
IMPACT *Harmless.*

Common Stoneflies

Perlidae

Yellowish brown to dark brown in general coloration, these often quite stout and flat-bodied stoneflies have minute remains of the nymphal gill tufts on the underside of the thorax near the bases of the legs. The front wings have a distinctive "double ladder" made up of numerous cross veins in the basal half. Males can be much smaller than the females.

FOUND *in a variety of flowing water bodies, such as rivers and streams with stony beds.*

♀

NYMPHS

The nymphs may take up to five years to become adult, and moult as many as thirty times.

dark pronotum

fully winged

▲ **PERLA BIPUNCTATA** *is very similar to* Dinocras cephalotes *but slightly larger; males are short-winged.*

♂

pale stripe on thorax

long cerci

▲ **DINOCRAS CEPHALOTES** *is a large, dark stonefly; females have a larger wingspan.*

ORDER *Plecoptera.*
FAMILY *Perlidae.*
NUMBER OF SPECIES *400.*
SIZE *2–5cm.*
FEEDING *Nymphs: predators. Adults: non-feeding*
IMPACT *Harmless.*

Predatory Stoneflies

Perlodidae

The commonest species in this family have yellowish or olive-green bodies and green wings, while others are dark brown or nearly black. The pronotum is rectangular in shape; the cerci are long. The rear, or anal, region of the hind wings is often enlarged with only a few lengthwise veins. Males of some species have short wings.

LIVE *near shallow streams with gravel or stone beds, often on chalky ground.*

NYMPHS

The long-legged nymphs appear to have a waxy texture and many lack gills.

yellowish body

▼ **ISOPERLA GRAMMATICA,** *or Yellow Sally, is a popular bait to catch trout.*

▼ **DIURA BICAUDATA,** *is a slender-legged stonefly mainly found in mountain streams.*

yellow-orange rear of head

♂

ORDER *Plecoptera.*
FAMILY *Perlodidae.*
NUMBER OF SPECIES *250.*
SIZE *1–3.2cm.*
FEEDING *Nymphs: predators, scavengers. Adults: non-feeding.*
IMPACT *Harmless.*

Willowflies

Taeniopterygidae

OCCUR *in streams of all kinds, where adults can be seen flying and running over waterside rocks and vegetation.*

These dark brown or black stoneflies have very long, slender antennae. The front wings may have a darkish broad band across them and the abdomen has a pair of very short tails. Although difficult to see, a good identification feature of these stoneflies is that the segments of the tarsi are all about the same length, whereas in closely related families the second segment is noticeably smaller.

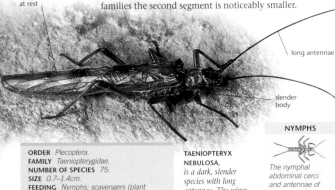

wings rolled at rest

long antennae

slender body

ORDER *Plecoptera.*
FAMILY *Taeniopterygidae.*
NUMBER OF SPECIES *75.*
SIZE *0.7–1.4cm.*
FEEDING *Nymphs: scavengers (plant fragments). Adults: mainly non-feeding.*
IMPACT *Harmless.*

TAENIOPTERYX NEBULOSA, *is a dark, slender species with long antennae. The wings are rolled around the body while at rest.*

NYMPHS

The nymphal abdominal cerci and antennae of these stoneflies are quite long.

Spring Stoneflies

Nemouridae

LIVE *around rocky, fast-flowing streams or springs and lakes.*

Also called brown stoneflies because of their typical body colour, these stoneflies are often stout-bodied and hold their wings rolled loosely around the body at rest. Several veins meet towards the tip of the front wings, giving the impression of an "X". The wings of some species are mottled and the abdomen has a pair of very short cerci.

NYMPHS

Spines and hairs cover the nymphs' bodies, and in some species they form distinctive patterns.

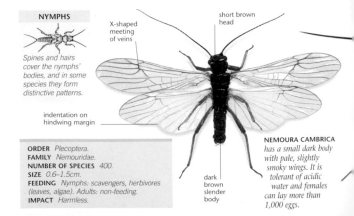

X-shaped meeting of veins

short brown head

indentation on hindwing margin

ORDER *Plecoptera.*
FAMILY *Nemouridae.*
NUMBER OF SPECIES *400.*
SIZE *0.6–1.5cm.*
FEEDING *Nymphs: scavengers, herbivores (leaves, algae). Adults: non-feeding.*
IMPACT *Harmless.*

dark brown slender body

NEMOURA CAMBRICA *has a small dark body with pale, slightly smoky wings. It is tolerant of acidic water and females can lay more than 1,000 eggs.*

True Crickets

Gryllidae

These insects are slightly flattened in body shape, with distinctive rounded heads and long, thin antennae, which are as long as or longer than the body. Crickets are rather drably coloured black or shades of brown. In winged species the front wings are held flat over the body at rest; males rub them together to produce songs. The end of the abdomen bears a pair of noticeable, often bristly, unsegmented cerci. In females the conspicuous ovipositor is cylindrical or needle-like.

FOUND in all manner of herbage in woods, hedgerows, grassland, and scrub.

♀

pale wing base

ovipositor

dark, shiny head

▲ GRYLLUS CAMPESTRIS, the Field Cricket, is a stocky insect with a big head and large hind legs. It makes burrows in grassland.

slender body

long antennae

▲ OECANTHUS PELLUCENS, the slender-bodied Italian Cricket, is a pale coloured fragile species and difficult to see among the bushes and trees where it lives.

folded hind wings

dull brown coloration

spines

▲ ACHETA DOMESTICA is a nocturnally active species. It is dull brown in colour and both sexes are fully winged.

short wings

▲ NEMOBIUS SYLVESTRIS, known as Wood Cricket, has short front wings and no hind wings.

mottled femur

bristly cerci

lightly banded antennae

▲ ARACHNOCEPHALUS VESTITUS, a wingless species, is distinctive as its head and thorax are narrower than other crickets'.

ORDER Orthoptera.
FAMILY Gryllidae.
NUMBER OF SPECIES 1,800.
SIZE 0.5–2.5cm.
FEEDING Nymphs and adults: herbivores, scavengers, predators.
IMPACT Some species can be crop pests.

NOTE

The male species sing mostly at night, by using their front wings, a series of small teeth on one wing rubbing over a scraper on the other.

Bush Crickets

Tettigoniidae

OCCUR *in a variety of habitats, both lush and sparsely vegetated, from ground level up to the treetops.*

NOTE

Bush cricket songs have been likened, among other things, to high-speed drills, watch winding, knife grinding, buzzing, and sliding a comb over a ruler's edge.

Highly distinctive due to their long, thread-like antennae and saddle-shaped pronotum, these brownish or greenish insects are sometimes known as long-horned grasshoppers. The wings are short in some species, but in fully-winged species the folded wings extend well beyond the end of the abdomen. The females have a conspicuous, laterally flattened ovipositor, which may be short and curved like a sickle or long like a sabre. The hind legs are greatly enlarged for jumping. Males make a species-specific song by rubbing the front wings together. Hearing organs are located at the top of the front tibiae, close to the "knee" joint.

small, brownish red spots all over body ♀

large, sword-like ovipositor

▼ **PLATYCLEIS ALBOPUNCTATA**, *the Grey Bush Cricket, is actually brownish with small pale spots. It lives mainly in dry, sunny places with little plant cover.* ♀

fully developed wings

▲ **LEPTOPHYES PUCTATISSIMA**, *the Speckled Bush Cricket, is common and widespread in well-vegetated areas such as woodland margins, hedgerows, and gardens. The wings are always very short.*

▼ **METRIOPTERA BRACHYPTERA** *is known as the Bog Bush Cricket, but also inhabits drier places such as heathland. Its song is a train of chirps that sound like "zrit".*

◀ **TETTIGONIA VIRIDISSIMA**, *the Great Green Bush Cricket, is a large but very well-camouflaged species. It is widespread throughout Europe in many habitats and feeds on insects.* ♂

brown stripe

♀

short wings

short wings

♀

sloping face

slender body

long wings

ORDER Orthoptera.
FAMILY Tettigoniidae.
NUMBER OF SPECIES 5,000.
SIZE 1.6–6cm.
FEEDING Nymphs and adults: herbivores, scavengers, predators.
IMPACT A few species can be plant pests.

▲ **CONOCEPHALUS DORSALIS**, *the Short-winged Conehead, is a slender species that favours moist habitats such as damp grassland, river edges, and the margins of salt marshes.*

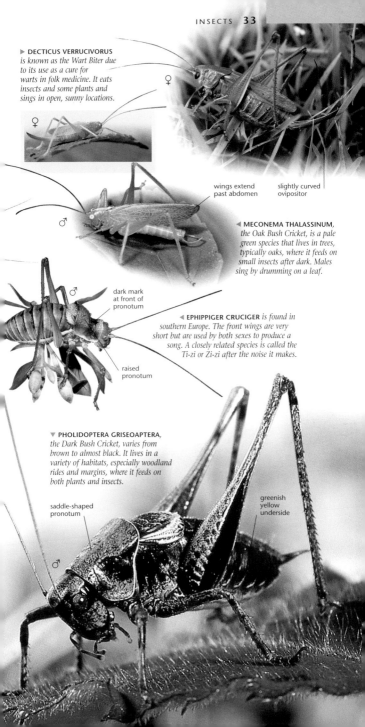

▶ **DECTICUS VERRUCIVORUS** *is known as the Wart Biter due to its use as a cure for warts in folk medicine. It eats insects and some plants and sings in open, sunny locations.*

♀

♀

♂

wings extend past abdomen

slightly curved ovipositor

◀ **MECONEMA THALASSINUM,** *the Oak Bush Cricket, is a pale green species that lives in trees, typically oaks, where it feeds on small insects after dark. Males sing by drumming on a leaf.*

♂

dark mark at front of pronotum

◀ **EPHIPPIGER CRUCIGER** *is found in southern Europe. The front wings are very short but are used by both sexes to produce a song. A closely related species is called the Ti-zi or Zi-zi after the noise it makes.*

raised pronotum

▼ **PHOLIDOPTERA GRISEOAPTERA,** *the Dark Bush Cricket, varies from brown to almost black. It lives in a variety of habitats, especially woodland rides and margins, where it feeds on both plants and insects.*

saddle-shaped pronotum

greenish yellow underside

♂

Grasshoppers and Locusts

Acrididae

NOTE

Females lay their eggs on the ground and surround them with a sticky secretion which dries and hardens to form a protective egg pod.

These insects are active during the day and prefer hot, sunny conditions. Most species are brownish or greenish with markings and patterns of all kinds. Two distinctive characteristics are the short antennae and the large saddle-shaped pronotum. The hind legs are greatly enlarged for jumping. The large hind wings are folded beneath the narrower and tougher front wings, but some species are short-winged. Many species have brightly coloured hind wings, which they can flash to startle enemies. Females are mostly larger than males, which sing by rubbing a row of small pegs on the inside of their hind femora against a hard, thickened vein on the edge of the front wings.

◀ **STENOBOTHRUS LINEATUS**, *the Stripe-winged Grasshopper, has a white stripe on the front wing. It likes dry habitats and has a buzzing song that changes pitch like a siren.*

red tip to abdomen in male

white mark on wing

◀ **CALLIPTAMUS ITALICUS**, *the Italian Grasshopper, flashes its red hind wings and hind tibiae when disturbed. Males make noises by rubbing their mandibles together.*

▼ **STETHOPHYMA GROSSUM**, *the Large Marsh Grasshopper, occurs in damp places. Males make a clicking noise by kicking their hind legs past their wings.*

camouflage coloration

yellow stripe along front of wings

very short wings

stout body

purple-red legs

▼ **OEDIPODA GERMANICA** *is well camouflaged against the stony habitats it favours. Its red hind wings are visible in flight.*

▲ **PODISMA PEDESTRIS**, *the Brown Mountain Grasshopper, is found in grassy or heathery alpine habitats.*

dark bands on wings

ORDER *Orthoptera.*
FAMILY *Acrididae.*
NUMBER OF SPECIES *9,000.*
SIZE *1–6cm.*
FEEDING *Nymphs and adults: herbivores (leaves and foliage).*
IMPACT *Some species are crop pests.*

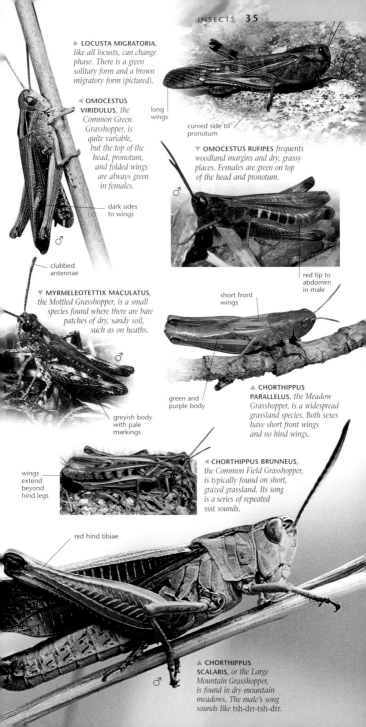

▶ **LOCUSTA MIGRATORIA,** *like all locusts, can change phase. There is a green solitary form and a brown migratory form (pictured).*

◀ **OMOCESTUS VIRIDULUS,** *the Common Green Grasshopper, is quite variable, but the top of the head, pronotum, and folded wings are always green in females.*

long wings

curved side to pronotum

dark sides to wings

♂

clubbed antennae

▼ **OMOCESTUS RUFIPES** *frequents woodland margins and dry, grassy places. Females are green on top of the head and pronotum.*

♂

red tip to abdomen in male

▼ **MYRMELEOTETTIX MACULATUS,** *the Mottled Grasshopper, is a small species found where there are bare patches of dry, sandy soil, such as on heaths.*

short front wings

♂

greyish body with pale markings

green and purple body

▲ **CHORTHIPPUS PARALLELUS,** *the Meadow Grasshopper, is a widespread grassland species. Both sexes have short front wings and no hind wings.*

wings extend beyond hind legs

◀ **CHORTHIPPUS BRUNNEUS,** *the Common Field Grasshopper, is typically found on short, grazed grassland. Its song is a series of repeated ssst sounds.*

red hind tibiae

♂

▲ **CHORTHIPPUS SCALARIS,** *or the Large Mountain Grasshopper, is found in dry mountain meadows. The male's song sounds like tsh-drr-tsh-drr.*

Mole Crickets

Gryllotalpidae

It would be very hard to confuse these brownish insects with anything else. Resembling miniature moles, they spend most of their life underground. Their body is very robust, cylindrical, and covered with short, velvety hairs. The legs are short and strong and the front legs are broad with strong teeth for digging. The head is narrower than the thorax, with short antennae and small eyes.

BURROW *in sand or soil near rivers, ponds, or lakes, emerging mainly to mate.*

short front wings

folded hind wings

powerful front legs for digging

NOTE

Mole crickets' front wings of these insects are modified with a special harp region to radiate the sound produced when the wings are rubbed together.

GRYLLOTALPA GRYLLOTALPA, *also known as the Mole Cricket, burrows just like a miniature mole. This insect is found especially where the soil is damp and sandy.*

stocky hind legs

ORDER *Orthoptera.*
FAMILY *Gryllotalpidae.*
NUMBER OF SPECIES *60.*
SIZE *2–5cm.*
FEEDING *Nymphs and adults: herbivores (plant roots), predators (worms, grubs).*
IMPACT *Some species can be crop pests.*

Pygmy Locusts

Tetrigidae

These poorly known insects look like small grasshoppers, but the pronotum extends backwards over the whole of the abdomen and tapers to a point. Most species are drably coloured greyish or brownish to match mossy or stony ground. The front wings are reduced to small, scale-like structures or are absent, while the hind wings are fully developed. The males do not sing.

PREFER *sunny, sparsely covered locations in damp habitats.*

elongated pronotum

pale mottling on sides

TETRIX UNDULATA, *the Common Groundhopper, varies in colour from pale brown to almost black. It is found in a variety of habitats.*

NOTE

As these insects do not sing to attract mates and are cryptically coloured to blend in with their background, it is not surprising that they are overlooked.

ORDER *Orthoptera.*
FAMILY *Tetrigidae.*
NUMBER OF SPECIES *1,200.*
SIZE *1–1.5cm.*
FEEDING *Nymphs and adults: scavengers, herbivores (decaying plants, algae, mosses).*
IMPACT *Harmless.*

Cave Crickets

Rhaphidophoridae

Also called wingless camel crickets, these insects lack wings and are hump-backed and drably coloured. They are dwarfed by their extremely long antennae and large hind legs. Mostly nocturnal in habit, many species are soft-bodied and may have reduced eyes. Females have a long, blade-like ovipositor.

FOUND *mainly in caves and caverns where there is food for them to eat.*

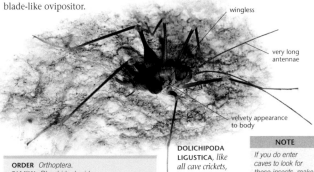

wingless

very long antennae

velvety appearance to body

DOLICHIPODA LIGUSTICA, *like all cave crickets, is a drab, brown species with very long antennae for feeling its way around in the dark and avoiding predators.*

NOTE

If you do enter caves to look for these insects, make sure you have a torch, that someone knows where you are, and do not go further than is safe.

ORDER *Orthoptera.*
FAMILY *Rhaphidophoridae.*
NUMBER OF SPECIES 500.
SIZE *1.5–2.2cm.*
FEEDING *Nymphs and adults: scavengers, herbivores.*
IMPACT *Harmless.*

Stick Insects

Bacillidae

These insects' legs and bodies are very long, slender, and cylindrical, making them resemble twigs and sticks. They feed mostly at night and hide from predators during the day by camouflaging themselves among foliage. Stick insects are usually green or brown and many are wingless. The antennae are shortish and the legs are generally equal in size.

USUALLY *found among grassy vegetation or on shrubs and trees, in dry habitats.*

◀ **BACILLUS ROSSIUS** *can be green or brown and females, which are larger than males, can reach just over 10cm in length.*

▲ **LEPTYNIA HISPANICA** *is found in dry grassy habitats in southwestern Europe, this species is pale yellowish brown or greenish; females may reach 6cm in length.*

front legs held together

pale lateral stripe

elongated abdomen

ORDER *Phasmatodea.*
FAMILY *Bacillidae.*
NUMBER OF SPECIES 300.
SIZE *3–10cm.*
FEEDING *Nymphs and adults: herbivores.*
IMPACT *Harmless.*

Striped Earwigs

Labiduridae

INHABIT *sand dunes, mud flats, and other coastal habitats; also along riverbanks and in piles of rubbish.*

Also known as long-horned earwigs due to their long antennae, these fairly robust insects are reddish brown in colour. The common species have longitudinal dark brown stripes down the pronotum and wing cases. The second tarsal segment of each leg is slightly elongated, not expanded sideways as in common earwigs (right). The forceps are large but not very curved.

strong forceps

groove at end of abdomen

very pale legs

♂

NOTE

Striped earwigs live under debris by day and excavate deep tunnels to lay their eggs. In defence, they can discharge a foul fluid from abdominal glands.

ORDER *Dermaptera.*
FAMILY *Labiduridae.*
NUMBER OF SPECIES 75.
SIZE 0.6–2cm.
FEEDING *Nymphs and adults: scavengers, predators, herbivores.*
IMPACT *Harmless.*

LABIDURA RIPARIA, *the Giant or Tawny Earwig, is found on riverbanks. It is nocturnal and partly or wholly predacious.*

Little Earwigs

Labiidae

HIDE *in compost heaps, rotting vegetation, piles of dung, and nettles, and under bark.*

These small, secretive earwigs are light yellowish brown or dull dark brown in colour, with pale legs; many species are covered with shortish golden hairs. The antennae have 11 to 15 segments and the second tarsal segment of each leg is cylindrical, not expanded as in common earwigs (right) or elongated like striped earwigs (above). Most species of little earwigs are fully winged; some are good fliers and are attracted to lights at night.

dark head

reddish brown front wings

♀

short forceps

NOTE

Lesser earwigs were introduced to the U.S.A. from Europe. The commonest species in this family, it is a good flier and is attracted to lights at night.

LABIA MINOR, *the Lesser Earwig, at less than 7mm long, is the smallest earwig in Europe. It is commonly found in compost heaps and rotting vegetation.*

ORDER *Dermaptera.*
FAMILY *Labiidae.*
NUMBER OF SPECIES 500.
SIZE *Up to 1.2cm (most species).*
FEEDING *Nymphs and adults: scavengers.*
IMPACT *Harmless.*

Common Earwigs

Forficulidae

These slender, nocturnal insects are reddish brown to dark brown with paler legs and thread-like antennae. The front wings are small and toughened, covering the folded, fan-shaped hind wings. The second tarsal segment of each leg is expanded sideways (compare this with striped and little earwigs, left). The body is flattened and the abdomen has a pair of forceps at the tip. Those of males are very curved and – as with all earwigs – used for courtship and defence; those of females are much straighter. Common earwigs are mainly omnivores, but some eat only plant matter.

CRAWL *through soil, leaf litter, crevices in rocks, or under bark, sometimes in large aggregations.*

long, curved forceps

▼ **FORFICULA AURICULARIA**
is a very common earwig. It is reddish brown in colour and the folded ends of the hind wings stick out from under the front wing.

teeth on inner edge of forceps

reddish brown, flattened abdomen

pale margins to pronotum

thread-like antennae

orange spot on front wings

reddish brown head

slender forceps

♀

♂

NOTE

Common earwigs rarely fly, perhaps due to the difficulty of folding their hind wings, but more likely because their lifestyle does not require flight often.

▲ **ANECHURA BIPUNCTATA**
is a scarce alpine species that can be found under stones. The males have strongly curved forceps, but the females' are straighter.

ORDER *Dermaptera.*
FAMILY *Forficulidae.*
NUMBER OF SPECIES *470.*
SIZE *1–1.5cm.*
FEEDING *Nymphs and adults: scavengers, predators, herbivores.*
IMPACT *Some species can be pests of crops.*

Praying Mantids

Mantidae

FOUND *in warm, dry vegetation of central and southern Europe where there is a good supply of insect prey.*

▼ **IRIS ORATORIO** *has brightly patterned hind wings that are flashed open as part of its threat display.*

Among the most easily recognized insects, the mantid has a mobile, triangular head which is broader than it is long and has large, widely separated eyes. The prothorax is elongated and the large front legs are adapted for catching prey. The front tibia can be folded back on the femur and both are armed with rows of alternating long and short spines. Females may have short wings; males are smaller and fully winged.

patterned hind wings ♂

prey-catching front legs

mobile head

elongated prothorax

♀

swollen, egg-filled abdomen

ORDER *Mantodea.*
FAMILY *Mantidae.*
NUMBER OF SPECIES *1,400.*
SIZE *2–9cm.*
FEEDING *Nymphs and adults: predators.*
IMPACT *Harmless.*

EGG CASE

papery covering

▲ **MANTIS RELIGIOSA** *can be both green and brown; males are smaller and slimmer.*

Empusid Mantids

Empusidae

FOUND *in warm southern parts of Europe in areas of long grass and scrub.*

EMPUSA PENNATA *is identified by its tall head crest and leaf-like body extensions; antennae of the females are thread-like.*

These greenish or brownish mantids are identified by the presence of a crest on top of the head, which makes the latter look diamond-shaped rather than triangular as in common praying mantids (above). The prothorax is very slender and the segments of the abdomen have lateral, leaf-like extensions. In some species, the femur of each leg may have small, leaf-like lobes.

feathery antennae

elongated prothorax

crest on head

♂

lobes on abdomen

♂

small lobes on legs

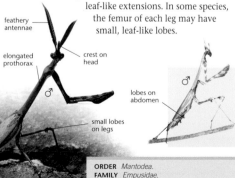

ORDER *Mantodea.*
FAMILY *Empusidae.*
NUMBER OF SPECIES *30.*
SIZE *2–7cm.*
FEEDING *Nymphs and adults: predators.*
IMPACT *Harmless.*

Blattellid Cockroaches

Blattellidae

Most of these smallish cockroaches are light to dark brown in colour with yellowish or reddish markings on the pronotum and wings. Most species are fully winged and the wings, when folded, reach the end of the abdomen. In some species and the females of others, the wings are short. However, all species show a marked reluctance to fly. Females of *Blattella germanica* produce an average of five egg cases containing about 40 eggs each. Rather than sticking the egg cases to objects, the female carries them around, protruding from her body, until they hatch.

THRIVE outdoors in leaf litter, debris, and rubbish dumps, as well as in houses, especially in summer.

egg case

black cerci

short, speckled wings

pale sides to pronotum

♀

▲ **ECTOBIUS PANZERI**, small pale to dark brown, this cockroach lives in sandy coastal regions and is not a pest. Females have pale legs with dark markings.

wings just shorter than abdomen

▲ **SUPELLA LONGIPALPA** is originally from Africa and is now a common pest in buildings. Males have longer wings and fly readily.

▶ **ECTOBIUS LAPPONICUS** is known as the Dusky Cockroach. This species lives in a variety of habitats among leaf litter, sometimes moving up into bushes.

♀

reddish head

light brown pronotum

spiny legs

wings just shorter than abdomen

black cerci

pale brown wings

two dark stripes on pronotum

◀ **BLATTELLA GERMANICA** is a common pest, found in factories, hotels, and restaurants where there is ample food.

egg case

♀

NOTE

Blatella germanica, like many species of cockroach, was introduced to Europe from Africa. Its presence is marked by a characteristic odour.

ORDER *Blattodea*.
FAMILY *Blattellidae*.
NUMBER OF SPECIES *1,750*.
SIZE *0.8–1.5cm.*
FEEDING *Nymphs and adults: scavengers.*
IMPACT *Blatella germanica* and *Supella longipalpa* *are major household pests.*

Blattids

Blattidae

NOTE

By day these insects hide in cracks and crevices, behind skirting boards, and under floors. They are very active and fast-running but fly only if very warm.

These cockroaches are broadly oval, with flattened bodies. In general, they are brown, reddish brown, or blackish brown in colour with darker or paler markings. Many species have a glossy or shiny appearance. The slender antennae are as long as the body and the underside of the middle and hind legs are spiny. Many species favour places such as houses, restaurants, bakeries, warehouses, sewers, and rubbish dumps; some species are common around ports and on ships.

yellow "ring" around pronotum

pale marks on sides of elytra

▼ **PERIPLANETA AMERICANA**
is found on ships and in food warehouses; females glue their egg cases to hidden surfaces.

▲ **PERIPLANETA AUSTRALASIAE**,
the Australian Cockroach, is very similar in habits and appearance to the blattids but has a continuous yellowish ring around the margin of the pronotum.

yellow patches at rear of pronotum

bristly legs

pronotum hides head

egg case

flattened body

▼ **BLATTA ORIENTALIS**,
known as Oriental or Common Cockroach, is dark brown to almost black in colour. The females have very short wings.

short wings

ORDER *Blattodea.*
FAMILY *Blattidae.*
NUMBER OF SPECIES *600.*
SIZE *2–4.5cm.*
FEEDING *Nymphs and adults: scavengers.*
IMPACT *Several species can be serious domestic pests.*

Subterranean or Damp-wood Termites

Rhinotermitidae

These soft-bodied, social insects are pale in colour. The rear margin of the pronotum of all castes (soldiers, workers, and reproductives) is rounded and may appear almost heart-shaped. The tarsi have three segments. Soldiers have a pale brown head about twice as long as it is broad and their mandibles lack teeth. The winged reproductive forms are dark brown.

FAVOUR *wood near to the soil, including roots, tree stumps, and building timbers.*

pale, soft-bodied worker

RETICULITERMES LUCIFUGUS *is one of two species of termite found in central and southern Europe.*

chews tunnels in soft wood

ORDER *Isoptera.*
FAMILY *Rhinotermitidae.*
NUMBER OF SPECIES *345.*
SIZE *4–8mm.*
FEEDING *Nymphs and adults: wood-feeders, dung-feeders.*
IMPACT *Can damage building timbers.*

Web Spinners

Embiidae

Web spinners are pale brownish to black, gregarious insects that make silken tunnels in soil, ground litter, and dead wood. They are elongated, with small eyes and thread-like antennae. Males may have two pairs of narrow wings, but females are always wingless. The legs are short and the front legs have distinctive swollen basal tarsal segments containing the silk glands.

LIVE *among leaf litter, under stones and dead wood, in southern Europe.*

EMBIA RAMBURI *is found in southern Europe. The female of this species is brown while the male is black.*

short legs

wings absent

swollen tarsus

NOTE

The liquid silk is produced from secretory glands on the tarsal segment. As the insect rubs its feet against a surface, a mat of silk is formed.

ORDER *Embioptera.*
FAMILY *Embiidae.*
NUMBER OF SPECIES *200.*
SIZE *0.3–2cm.*
FEEDING *Nymphs and adults: scavengers, herbivores (moss, lichen).*
IMPACT *Harmless.*

Booklice

Liposcelidae

These small, light to yellowish brown insects have squat, slightly flattened bodies and are quite difficult to see. The hind legs are larger than the first two pairs and the hind femora are very enlarged, allowing the insects to make small jumps. The tarsi have three segments The head, which is large in comparison to the rest of the body and appears to bulge at the front, carries a pair of small compound eyes, chewing mouthparts, and shortish, thread-like antennae. Most species are wingless; when present, the wings have rounded ends.

INFEST houses and collections of stored plants and insects; also found in scrub and woods under bark and among leaf litter.

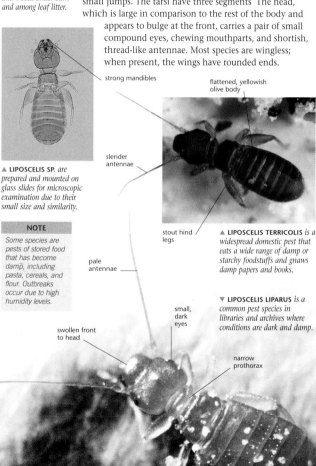

strong mandibles

slender antennae

▲ LIPOSCELIS SP. are prepared and mounted on glass slides for microscopic examination due to their small size and similarity.

NOTE

Some species are pests of stored food that has become damp, including pasta, cereals, and flour. Outbreaks occur due to high humidity levels.

pale antennae

flattened, yellowish olive body

stout hind legs

▲ LIPOSCELIS TERRICOLIS is a widespread domestic pest that eats a wide range of damp or starchy foodstuffs and gnaws damp papers and books.

▼ LIPOSCELIS LIPARUS is a common pest species in libraries and archives where conditions are dark and damp.

small, dark eyes

swollen front to head

narrow prothorax

ORDER Psocoptera.
FAMILY Liposcelidae.
NUMBER OF SPECIES 150.
SIZE 0.5–1.5mm.
FEEDING Nymphs and adults: scavengers, fungi-feeders.
IMPACT May be pests of stored produce.

Common Barklice

Psocidae

Most common barklice have dull brown, grey, or blackish coloration and many have pale markings. The antennae have 13 segments. The wings, which are hairless, may be mottled with brown or have rows of smoky spots or irregular patches. The thorax is humped in side view and often shiny. These insects may occur in "herds" of many hundreds or even thousands.

FOUND *on the bark, twigs, and branches of various trees and shrubs, and on the foliage of conifers.*

PSOCOCERASTIS GIBBOSA *lives on a number of trees and is the largest member of its genus in Britain.*

transparent wings with dark veins

large, bulging eyes

NOTE

Some species have specialized feeding preferences; for example, eating only a few species of lichen. Others scavenge all types of organic detritus.

ORDER *Psocoptera.*
FAMILY *Psocidae.*
NUMBER OF SPECIES *500.*
SIZE *1–6mm.*
FEEDING *Nymphs and adults: scavengers, fungi-feeders, herbivores (pollen, algae).*
IMPACT *Harmless.*

Bird Lice

Menoponidae

These small, wingless ectoparasites are pale brown in colour. The head is triangular and expanded behind the eyes. It has biting mandibles and short, slightly clubbed antennae that can be concealed in grooves on the underside of the head. The abdomen is oval and the legs are short and stout, each with claws for gripping their host's feathers. All species feed on skin and feather fragments, supplemented with blood.

OCCUR *only on the plumage and skin of a variety of birds.*

NOTE

Bird lice attach their eggs singly to their host's feathers with a water-insoluble glue-like substance. Most have specific hosts; some attack several bird species.

broad head

stout legs

two claws on each leg

pale body hairs

oval abdomen

ORDER *Phthiraptera.*
FAMILY *Menoponidae.*
NUMBER OF SPECIES *650.*
SIZE *1–6mm.*
FEEDING *Nymphs and adults: parasites (skin, feathers, blood).*
IMPACT *Some species are pests of poultry.*

MENACANTHUS STRAMINEUS, *the Chicken Body Louse, infests poultry, often leading to feather loss and infections.*

Bird-chewing Lice

Philopteridae

These pale, yellowish brown lice have a relatively large head with prominent mandibles. The antennae have five segments. The thorax is short with the middle and hind thorax segments fused together. The legs are short and similarly sized, and each has a pair of claws. The abdomen is slightly flattened and may be pear-shaped in species that live on the short feathers of birds' heads and necks; species found on the wing feathers are more elongated.

REMAIN *permanently on their bird hosts and are never free-living.*

NOTE

These insects are difficult to observe in the wild. One way to see them is to examine the wings of freshly dead birds under a hand lens.

COLUMBICOLA CLAVIFORMIS, *the Pigeon Louse, is found on feathers, often in small groups, and usually aligned with the direction of the feather barbs.*

relatively large head

slender, elongated body

yellowish brown coloration

ORDER *Phthiraptera.*
FAMILY *Philopteridae.*
NUMBER OF SPECIES *2,700.*
SIZE *Up to 3mm.*
FEEDING *Nymphs and adults: parasites (skin and feathers).*
IMPACT *Parasites of wild birds.*

Mammal-chewing Lice

Trichodectidae

Generally pale brown in colour, these lice have large, squarish heads with distinctive mandibles. The antennae are conspicuous, short, and have three segments. The legs are short, each with a single tarsal claw. Females have oval, blunt-ended abdomens, while those of males are more pointed towards the rear and carry prominent genitalia.

FOUND *on mammalian hosts in a variety of habitats, including fields and farms.*

shortish legs

short antennae

jaws

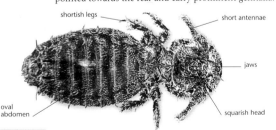

oval abdomen

squarish head

NOTE

Some species are pests of domestic animals. They can cause severe irritation and loss of hair and fur by inducing prolonged scratching.

ORDER *Phthiraptera.*
FAMILY *Trichodectidae.*
NUMBER OF SPECIES *360.*
SIZE *1–3mm.*
FEEDING *Nymphs and adults: parasites (skin, hair, secretions, blood).*
IMPACT *Infest wild and domestic animals.*

TRICHODECTES CANIS *feeds on bits of skin and fur. The louse looks blue here as it has been stained and mounted on a glass slide to enable detailed examination.*

Human Lice

Pediculidae

These lice are small and pale with narrow heads and
pear-shaped, flattened bodies. The mouthparts are
modified for piercing and sucking. The legs are short,
strong, and inwardly curved. Each has a large claw for
grasping and climbing through hair.
Human head and body lice appear
to differ only in the area of
the body they occupy.

LIVE *on humans on
hair and among items
of clothing.*

body engorged
with blood

NOTE

*There is evidence
that head lice are
becoming resistant
to insecticidal
treatments. They
pass from person to
person by close
head contact.*

ORDER *Phthiraptera.*
FAMILY *Pediculidae.*
NUMBER OF SPECIES *2.*
SIZE *1.5–3.5mm.*
FEEDING *Nymphs and adults: parasites.*
IMPACT *Body lice transmit diseases
to humans.*

small head

PEDICULUS HUMANUS, *the Human Head Louse,
lives entirely in hair and attaches its eggs, called
nits, to hair shafts with a strong glue. It is
prevalent among young school children.*

Pubic Lice

Pthiridae

Also called the Crab Louse, this pale to translucent louse
has a squat, flat body and a head that is much narrower
than the thorax. The middle and hind legs are
especially stout with strong curved claws for
gripping pubic hair shafts. The
family includes the Human
Pubic Louse, *Pthirus pubis*,
and the Gorilla Pubic
Louse, *P. gorillae*.

OCCUR *on the bodies
of humans (also on
gorillas in Africa).*

conspicuous
eye

PTHIRUS PUBIS
*lives on human pubic
hairs and is passed on
through intimate contact.
These slow-moving
lice cannot jump,
and feed on
blood.*

pubic
hair
shaft

strong
middle
and hind
claws

NYMPH

flattened body

NOTE

*This species is
found all over the
world wherever
there are humans. It
is unpleasant, but is
not known
to transmit any
diseases.*

ORDER *Phthiraptera.*
FAMILY *Pthiridae.*
NUMBER OF SPECIES *2.*
SIZE *1.5–3mm.*
FEEDING *Nymphs and adults: parasites
(blood).*
IMPACT *Parasites of humans and gorillas.*

Bark Bugs

Aradidae

Also known as flat bugs, these insects have a very flat, oval shape and are reddish brown or dark in colour. The surface of the body looks roughened due to the presence of many small dimples and bumps. The distinctive head narrows behind the eyes; it has short, stout antennae with four segments and a very short rostrum, also with four segments. Bark bugs have short legs and many species are wingless.

stout antennae

dimpled surface

flattened body

ARADUS DEPRESSUS feeds on fungal threads and fruiting bodies. It lives under the bark of birch, oak, beech, and some other deciduous trees.

NOTE

Most bark bugs live on trees, but some live in leaf litter on forest floors. One species is found on old Scots Pine trees, where it feeds on sap.

ORDER Hemiptera.
FAMILY Aradidae.
NUMBER OF SPECIES 1,800.
SIZE 3–6mm.
FEEDING Nymphs and adults: scavengers, fungi-feeders.
IMPACT Harmless.

Acanthosomatids

Acanthosomatidae

Typically greenish or reddish brown with dark markings, acanthosomatids have broad bodies that taper slightly to the rear, behind the broad pronotum. The relatively small head has antennae with five segments, and can appear sunk into the front margin of the pronotum. The scutellum is large and triangular. The tarsi have two segments.

▼ **ACANTHOSOMA HAEMORRHOIDALE** is mainly found on hawthorn, where it feeds on buds and berries. It also feeds on other deciduous tree species, such as hazel.

broad pronotum

pronotum pointed at sides

large, triangular scutellum

▲ **ELASMUCHA GRISEA**, the Parent Bug, shows maternal behaviour, the females guarding their eggs and newly hatched nymphs from predators.

ORDER Hemiptera.
FAMILY Acanthosomatidae.
NUMBER OF SPECIES 250.
SIZE 0.8–1.3cm.
FEEDING Nymphs and adults: herbivores.
IMPACT Harmless.

Burrowing Bugs

Cydnidae

These small bugs are broadly oval and slightly convex in shape. They are generally shiny black or dark reddish brown, often with blue tinges and white markings. The head can appear sunk into the pronotum. The antennae have five segments. The front tibiae are flattened, and the tibia of all legs are distinctively spiny.

FOUND *on foliage or among roots near the base of susceptible host plants, mainly in woodland, hedgerows, and open ground.*

▼ **SEHIRUS BIGUTTATUS** *is an oval, black, shiny bug with two yellowish spots on the front wings and blackish brown legs. It is found throughout Europe.*

pale spot on elytra

small head

spiny legs

oval outline

▲ **CYDNUS ATTERIMUS** *is matt black with a pitted surface. Its wing membranes are whitish or yellowish brown.*

ORDER Hemiptera.
FAMILY Cydnidae.
NUMBER OF SPECIES 400.
SIZE 4–9mm.
FEEDING Nymphs and adults: herbivores.
IMPACT Harmless.

Scutellerids

Scutelleridae

These rounded, almost beetle-like bugs are convex in side view and are yellowish to black with pale to dark brown markings. They are similar to shield bugs, but have a much larger scutellum that covers the abdomen and completely covers the membranous wings. The head is triangular or broad, and the antennae have five segments. All scutellerids are plant suckers. Some have attained pest status by the damage they cause to grain crops, and cotton in particular.

LIVE *in damp, marshy habitats and coastal areas; some on arable farmland.*

very large, parallel-sided scutellum

NOTE

When the Tortoise Bug takes off, the wings are folded out from under the large, shield-like scutellum, from which it gets its common name.

triangular head

EURYGASTER MAURA, *the European Tortoise Bug, is a generalist feeder on many grasses and sometimes attacks cereal crops. It is not as serious a pest as some other scutellerids.*

ORDER Hemiptera.
FAMILY Scutelleridae.
NUMBER OF SPECIES 400.
SIZE 5–12mm.
FEEDING Nymphs and adults: herbivores.
IMPACT A few species can be pests; Eurygaster maura damages cereal crops.

Stink Bugs

Pentatomidae

NOTE

The eggs are laid in small, regular or hexagonal clusters. In many species the females guard the eggs and nymphs, standing over them when danger strikes.

Also known as shield bugs due to their distinctive shape, stink bugs can produce powerful defensive odours (which may be strong enough to induce headaches) from glands on the thorax. Many species are brown and green, but others are very conspicuously marked black and red. The head can appear partly sunk into the pronotum, which is broad and may have sharply angled corners. The antennae typically have five segments, while the tarsi have three. The scutellum reaches midway down the abdomen.

▼ **GRAPHOSOMA ITALICUM** *has bright coloration that warns of its unpalatability. It occurs mainly in sunny, flower-rich habitats in southern Europe.*

unbroken red and black stripes

banded head

large scutellum

unmarked black legs

metallic sheen

sharply angled pronotum

yellowish marking down pronotum

distinctive pattern on wings

▲ **EURYDEMA OLERACEA** *is known as the Brassica Bug because it can be a pest of crops from the cabbage and cress families. Its coloration may be quite variable.*

▶ **EURYDEMA DOMINULUS** *can be red or orange in colour and feeds on plants in the cress family. It may also be a pest of cultivated brassicas.*

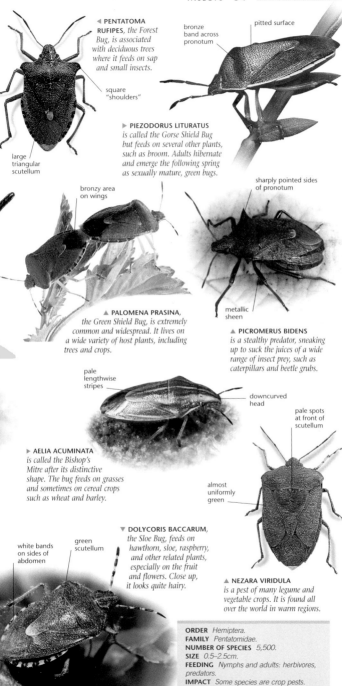

◀ **PENTATOMA RUFIPES**, the Forest Bug, is associated with deciduous trees where it feeds on sap and small insects.

square "shoulders"

large triangular scutellum

bronze band across pronotum

pitted surface

▶ **PIEZODORUS LITURATUS** is called the Gorse Shield Bug but feeds on several other plants, such as broom. Adults hibernate and emerge the following spring as sexually mature, green bugs.

bronzy area on wings

sharply pointed sides of pronotum

▲ **PALOMENA PRASINA**, the Green Shield Bug, is extremely common and widespread. It lives on a wide variety of host plants, including trees and crops.

metallic sheen

▲ **PICROMERUS BIDENS** is a stealthy predator, sneaking up to suck the juices of a wide range of insect prey, such as caterpillars and beetle grubs.

pale lengthwise stripes

downcurved head

pale spots at front of scutellum

▶ **AELIA ACUMINATA** is called the Bishop's Mitre after its distinctive shape. The bug feeds on grasses and sometimes on cereal crops such as wheat and barley.

almost uniformly green

white bands on sides of abdomen

green scutellum

▼ **DOLYCORIS BACCARUM**, the Sloe Bug, feeds on hawthorn, sloe, raspberry, and other related plants, especially on the fruit and flowers. Close up, it looks quite hairy.

▲ **NEZARA VIRIDULA** is a pest of many legume and vegetable crops. It is found all over the world in warm regions.

ORDER Hemiptera.
FAMILY Pentatomidae.
NUMBER OF SPECIES 5,500.
SIZE 0.5–2.5cm.
FEEDING Nymphs and adults: herbivores, predators.
IMPACT Some species are crop pests.

Squash Bugs

Coreidae

Squash bugs are so named because some species feed on squash plants. Most are roughly oval in shape and dull brown. In some species, the abdomen is flattened, projects sideways, and may be lobed and angular. The head is very much narrower and shorter than the pronotum. The antennae have four segments. The hind part of the front wings has a distinctive pattern of parallel veins. All squash bugs are herbivorous as adults and nymphs, eating shoots, buds, fruits, and unripe seeds of their food plants.

DISTRIBUTED *wherever their host plants grow, especially in grassland, heathland, and light woodland.*

NOTE

When threatened, some large species of squash bug produce unpleasant or fruity-smelling secretions from special glands in the thorax.

white tubercles

▼ **SYROMASTUS RHOMBEUS**
inhabits dry, sandy places. The lack of wings and presence of dorsal gland openings show that this specimen is a nymph.

▶ **CORIOMERIS DENTICULATUS**
is a relatively slender squash bug with many short spines. It feeds on leguminous plants on well-drained soils.

scent gland opening

NYMPH

thickened antennae

distinctive veins on wing membrane

broad abdomen

pronotum broad at front

centre of antenna is orange

forward-pointing spines

◀ **COREUS MARGINATUS**
has a noticeably broad abdomen. Nymphs feed on dock plants; adults feast on fruit prior to hibernating.

ORDER *Hemiptera.*
FAMILY *Coreidae.*
NUMBER OF SPECIES *2,000.*
SIZE *1–1.8cm.*
FEEDING *Nymphs and adults: herbivores.*
IMPACT *Mainly harmless, although a few species are pests of crops and vegetables.*

Scentless Plant Bugs

Rhopalidae

These pale, light brown or greenish bugs are similar to squash bugs (left). The head is quite broad but narrower than the hind margin of the pronotum, and the antennae have four segments. The body can be covered with punctures or tiny pits and may be quite hairy.

USUALLY *found among weeds and rough vegetation in old fields, by roadsides, and in other disturbed areas.*

▼ **RHOPALUS SUBRUFUS** *browses on low-growing plants in light woodland, rides, and clearings. It has distinctive bulging eyes.*

► **MYRMUS MIRIFORMIS** *feeds on grasses, especially the unripe seeds. Males may be green or brown.*

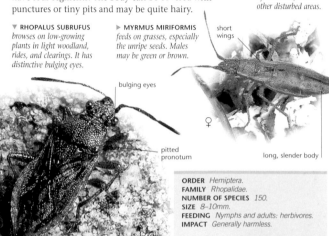

short wings

bulging eyes

♀

pitted pronotum

long, slender body

ORDER Hemiptera.	
FAMILY Rhopalidae.	
NUMBER OF SPECIES 150.	
SIZE 8–10mm.	
FEEDING Nymphs and adults: herbivores.	
IMPACT Generally harmless.	

Fire Bugs

Pyrrhocoridae

These insects are also known as red bugs on account of their bright red and black coloration. Similar in outline to some seed bugs (p.54), fire bugs have triangular heads with prominent eyes, a long, slender, four-segmented rostrum, and antennae with four segments. Short-winged forms are common, but fully winged individuals also occur.

LIVE *on plants in the family Malvaceae, such as cotton, mallow, and hibiscus.*

NOTE

The species pictured overwinters in crevices and in the soil as adults and emerge in the spring. The nymphs have black wing pads.

two black dots on wings

ORDER Hemiptera.	
FAMILY Pyrrhocoridae.	
NUMBER OF SPECIES 300.	
SIZE 0.8–1.4cm.	
FEEDING Nymphs and adults: herbivores.	
IMPACT Some species in the genus Dysdercus are serious pests of cotton crops.	

PYRRHOCORIS APTERUS, *commonly known as the Fire Bug, is a gregarious, flightless species widespread in central and southern Europe.*

end of abdomen exposed

Seed Bugs

Lygaeidae

FOUND *close to the ground in leaf litter, under stones, or among low-growing vegetation.*

Also known as ground bugs, these bugs are dull-coloured, being mainly pale yellow, brown, or black, although a few species are bright red and black. The body is quite tough and flattened and is either elongate or oval. The head is typically triangular but can be very broad in some species. The antennae arise from well down the sides of the head, below the prominent eyes. Many of the ground-living species may be short-winged or wingless. The femora of the front legs may be swollen, with stout spines. As their name suggests, seed bugs are mostly seed-feeders, using the strong, toothed or spined front legs to grasp their food.

bulging eyes

◀ **SCOLOPOSTETHUS THOMSONI** *favours habitats with lush vegetation such as nettles. It sucks soft plant parts and seeds and sometimes attacks small insects.*

bright warning coloration

▲ **LYGAEUS SAXATILIS** *is similar to L. equestris (below) but lacks white wing markings. Both species like sunny locations.*

mating pair

▼ **LYGAEUS EQUESTRIS** *is a large and distinctively marked bug common in central and southern Europe. It feeds at dandelions and other flowers.*

flattened body

broad head

white markings on wing membranes

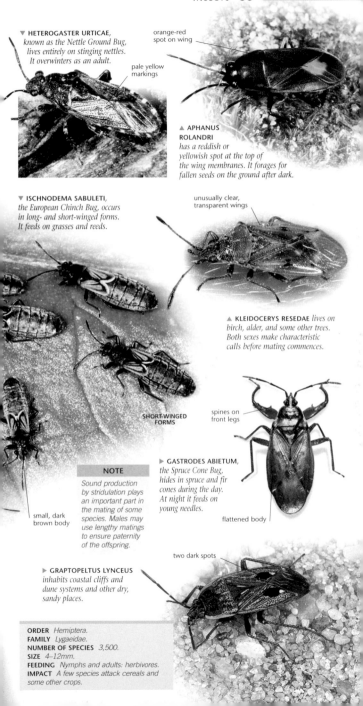

▼ **HETEROGASTER URTICAE,** *known as the Nettle Ground Bug, lives entirely on stinging nettles. It overwinters as an adult.*

orange-red spot on wing

pale yellow markings

▲ **APHANUS ROLANDRI** *has a reddish or yellowish spot at the top of the wing membranes. It forages for fallen seeds on the ground after dark.*

▼ **ISCHNODEMA SABULETI,** *the European Chinch Bug, occurs in long- and short-winged forms. It feeds on grasses and reeds.*

unusually clear, transparent wings

▲ **KLEIDOCERYS RESEDAE** *lives on birch, alder, and some other trees. Both sexes make characteristic calls before mating commences.*

spines on front legs

SHORT-WINGED FORMS

NOTE

Sound production by stridulation plays an important part in the mating of some species. Males may use lengthy matings to ensure paternity of the offspring.

small, dark brown body

▶ **GASTRODES ABIETUM,** *the Spruce Cone Bug, hides in spruce and fir cones during the day. At night it feeds on young needles.*

flattened body

two dark spots

▶ **GRAPTOPELTUS LYNCEUS** *inhabits coastal cliffs and dune systems and other dry, sandy places.*

ORDER *Hemiptera.*
FAMILY *Lygaeidae.*
NUMBER OF SPECIES *3,500.*
SIZE *4–12mm.*
FEEDING *Nymphs and adults: herbivores.*
IMPACT *A few species attack cereals and some other crops.*

Stilt Bugs

Berytidae

FOUND among weeds and tall grass in meadows and woods, and around the margins of ponds.

These pale, reddish or yellowish brown to grey bugs look very delicate. They have elongated – sometimes very slender – bodies and are named for their long, thin, spindly legs and the way in which they appear to "stilt-walk" with their bodies held high. Their antennae are also long and thin; the first of the four antennal segments is long, while the last segment is short and swollen at the tip. The rostrum has four segments and the knees can be slightly swollen. Stilt bugs are generally slow-moving, often "freezing" when disturbed.

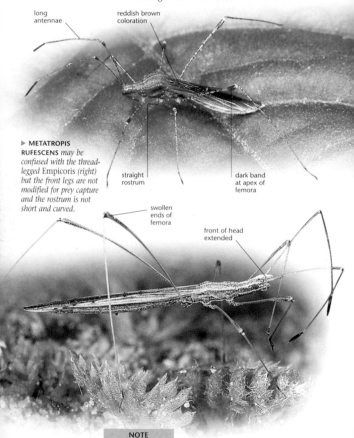

long antennae

reddish brown coloration

▶ **METATROPIS RUFESCENS** *may be confused with the thread-legged* Empicoris *(right) but the front legs are not modified for prey capture and the rostrum is not short and curved.*

straight rostrum

dark band at apex of femora

swollen ends of femora

front of head extended

▲ **NEIDES TIPULARIUS** *is found in heathland and dry, weedy fields where it feeds on a variety of plants. Adults find dry places to overwinter and emerge in spring.*

NOTE

Finding stilt bugs might take a bit of practice as they are quite small and often freeze motion-less when disturbed, looking just like a bit of dry plant.

ORDER Hemiptera.
FAMILY Berytidae.
NUMBER OF SPECIES 180.
SIZE 6–10mm.
FEEDING Nymphs and adults: herbivores, predators.
IMPACT Harmless.

Assassin Bugs

Reduviidae

Most of these bugs are yellowish brown, grey, or blackish, but some are reddish orange. The body shape varies from robust and oval to very elongated and slender with thread-like legs. The head has a transverse groove between the eyes and the antennae; the latter are often bent after the long, first segment, have four main segments, and many subsegments. The rostrum has three segments and is distinctively short and curved. The front legs are often enlarged and used to grasp prey.

OCCUR on vegetation of all kinds and sometimes in houses where their prey is present.

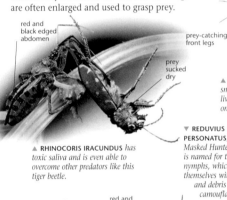

prey-catching front legs

red and black edged abdomen

prey sucked dry

▲ EMPICORIS VAGABUNDUS, a small thread-legged assassin bug, lives mainly in trees where it preys on small soft-bodied insects.

▲ RHINOCORIS IRACUNDUS has toxic saliva and is even able to overcome other predators like this tiger beetle.

▼ REDUVIUS PERSONATUS, the Masked Hunter, is named for the nymphs, which cover themselves with dust and debris as camouflage.

NYMPH

red and black wings

shiny black head and pronotum

brownish body

enlarged pronotum

▲ PIRATES HYBRIDUS is a ground-active assassin bug with a shiny black head and pronotum and distinctively marked wings.

broad abdomen

prey-catching front legs

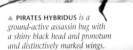

NOTE

Assassin bugs can make faint sounds by rubbing the tip of their rostrum along a special ridged groove on the underside of the thorax.

ORDER Hemiptera.
FAMILY Reduviidae.
NUMBER OF SPECIES 6,000.
SIZE 0.6–1.6cm.
FEEDING Nymphs and adults: predators.
IMPACT If handled roughly, larger species may bite, piercing human skin.

▲ PHYMATA CRASSIPES is a squat and odd looking ambush bug. It rests on flowers to seize insects as it flies in to feed.

Damsel Bugs

Nabidae

Damsel bugs are highly active, slender-bodied predators. They are usually dull brown or straw-coloured with a variety of markings, but a few are black and red. The head is relatively elongated and has thin antennae with four or five segments; the rostrum has four segments. The front femora are thickened and armed with short spines to grip prey. Many species have short- and fully-winged forms.

FOUND on the ground or among vegetation, wherever small insect prey is plentiful.

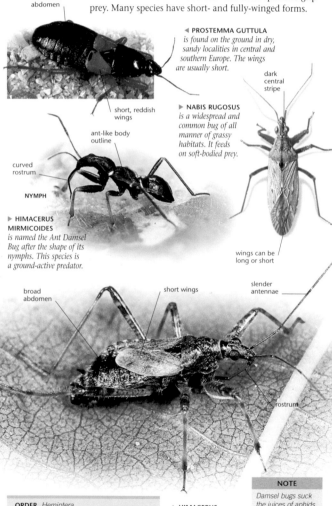

slim black abdomen

◀ **PROSTEMMA GUTTULA** is found on the ground in dry, sandy localities in central and southern Europe. The wings are usually short.

short, reddish wings

▶ **NABIS RUGOSUS** is a widespread and common bug of all manner of grassy habitats. It feeds on soft-bodied prey.

dark central stripe

ant-like body outline

curved rostrum

NYMPH

▶ **HIMACERUS MIRMICOIDES** is named the Ant Damsel Bug after the shape of its nymphs. This species is a ground-active predator.

wings can be long or short

broad abdomen

short wings

slender antennae

rostrum

ORDER Hemiptera.
FAMILY Nabidae.
NUMBER OF SPECIES 400.
SIZE 3–11mm.
FEEDING Nymphs and adults: predators.
IMPACT Larger species can deliver a painful bite that may pierce human skin.

▲ **HIMACERUS APTERUS**, the Tree Damsel Bug, lives in a range of deciduous trees, where it feeds on small insects such as aphids.

NOTE

Damsel bugs suck the juices of aphids, caterpillars, and a range of soft-bodied insects. Nymphs seek their first, very small meal straight after hatching.

Lace Bugs

Tingidae

These small, greyish or brownish bugs are distinguished by the delicate lace-like or net-like patterning and sculpturing on the upper surface. The pronotum and front wings may be elaborately ridged and pitted, while the former can extend over the head like a hood, reaching to the sides and backwards to cover the scutellum. The antennae and rostrum have four segments.

HIDE *under the leaves or inside the flowers of herbaceous plants, mostly in open places; some species on trees and shrubs.*

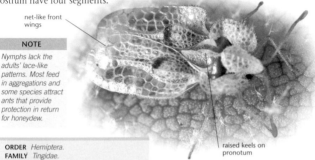

net-like front wings

NOTE

Nymphs lack the adults' lace-like patterns. Most feed in aggregations and some species attract ants that provide protection in return for honeydew.

raised keels on pronotum

ORDER *Hemiptera.*
FAMILY *Tingidae.*
NUMBER OF SPECIES *2,000.*
SIZE *2–4mm.*
FEEDING *Nymphs and adults: herbivores.*
IMPACT *Some species can be crop pests, causing yellow spots on foliage and leaf drop.*

CORYTHUCA CILIATA,
the Sycamore Lace Bug, which also attacks plane trees, can be a pest. It originated in North America and is now widespread in Europe.

Flower Bugs

Anthocoridae

Also known as minute pirate bugs, these tiny, flattened insects are blackish or brownish in colour, with paler markings. The body may be elongated or oval and shiny or dull. The head is pointed, the antennae have four segments, and the rostrum has three segments. Most species are fully winged; the rear part of the front wings has no closed cells and few or no veins.

OCCUR *on flowers, as the name suggests, but often in leaf litter, foliage, and fungi or under bark in woods.*

NOTE

These bugs feed on tiny insects, eggs, and larvae. A few species may be found in bird nests, bat caves, mammal burrows, grain stores, and houses.

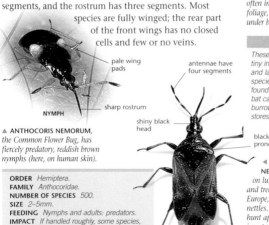

pale wing pads

antennae have four segments

sharp rostrum

NYMPH

shiny black head

black pronotum

▲ **ANTHOCORIS NEMORUM,**
the Common Flower Bug, has fiercely predatory, reddish brown nymphs (here, on human skin).

◄ **ANTHOCORIS NEMORUM** *lives on lush vegetation and trees throughout Europe, especially on nettles. The adults hunt aphids and soft insect prey.*

ORDER *Hemiptera.*
FAMILY *Anthocoridae.*
NUMBER OF SPECIES *500.*
SIZE *2–5mm.*
FEEDING *Nymphs and adults: predators.*
IMPACT *If handled roughly, some species, such as Anthocoris nemorum, will try to bite.*

Plant Bugs

Miridae

LIVE *in almost every habitat from ground level to the treetops.*

This family is the largest group of true bugs in the world. Plant bugs have a delicate structure and are variously coloured green, brown, red, and black, with a great diversity of markings. The rostrum and the antennae have four segments and the hind part of the front wings, or membrane, has one or two distinctive closed cells. Most species are fully winged, although short-winged and wingless forms occur. Diverse in their biology, plant bugs are mostly herbivores, eating seeds, fruit, leaves, and plant juices. Others are scavengers or are predators of aphids, mealy bugs, mites, and soft-bodied prey.

mainly green

◄ **LYGOCORIS PABULINUS,** *the Common Green Plant Bug, is a serious pest of a wide range of plants, including fruit such as raspberries, pears, and apples.*

brown membrane

orange-yellow patch on scutellum

▲ **CAMPLYONEURA VIRGULA** *is a tree-living predator that hunts bark lice, aphids, and other soft-bodied prey. Despite its fragile appearance, it can bite if handled.*

shiny red upperside

swollen and hairy segments

► **HETEROTOMA MERIOPTERA** *is recognizable by its antennae, the first two segments of which are swollen. It lives among nettles and other rank vegetation.*

▲ **PANTILIUS TUNICATUS** *feeds on hazel, birch, and alder trees. Adults are yellowish green when they first appear, becoming reddish and darker as they get older.*

pink veins

pale green legs

▼ **NOTOSTIRA ELONGATA** *is a common grass bug, found on rough, grassy verges. Females are green with a swollen abdomen; males are darker and more slender.*

swollen abdomen

♀

slender body

◄ **STENODEMA LAEVIGATUM** *has a slender, elongated body and can be found on a variety of grasses, where the nymphs and adults feed on the flower-heads and unripe seeds.*

ORDER *Hemiptera.*
FAMILY *Miridae.*
NUMBER OF SPECIES *7,000.*
SIZE *2–12mm.*
FEEDING *Nymphs and adults: herbivores, predators, scavengers.*
IMPACT *Several species attack crops.*

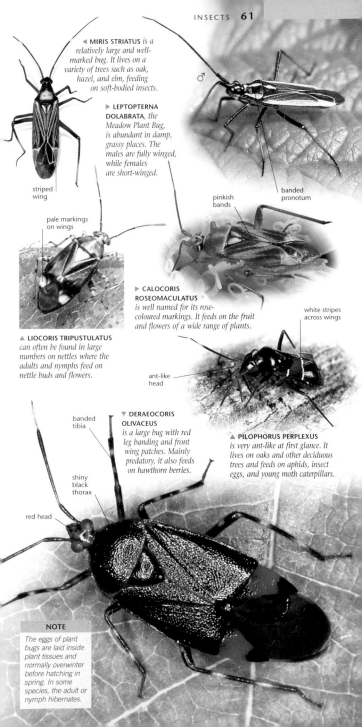

◀ **MIRIS STRIATUS** *is a relatively large and well-marked bug. It lives on a variety of trees such as oak, hazel, and elm, feeding on soft-bodied insects.*

▶ **LEPTOPTERNA DOLABRATA,** *the Meadow Plant Bug, is abundant in damp, grassy places. The males are fully winged, while females are short-winged.*

striped wing

pale markings on wings

banded pronotum

pinkish bands

▶ **CALOCORIS ROSEOMACULATUS** *is well named for its rose-coloured markings. It feeds on the fruit and flowers of a wide range of plants.*

white stripes across wings

ant-like head

▲ **LIOCORIS TRIPUSTULATUS** *can often be found in large numbers on nettles where the adults and nymphs feed on nettle buds and flowers.*

banded tibia

▼ **DERAEOCORIS OLIVACEUS** *is a large bug with red leg banding and front wing patches. Mainly predatory, it also feeds on hawthorn berries.*

shiny black thorax

red head

▲ **PILOPHORUS PERPLEXUS** *is very ant-like at first glance. It lives on oaks and other deciduous trees and feeds on aphids, insect eggs, and young moth caterpillars.*

NOTE

The eggs of plant bugs are laid inside plant tissues and normally overwinter before hatching in spring. In some species, the adult or nymph hibernates.

Bed Bugs

Cimicidae

FEED on their mammal and bird hosts at night; during the day, they hide in crevices, in and under wallpaper and skirting floorboards.

Unlike lice, these blood-sucking bugs do not keep in permanent contact with their hosts. They are oval and flattened in shape, with vestigial (very reduced) front wings and no hind wings. Generally orange or reddish brown in colour, they have a sparse covering of pale hairs. The head is not very large and carries the sharp rostrum, or beak, which lies in a groove along the underside of the body when not in use. The antennae have four segments.

lobe on pronotum

tiny vestigial wings

flattened, reddish brown body

CIMEX LECTULARIUS is a bed bug that does not live on its host; it feeds on blood at night, returning to hiding places during the day.

ORDER Hemiptera.
FAMILY Cimicidae.
NUMBER OF SPECIES 90.
SIZE 3–6mm.
FEEDING Nymphs and adults: parasites, blood-suckers.
IMPACT Parasites of mammals and birds.

Water Measurers

Hydrometridae

FOUND in quiet pools, marshes, and swamps, including stagnant and even brackish water. Stay at the water's edge or on floating plants.

Also called marsh-treaders, these delicate, reddish to dark brown bugs are very slender, with thread-like legs. The eyes are fairly large and bulge out from the sides of the elongated head. The antennae and rostrum have four segments. Most species are wingless, but short-winged or fully-winged forms occur in some species. Water measurers are slow-moving and take small prey.

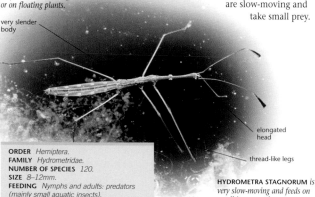

very slender body

elongated head

thread-like legs

ORDER Hemiptera.
FAMILY Hydrometridae.
NUMBER OF SPECIES 120.
SIZE 8–12mm.
FEEDING Nymphs and adults: predators (mainly small aquatic insects).
IMPACT Harmless.

HYDROMETRA STAGNORUM is very slow-moving and feeds on small insects and crustaceans such as water fleas.

Water Crickets

Veliidae

These bugs are also called small water striders and resemble pond skaters (below), but are generally much smaller, more robust, and have shorter, stouter legs. Most are brownish with orange undersides and orange or silver markings. The antennae and rostrum have four segments. Some species are fully-winged; others can be short-winged or wingless.

LIVE *among vegetation or on the surface of still or slow-moving water in ponds, lakes, and damp forests.*

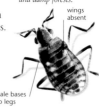

wings absent

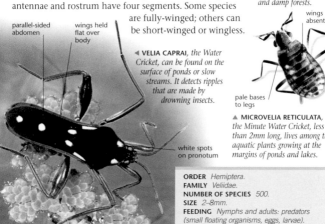

parallel-sided abdomen

wings held flat over body

◀ **VELIA CAPRAI**, *the Water Cricket, can be found on the surface of ponds or slow streams. It detects ripples that are made by drowning insects.*

pale bases to legs

▲ **MICROVELIA RETICULATA**, *the Minute Water Cricket, less than 2mm long, lives among the aquatic plants growing at the margins of ponds and lakes.*

white spots on pronotum

ORDER *Hemiptera.*
FAMILY *Veliidae.*
NUMBER OF SPECIES *500.*
SIZE *2–8mm.*
FEEDING *Nymphs and adults: predators (small floating organisms, eggs, larvae).*
IMPACT *Harmless.*

Pond Skaters

Gerridae

Also known as water striders, these fast-moving and often wingless bugs are adapted to living on the surface of water. They are dark brown or blackish, with a covering of velvety hairs. The antennae and rostrum have four segments. The front legs are short for grasping prey, while the middle and hind legs are more elongated. Ripple-sensitive hairs on the legs locate struggling prey.

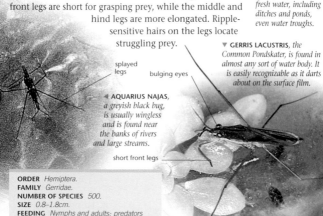

WALK *on the surface film of any available fresh water, including ditches and ponds, even water troughs.*

splayed legs

bulging eyes

▼ **GERRIS LACUSTRIS**, *the Common Pondskater, is found in almost any sort of water body. It is easily recognizable as it darts about on the surface film.*

◀ **AQUARIUS NAJAS**, *a greyish black bug, is usually wingless and is found near the banks of rivers and large streams.*

short front legs

ORDER *Hemiptera.*
FAMILY *Gerridae.*
NUMBER OF SPECIES *500.*
SIZE *0.8–1.8cm.*
FEEDING *Nymphs and adults: predators (dead or dying insects).*
IMPACT *Harmless.*

Water Scorpions

Nepidae

FOUND *in either still or slow-moving water, with some species in muddy shallows and others in deeper water.*

These brownish bugs are also known as water stick insects due to their shape. They may be oval, flattened with short legs, or cylindrical and elongated with relatively long legs. The head has rounded eyes and a short, curved rostrum. The front legs are modified for catching prey. There is a distinctive breathing siphon at the rear that may be as long as the body.

breathing siphon

enlarged femur

▼ **RANATRA LINEARIS,** *the yellowish brown Water Stick Insect, is a predator and attacks even small vertebrates.*

wings folded over broad body

narrow body

front legs gripping prey

▲ **NEPA CINEREA,** *or the Water Scorpion, has a long breathing siphon at its rear end. It also has powerful front legs.*

ORDER *Hemiptera.*
FAMILY *Nepidae.*
NUMBER OF SPECIES *250.*
SIZE *1.8–3cm.*
FEEDING *Nymphs and adults: predators.*
IMPACT *Generally harmless, but sometimes bite if handled.*

Saucer Bugs

Naucoridae

MOVE *slowly on the bottom of static or moving water bodies, or climb about on submerged vegetation.*

Also known as creeping water bugs, these flat, streamlined insects have a smooth, rounded or oval body. Most species are dark greyish green or brown. The front legs are adapted for capturing prey, with curved, sickle-like tibiae that fold back like a jack-knife on to the enlarged femora. The hind legs have rows of specialized swimming hairs.

head appears sunk into prothorax

NOTE

Saucer bugs lack a breathing siphon: supplies of oxygen are obtained at the water surface and retained in the space under the wings.

broad, flat body

ORDER *Hemiptera.*
FAMILY *Naucoridae.*
NUMBER OF SPECIES *400.*
SIZE *1–1.5cm.*
FEEDING *Nymphs and adults: predators (mainly larvae, crustaceans, snails).*
IMPACT *Occasionally bite if handled.*

hairs on legs

ILYOCORIS CIMICOIDES *or the Saucer Bug, is a flattened greyish green insect that has wings, but cannot fly. Instead, it uses the space beneath the wings to store air.*

Backswimmers

Notonectidae

These compact, wedge-shaped bugs swim upside-down in water and when resting at the surface they hang from the end of their abdomen. The surface of their back is typically pale-coloured and convex, with a ridge or keel running down the middle. Their underside is dark brown to black. The eyes are large, dark, and shiny. The stout rostrum and the very short antennae have four segments. Used for propulsion, the oar-like hind legs, are fringed with hairs.

Backswimmers are often called "water boatmen", but this name should be reserved for the Corixidae (p.66).

FAVOUR *still, open stretches of water such as lake margins, pools, and stream edges.*

short rostrum

dark underside

▶ **NOTONECTA LUTEA**
favours long-established water bodies. When not swimming it hangs from the surface film, its abdominal tip just breaking the surface.

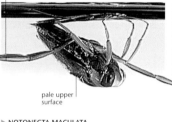

hair fringes

pale upper surface

◀ **NOTONECTA GLAUCA,**
the Common Backswimmer, is widespread and can be found in ponds, lakes, and even canals or ditches.

NOTE

The presence of these predators prevents egg-laying in certain mosquitoes, which can detect the chemical released in water by these bugs.

oar-like hind leg

mottled reddish wings

▶ **NOTONECTA MACULATA**
is found in the northern hemisphere and feeds on prey trapped by the surface film in temporary habitats.

pale pronotum

dark, shiny eyes

ORDER *Hemiptera.*
FAMILY *Notonectidae.*
NUMBER OF SPECIES 350.
SIZE 0.8–1.6cm.
FEEDING *Nymphs and adults: predators (varied prey up to size of small fish).*
IMPACT *May bite if handled.*

Water Boatmen

Corixidae

FOUND *in still and slow-moving water in ponds, lakes, and occasionally streams.*

Superficially similar to backswimmers (p.65), these streamlined bugs are generally dark reddish- or yellowish brown, often with fine transverse markings. The upper body surface is flattened without a central keel and the under body is pale. Corixids do not swim upside-down. The short head has large dark eyes, short antennae, and a short, stout rostrum. The front legs have scoop-shaped ends for feeding; the middle legs are used for holding plants; and the clawless back legs are fringed with hairs.

NOTE

While underwater, corixids carry bubbles of air under their wings where the concave, dorsal surface of the abdomen acts as a reservoir.

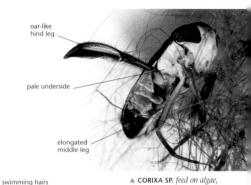

oar-like hind leg

pale underside

elongated middle leg

▼ **CORIXA PUNCTATA** *is common and has a wide distribution. Typically, the back is patterned and dark, while the underside is pale. This species flies and is attracted to lights at night.*

▲ **CORIXA SP.** *feed on algae, diatoms, and plant debris at the bottom of well-vegetated ponds, using their hair-fringed front legs to filter through the debris.*

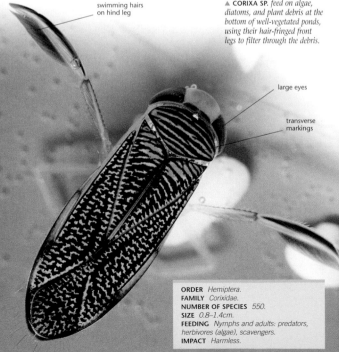

swimming hairs on hind leg

large eyes

transverse markings

ORDER *Hemiptera.*
FAMILY *Corixidae.*
NUMBER OF SPECIES 550.
SIZE *0.8–1.4cm.*
FEEDING *Nymphs and adults: predators, herbivores (algae), scavengers.*
IMPACT *Harmless.*

Cicadas

Cicadidae

Cicadas are blackish, brown, or green in colour, and may
have dark markings or be cryptically patterned. They are
recognizable by their blunt head, broadly tapered body
shape, and the loud songs made by males. The eyes are
large and the antennae are short. The longitudinal wing
veins do not reach the wing margins. Each species has a
unique song, usually produced by a pair of organs, called
tymbals, on the underside of the first abdominal segment.
Nymphs burrow into the soil after hatching, using their
strong front legs. They
take 4–17 years to reach
adulthood, crawling up
trees for their final moult.

OCCUR on a wide
range of host shrubs
and trees; nymphs live
underground on roots.

bulging eyes

NOTE

The characteristic
buzzing noise is
made by a stiff
membrane that is
rapidly clicked in
and out. Usually,
it is the males that
sing during the day.

stiff, clear
wings

▲ TIBICINA HAEMATODES feeds
on the sap of various trees. It is
found in central and southern
parts of Europe.

reddish wing
veins

◀ CICADETTA
MONTANA has three
spines on the inside
of the front femur.
It is found in scrub
and woodland.

dark thorax

black spots
on wings

grey body

▼ CICADA ORNI is
large, and distinctively
grey with small, dark
spots on the wings.

ORDER Hemiptera.
FAMILY Cicadidae.
NUMBER OF SPECIES 2,500.
SIZE 1.8–4.2cm.
FEEDING Nymphs and adults: herbivores.
IMPACT Can damage trees through feeding
and egg-laying.

Froghoppers

Cercopidae

These squat, round-eyed bugs are good jumpers and very similar to spittle bugs (below). Most species are brown, grey, or drab, but some are black with vivid red or orange markings. The head has rounded eyes and is narrower than the thorax, which can look hexagonal or angular. Like spittle bugs (below), the nymphs produce frothy excrement to reduce evaporation and provide protection from predators.

INHABIT well-vegetated areas such as woods, meadows, and scrub, occurring on a variety of shrubs, trees, and herbaceous plants.

◀ **CERCOPIS VULNERATA** *is a very conspicuous species, with bright warning coloration to deter potential predators.*

▼ **CERCOPIS ARCUATA** *is one of several similar-looking froghoppers widespread across Europe. In this species, males are larger than females.*

angular thorax

bold red markings

round spot

wavy red band

ORDER *Hemiptera.*
FAMILY *Cercopidae.*
NUMBER OF SPECIES *2,400.*
SIZE *0.5–2cm. Most under 1.4cm.*
FEEDING *Nymphs and adults: herbivores (plant juices); nymphs feed on root sap.*
IMPACT *Some species are crop pests.*

Spittle Bugs

Aphrophoridae

Spittle bugs vary from pale to dark brown with lighter mottling and markings. Some species have many colour forms. The head is almost as wide as the pronotum, the front of which is arched or curved forwards. The hind tibiae have one or two strong spines and a circle of smaller spines at their ends. These bugs are good jumpers.

COMMON in nearly all habitats on a wide range of woody and herbaceous plants.

variable colour and pattern

NOTE

Nymphs produce cuckoo spit: a frothy protective covering. This is made by blowing watery excrement through a modified anus.

CUCKOO SPIT

PHILAENUS SPUMARIUS, *the Meadow Spittle Bug or Common Froghopper, lives on many plants. The nymphs' foamy mass is a familiar sight in sheltered habitats.*

broad, thick-set head

ORDER *Hemiptera.*
FAMILY *Aphrophoridae.*
NUMBER OF SPECIES *850.*
SIZE *6–10mm.*
FEEDING *Nymphs and adults: herbivores (leaves, shoots, stems, and plant sap).*
IMPACT *Some species are minor crop pests.*

Treehoppers

Membracidae

Treehoppers, or thorn bugs, are mainly green or brown to blackish. They are easily recognized by the large pronotum, which extends sideways and backwards to cover part of the abdomen. The head, with hair-like antennae, is blunt, downward-facing, and much smaller than the pronotum. The enlarged hind legs allow these insects to make short jumps.

OCCUR *on all kinds of shrubs, trees, and other vegetation. Most are specific to a host plant.*

lateral extension

extended pronotum

▼ **STICTOCEPHALUS BISONIA**, *the Buffalo Treehopper, is a North American species now established in Europe.*

broad, horned pronotum

head tucked under

▲ **CENTROTUS CORNUTUS**, *the Horned Treehopper, has a very long projection on its pronotum that extends backwards.*

> **ORDER** Hemiptera.
> **FAMILY** Membracidae.
> **NUMBER OF SPECIES** 2,500.
> **SIZE** 6–10mm.
> **FEEDING** Nymphs and adults: herbivores.
> **IMPACT** The Buffalo Treehopper damages a variety of trees, including apple trees.

Planthoppers

Delphacidae

These small bugs are mostly brown or greenish. Their body is elongated and almost parallel-sided. The antennae are short and often arise from a small indentation on the lower edge of the eyes. A distinctive feature of these insects is a flat, moveable spur at the end of the hind tibiae. Most species have short-winged and fully winged forms.

ABUNDANT *at or near ground level in grassy areas, meadows, and woodland margins, especially near water.*

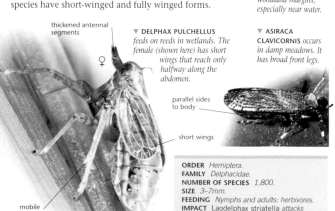

thickened antennal segments

♀

▼ **DELPHAX PULCHELLUS** *feeds on reeds in wetlands. The female (shown here) has short wings that reach only halfway along the abdomen.*

▼ **ASIRACA CLAVICORNIS** *occurs in damp meadows. It has broad front legs.*

parallel sides to body

short wings

mobile spur

> **ORDER** Hemiptera.
> **FAMILY** Delphacidae.
> **NUMBER OF SPECIES** 1,800.
> **SIZE** 3–7mm.
> **FEEDING** Nymphs and adults: herbivores.
> **IMPACT** Laodelphax striatella attacks wheat, maize, and oats.

Leafhoppers

Cicadellidae

ABUNDANT *virtually everywhere, especially in lush, well-vegetated habitats.*

Leafhoppers are generally slender with broad or triangular heads and large eyes. Many species are green or brown in colour and may have brightly striped markings. The body has parallel sides or tapers towards the rear end. One of the most characteristic features of these bugs is their excellent jumping ability. The hind legs are enlarged and the hind tibiae are slightly flattened and distinctive in having three or four regular rows of very conspicuous spines arranged along their length. All leafhoppers are herbivores: most species suck the juices of plants' phloem vessels (the main transport vessels in plants), while others suck the contents of individual plant cells.

▼ **EUPELIX CUSPIDATA** *occurs in dry, grassy areas and is recognized by its large, shovel-shaped head.*

spiny hind leg

front of head pointed

▼ **GRAPHOCEPHALA FENNAHI,** *the Candy-striped Leafhopper, is native to the USA but is now quite widespread in Europe on rhododendrons.*

black stripe through eye

▼ **LEDRA AURITA** *is a large, flat-bodied species with distinctive horns on the sides of the pronotum. It is well camouflaged against the lichen-covered bark of the oak trees on which it lives.*

net-like pattern of veins

camouflaged coloration

horns on pronotum

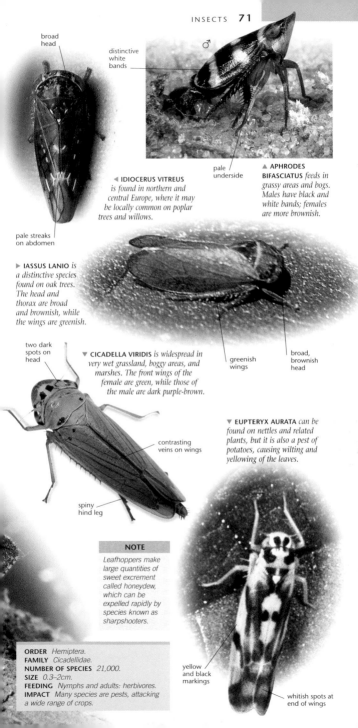

◀ **IDIOCERUS VITREUS** is found in northern and central Europe, where it may be locally common on poplar trees and willows.

broad head

distinctive white bands

♂

pale underside

pale streaks on abdomen

▲ **APHRODES BIFASCIATUS** feeds in grassy areas and bogs. Males have black and white bands; females are more brownish.

▶ **IASSUS LANIO** is a distinctive species found on oak trees. The head and thorax are broad and brownish, while the wings are greenish.

two dark spots on head

▼ **CICADELLA VIRIDIS** is widespread in very wet grassland, boggy areas, and marshes. The front wings of the female are green, while those of the male are dark purple-brown.

greenish wings

broad, brownish head

contrasting veins on wings

spiny hind leg

▼ **EUPTERYX AURATA** can be found on nettles and related plants, but it is also a pest of potatoes, causing wilting and yellowing of the leaves.

NOTE

Leafhoppers make large quantities of sweet excrement called honeydew, which can be expelled rapidly by species known as sharpshooters.

yellow and black markings

whitish spots at end of wings

ORDER Hemiptera.
FAMILY Cicadellidae.
NUMBER OF SPECIES 21,000.
SIZE 0.3–2cm.
FEEDING Nymphs and adults: herbivores.
IMPACT Many species are pests, attacking a wide range of crops.

Plant Lice, Greenfly, or Aphids

Aphididae

These small, slow-moving, soft-bodied insects make up one of the most destructive insect families. They reproduce with phenomenal speed and cause immense damage to crops and garden plants. Most species are green, but some may be pink, black, or brown. The antennae have between four and six segments. The pear-shaped abdomen ends in a short, pointed tail – the cauda – and usually has a pair of projecting tubes, or cornicles, from which a defensive secretion can be produced. In some species the entire body may be coated with a white waxy secretion. When present, the wings are held tent-like over the body and are clear or sometimes have darkish markings; the hind wings are much smaller than the front wings.

FOUND on almost all plant types, including the roots, in most habitats.

▼ **THECABIUS AFFINIS** is a woolly aphid which causes distortion and folding of the leaves of poplar and also the leaves of some buttercups.

NOTE

Aphid excrement (honeydew) is rich in sugar, attracting ants which feed on it. In return the ants protect the aphids from enemies such as parasitic wasps.

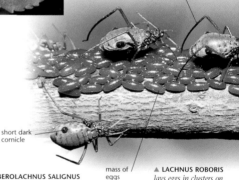

long hind legs

short dark cornicle

mass of eggs

▼ **TUBEROLACHNUS SALIGNUS** is a large and widespread aphid occurring on willow. The back of the fourth abdominal segment has a single projection called a tubercle.

▲ **LACHNUS ROBORIS** lays eggs in clusters on oak branches. The aphids live in colonies and are attended by ants, which feed on their honeydew.

▼ **PERIPHYLLUS ACERICOLA** lives on the leaves of sycamore trees. The nymphs have a resting period in the height of summer.

winged adult

aggregation of aphids

two or three spirals

▲ **PEMPHIGUS SPIROTHECAE**
lives inside elongated, spiral galls, which it induces on the leaf stalks of Black Poplar.

▶ **MACROSIPHUM ROSAE**, *the Rose Aphid, may be pink or green. This common garden pest feeds on roses in spring; later, a winged generation flies to teasels or scabious.*

pear-shaped abdomen

green individual

long cornicles

▼ **TUBERCULOIDES ANNULATUS** *is a small yellow, greenish, or pinkish aphid that lives underneath oak leaves.*

drop of honeydew

soft body

▼ **APHIS FABAE**, *the Black Bean Aphid or Blackfly, attacks beans and other plants during the summer.*

black body with short cornicles

ORDER *Hemiptera.*
FAMILY *Aphididae.*
NUMBER OF SPECIES *2,250.*
SIZE *2–5mm.*
FEEDING *Nymphs and adults: herbivores.*
IMPACT *Many species are pests of crops and garden plants.*

Adelgids

Adelgidae

FOUND on coniferous trees such as larch, spruce, and fir.

These very small, pale brown insects are closely related to aphids (pp.72–73), with fully winged and wingless forms. The front wings have a darkened pterostigma and very few veins. The blunt-ended abdomen has no abdominal projections, or cornicles. Wingless females have a covering of powdery wax.

> **NOTE**
>
> The galls induced by adelgids damage and deform young conifers, and can ruin the shape of those grown as a crop for Christmas.

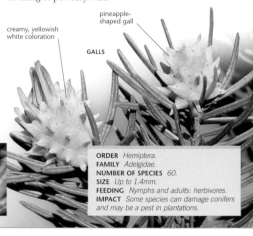

creamy, yellowish white coloration

pineapple-shaped gall

GALLS

ADELGES ABIETIS lays its eggs at the base of needles near the ends of branches, inducing the growth of a gall.

very dry, tough old gall

ORDER Hemiptera.
FAMILY Adelgidae.
NUMBER OF SPECIES 60.
SIZE Up to 1.4mm.
FEEDING Nymphs and adults: herbivores.
IMPACT Some species can damage conifers and may be a pest in plantations.

Jumping Plant Lice

Psyllidae

OCCUR in a variety of habitats wherever their host plants occur.

These variously coloured bugs look superficially like small leafhoppers (pp.70–71), but have longer antennae with ten segments. The mouthparts take the form of a beak in three segments. Both sexes have two pairs of broadly oval wings held together roof-like over the body. The front wings may be clear or clouded with smoky patterns. The hind legs are slightly enlarged, enabling psyllids to jump.

wings held together, roof-like, over body

striped thorax

> **NOTE**
>
> Psyllids lay stalked eggs on or inside plants, where some may induce the formation of galls or deform the leaves. The nymphs live in aggregations.

red eyes

dark marks at wingtips

PSYLLOPSIS FRAXINI is a boldly marked plant louse that lives on ash trees. The feeding activities of its woolly larvae cause the edges of leaves to become reddish and swollen.

ORDER Hemiptera.
FAMILY Psyllidae.
NUMBER OF SPECIES 1,500.
SIZE 2–4mm.
FEEDING Nymphs and adults: herbivores.
IMPACT Some species are pests of pear and apple trees; others attack carrots and onions.

Phylloxerans

Phylloxeridae

Phylloxerans are minute, greenish or pale brown, aphid-like insects. Females may be winged or wingless, although the former are rare in Europe. When present, the white wings are held flat over the body at rest. The head has a pair of small dark eyes and the antennae have three segments. The abdomen has no "tails" (cauda) or projections (cornicles).

LIVE *on the roots and leaves of susceptible plants, such as oak trees and vines.*

small yellowish eggs

adult female

NOTE

Vine Phylloxerans, Viteus vitifoliae, were introduced from North America in 1858–1862, causing immense damage to Europe's vineyards.

ORDER *Hemiptera.*
FAMILY *Phylloxeridae.*
NUMBER OF SPECIES 55.
SIZE *0.8–1.6mm.*
FEEDING *Nymphs and adults: herbivores.*
IMPACT Viteus vitifoliae *is an extremely serious pest of cultivated vines.*

PHYLLOXERA QUERCUS *is one of several similar species found on oak tree foliage. Early in the year, the wingless females can be seen on the undersides of leaves, surrounded by eggs.*

Whiteflies

Aleyrodidae

Whiteflies are very small, white, moth-like insects with two pairs of relatively broad wings that are usually white with a distinctive dusting of white, powdery wax. The hind and front wings are of the same size and, when resting, are held horizontally over the body. The head has a pair of antennae with seven segments. Females lay their eggs on tiny stalks on the undersides of leaves.

THRIVE *on both wild and cultivated plants in a range of habitats, including greenhouses.*

▼ **TRIALEURODES VAPORARIORUM,** *the Glasshouse Whitefly, is a pest of glasshouse crops such as tomatoes.*

▼ **ALEYRODES PROLETELLA** *attacks brassica species such as cabbages. It can be found at almost any time of year.*

white legs and antennae

white wings covered in powdery wax

empty skin

freshly emerged adult

dark spots on wings

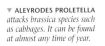

ORDER *Hemiptera.*
FAMILY *Aleyrodidae.*
NUMBER OF SPECIES 1,200.
SIZE 1–3mm.
FEEDING *Nymphs and adults: herbivores.*
IMPACT *May be pests of glasshouse crops and plants in the cabbage family.*

Soft, Wax, and Tortoise Scales

Coccidae

FOUND *on host plants, both in the wild and in fields, orchards, and greenhouses; also feed on houseplants.*

These scale insects are very variable in form, but females are usually oval and flattened with a hard, smooth, or waxy body. Wax-covered species appear white, while others may be brownish. Females are almost always sedentary on their host plant. They reproduce mainly by parthenogenesis, without the need for males. Males, which are rarely seen, may be winged or wingless and are short-lived.

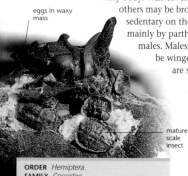

eggs in waxy mass

mature scale

mature scale insect

◀ **PULVINARIA REGALIS** *is known as the Horse Chestnut Scale; females reproduce without males and lay as many as 3,000 eggs.*

reddish brown body

▶ **PARTHENOLECANIUM CORNI**, *the Brown Scale, is a pest of some fruit trees and around 300 ornamental plant species.*

ORDER *Hemiptera.*
FAMILY *Coccidae.*
NUMBER OF SPECIES *1,250.*
SIZE *2–6mm.*
FEEDING *Nymphs and adults: herbivores.*
IMPACT *Many species are pests of crops, gardenplants, and houseplants.*

Mealy Bugs

Pseudococcidae

OCCUR *wherever their host plant grows, in the wild or in glasshouses.*

Unlike related families of scale insects, mealy bugs have functional legs at all stages of their life history (in others, there is a sedentary stage). The sexes are very different. Females are elongated, wingless, covered with a wax coating, and possess sucking mouthparts. Males have a pair of wings, so look like typical insects, but lack developed mouthparts.

NOTE

Mealy bugs are sap-suckers and infest all parts of their host plant. Some species lay eggs in a mass of downy wax; others give birth to live nymphs.

long tail filaments

soft, waxy body

PSEUDOCOCCUS LONGISPINUS, *the Long-tailed Mealy Bug, is a pest of apple, pear, and citrus trees and also attacks crops and garden and house plants.*

ORDER *Hemiptera.*
FAMILY *Pseudococcidae.*
NUMBER OF SPECIES *2,000.*
SIZE *1.5–4mm.*
FEEDING *Nymphs and adults: herbivores.*
IMPACT *Some species are pests of crops, gardenplants, and houseplants.*

Common Thrips

Thripidae

The wings of these pale yellow, brown, or blackish thrips are narrower than in banded thrips and their ends are more pointed. The body appears flattened and the antennae usually have seven or eight segments. The front wings may have one or two longitudinal veins. In females the ovipositor curves downwards, not upwards.

FAVOUR the leaves and flowers of a vast range of plants, often including crops.

▼ **TAENIOTHRIPS SIMPLEX** can be a serious pest on Gladiolus and related flowers, leaving pale speckled marks on the flowers.

▶ **LIMOTHRIPS CEREALIUM**, or the Grain Thrips, is a cosmopolitan species that attacks grasses and cereals.

pale wings

wings not overlapped at rest

flattened body

ORDER Thysanoptera.
FAMILY Thripidae.
NUMBER OF SPECIES 1,500.
SIZE 0.7–2mm.
FEEDING Nymphs and adults: herbivores.
IMPACT Some species cause serious damage to field crops by feeding.

Tube-tailed Thrips

Phlaeothripidae

Most of these small insects are dark brown or black, but they often have lighter or mottled wings. They are more stout-bodied than other thrips and the end of the abdomen is distinctly pointed. The antennae have eight segments. The wings overlap each other when folded and have no longitudinal veins. The females do not have an ovipositor.

LIVE on a wide variety of herbaceous plants, shrubs, and trees in well-vegetated places.

nymph

wings overlapped at rest

PHLAEOTHRIPS ANNULIPES is a common species that feeds by sucking the juices from fungal hyphae and spores.

tube-like tail

ORDER Thysanoptera.
FAMILY Phlaeothripidae.
NUMBER OF SPECIES 2,700.
SIZE 1.5–4.5mm.
FEEDING Nymphs and adults: herbivores, fungi-feeders, predators.
IMPACT Harmless.

Alderflies

Sialidae

Alderflies are day-flying insects with stout, dark brown to blackish grey bodies and a brownish or greyish tint to the wings, which are held together, tent-like, over the body. The head is blunt with large eyes and long, thread-like antennae. The pronotum is squarish. The front and hind wings are similarly sized with prominent dark veins that are not forked close to the wing margins.

LARVAE

The aquatic larvae have powerful jaws and seven pairs of feathery abdominal gills on each side.

SIALIS LUTARIA, *the Alderfly, is often seen in late spring and early summer, perching on trees and other plants near to or overhanging water.*

thread-like antennae

drab, dusky wings

egg mass

NOTE

The short-lived females lay masses of eggs on waterside reeds or stones. The newly-hatched larvae crawl into the water on their well-developed legs.

ORDER Megaloptera.
FAMILY Sialidae.
NUMBER OF SPECIES 75.
SIZE 1.8–2.2cm.
FEEDING Larvae: predators (small aquatic insects and worms). Adults: non-feeding.
IMPACT Harmless.

Snakeflies

Raphidiidae

▼ **RAPHIDIA NOTATA** *inhabits deciduous woodland, especially with oak trees. The larvae are often found in rotting stumps.*

These shiny, dark brown insects have an elongated prothorax on which the head can be raised. The head is broadest across the eyes and tapers behind. The clear wings have a pterostigma and a prominent network of veins, which fork close to the wing margins. Females are a little larger than males, with a long ovipositor.

♀

elongated prothorax

clear wings with dark veins

▶ **RAPHIDIA XANTHOSTIGMA** *lives in woodland, where the larvae hunt small insects under bark. The sexes are identical, except for the female's ovipositor.*

head narrows to rear

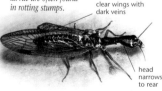

LARVAE

The slender larvae lack abdominal gills and have short, curved mandibles like those of adults.

long ovipositor

ORDER Raphidioptera.
FAMILY Raphidiidae.
NUMBER OF SPECIES 85.
SIZE 1.4–2cm.
FEEDING Larvae and adults: predators (mainly aphids and soft-bodied insects).
IMPACT Harmless.

Osmylids

Osmylidae

Sometimes called giant lacewings, these brownish insects are scavengers that also feed on nectar. They are relatively slender-bodied and have distinctively broad wings with dark spots and blotches and many cross veins; despite their large wings, they are weak fliers. The reddish head has prominent eyes and slender, thread-like antennae. The prothorax is slightly elongated. The legs are yellowish brown.

CONFINED *to the margins of streams in woodland.*

LARVAE

The semiaquatic larvae are predators and are armed with straight, needle-like mouthparts.

dark blotches on wings

pale yellow legs

◄ **OSMYLUS CHRYSOPS** *flies after dark near slow-flowing streams, and rests near the water on foliage during the day.*

dark, spotted wings

▲ **OSMYLUS FULVICEPHALUS,** *the Giant Lacewing, prefers wet, shady places such as woodland streams. Adults hunt prey after dark; larvae feed on insect larvae among mosses.*

ORDER *Neuroptera.*
FAMILY *Osmylidae.*
NUMBER OF SPECIES *150.*
SIZE *3.8–5.2cm (wingspan).*
FEEDING *Larvae: predators. Adults: liquid-feeders (nectar), scavengers.*
IMPACT *Harmless.*

Mantispids

Mantispidae

These relatively small insects are also known as mantisflies because their front legs are exactly like those of praying mantids (p.40). The first segment of the thorax is very elongated and the enlarged front femora are armed with spines onto which the tibiae can fold. The wings are held together over the body, not flat as in mantids.

FOUND *mainly in warm, lightly wooded areas of central and southern Europe.*

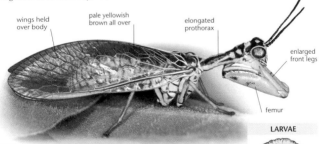

wings held over body

pale yellowish brown all over

elongated prothorax

enlarged front legs

femur

LARVAE

The larvae have three pairs of legs on the thorax, and become maggot-like as they mature.

ORDER *Neuroptera.*
FAMILY *Mantispidae.*
NUMBER OF SPECIES *300.*
SIZE *2–2.5cm (wingspan).*
FEEDING *Larvae: parasites, predators (spiders' eggs). Adults: predators (insects).*
IMPACT *Harmless.*

MANTISPA STYRIACA *has highly distinctive enlarged front legs for catching small flies. It is found in dry, shaded habitats in central and southern Europe.*

Brown Lacewings

Hemerobiidae

These drab, brownish or greyish insects hold their oval wings roof-like over the body. The wings can be clear or dusky and are mottled or speckled with dark brown spots and markings. There are many long veins; those close to the wing margins are forked. The antennae are thread-like and may be as long as the wing length.

COMMON *inhabitants of deciduous woods, hedgerows, and gardens; mainly on low vegetation.*

hooked wingtip

slender antennae

wings hide body at rest

translucent brown wings

LARVAE

The larvae taper at both ends and lack warts or tubercles. They possess stout, curved mandibles.

▶ **HEMEROBIUS HUMULINUS** *is one of several similar-looking species with pale or translucent wings found in broadleaved woodland.*

▲ **DREPANEPTERYX PHALAENOIDES** *resembles a dead leaf when perched among foliage, due to its brown, wavy-edged wings.*

ORDER *Neuroptera.*
FAMILY *Hemerobiidae.*
NUMBER OF SPECIES *900.*
SIZE *1.6–2.4cm (wingspan).*
FEEDING *Larvae and adults: predators.*
IMPACT *Beneficial, as they consume large numbers of aphids and other insect pests.*

Common Lacewings

Chrysopidae

These delicate insects generally have a green body and wings and are sometimes known as green lacewings. The wings are often iridescent with delicate tints of pink, green, and blue, have many forked veins, lack markings, and are held roof-like over the body. The eyes are golden, brassy, or reddish and appear to shine. The antennae are long and slender.

FOUND *in all types of vegetation, including along woodland edges and hedgerows.*

green tint to wings

zigzag vein

long antennae

brassy, shining eye

LARVAE

Stouter and broader than the larvae of brown lacewings, with more slender mandibles, and warts and tubercles on their backs.

eggs on stalks

EGGS

CHRYSOPA CARNEA *is common anywhere with enough vegetation and a plentiful supply of aphids. It often enters attics and outbuildings to hibernate.*

ORDER *Neuroptera.*
FAMILY *Chrysopidae.*
NUMBER OF SPECIES *1,600.*
SIZE *2–3.8cm (wingspan).*
FEEDING *Larvae and adults: predators.*
IMPACT *Prey on insect pests; Chrysopa carnea is reared as a biological control agent.*

Antlions

Myrmeleontidae

Adult antlions are large, slender-bodied, mostly nocturnal insects resembling damselflies (pp.23–24). The body varies from yellow or green to dark brown, with darker markings. The head is much broader than the pronotum and the eyes are conspicuous. The thickened antennae are club-ended. The long, narrow, richly-veined wings are clear or marked with brown or black.

OCCUR *mainly in sand dunes, scrub grassland, and open woodland in central and southern Europe.*

mottled wings

LARVAE

In many species, the powerful-jawed larvae dig pits in loose sand to trap prey, waiting at the bottom for victims.

clubbed antennae

hairy thorax

▼ EUROLEON NOSTRAS *is a fairly widespread species of warm, shaded places. Adults closely resemble damselflies, but with thicker antennae.*

lightly spotted wings

▲ PALPARES LIBELLULOIDES *is diurnal and looks like a large, fluttering dragonfly. It lives in Mediterranean scrub.*

ORDER *Neuroptera.*
FAMILY *Myrmeleontidae.*
NUMBER OF SPECIES *1,000.*
SIZE *6–11cm (wingspan).*
FEEDING *Larvae: predators (insects). Adults: mainly predators, also herbivores (pollen).*
IMPACT *Harmless.*

Owlflies

Ascalaphidae

Owlflies are reddish brown to black with stout bodies, large, dark eyes, and distinctive richly-veined wings. They resemble dragonflies (pp.25–28), but hold their wings roof-like over the body at rest. The slender antennae are very long and club-ended. The wings have dark brown, yellow, and white markings, often at the bases or tips.

LIVE *in a variety of grassland habitats and in warm, dry woodland.*

long, clubbed antennae

broad pale area on wings

dark, hairy body

◀ LIBELLOIDES LONGICORNIS *lives in southern Europe and catches insect prey on the wing in warm, grassy areas.*

yellow veins

LARVAE

Owlfly larvae have oval, flat bodies with expansions at the abdomen sides, and wide-opening jaws.

ORDER *Neuroptera.*
FAMILY *Ascalaphidae.*
NUMBER OF SPECIES *450.*
SIZE *4–6cm (wingspan).*
FEEDING *Larvae and adults: predators.*
IMPACT *Harmless.*

▲ LIBELLOIDES COCCAJUS *is hairy and black, with bright yellow legs. The upper surface of the hind wings has a large dark yellow area, reaching from the base to the rear angle.*

Ground Beetles

Carabidae

These beetles are active hunters with long, slender legs and powerful jaws; most species are nocturnal. They may be dull or shiny. The majority are brown or black, often with a metallic sheen, although a few species are green, red, and black or have yellow or green markings. The body is long, parallel-sided, and slightly flattened, with striations running along the elytra. The head has thread-like antennae, conspicuous eyes, and toothed jaws. The head, thorax, and abdomen tend to be clearly differentiated.

LARVAE

Most larvae live in soil or debris and are black or dark brown with long bodies that taper at both ends. They use enzymes to digest prey, then suck in the resulting liquid.

4 pale spots

▲ **DROMIUS QUADRIMACULATUS** *is easily recognized by its dark elytra with four yellowish brown spots. It hides under tree bark.*

reddish legs

▲ **HARPALUS RUFIPES** *occurs in cultivated land, waste ground, and gardens. It forages after dark for seeds, sometimes attacking strawberries.*

▼ **BRACHINUS CREPITANS** *hides under stones in dry locations. Like all bombardier beetles, it can fire hot chemicals from its rear end in defence.*

bluish or greenish elytra

reddish brown head, thorax, and legs

flattened body

▲ **NEBRIA BREVICOLLIS** *is found in many habitats, but is most common under stones and logs in woodland and hedgerows.*

metallic violet sheen

▼ **CARABUS VIOLACEUS**, *better known as the Violet Ground Beetle, is a large, widespread species that feeds on a range of invertebrates, including slugs. It is commonest in woodland.*

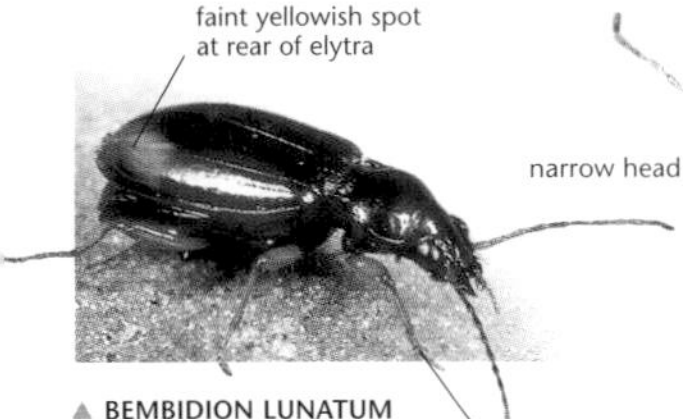

faint yellowish spot
at rear of elytra

narrow head

▲ **BEMBIDION LUNATUM**
*is common and widespread near
water across Europe. There are
many similar species.*

yellow legs

▲ **CYCHRUS CARABOIDES**
*crawls under moss and bark on
old tree stumps in woodland. It
emerges after dark to hunt snails.*

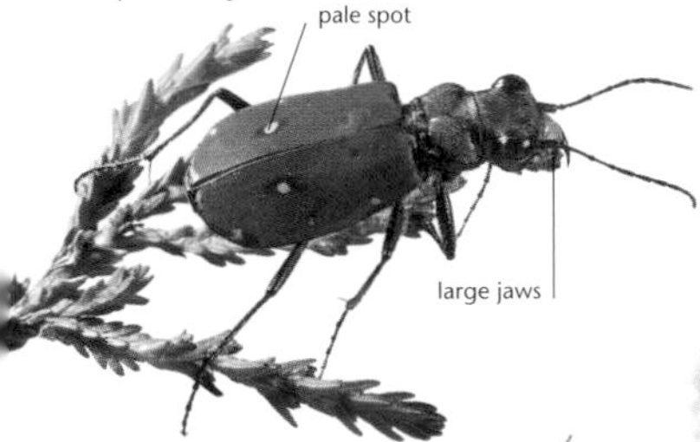

pale spot

◀ **CICINDELLA CAMPESTRIS**, *the
Green Tiger Beetle, is an active
flier and very fast runner. It likes
hot, sunny, open areas.*

large jaws

pale, circular
spots

bronze sheen
to elytra

large
eyes

▲ **ELAPHRUS RIPARIUS** *is
unmistakable due to its rows
of pale spots. It forages on bare
ground near ponds and streams.*

broad
body

▲ **NOTIOPHILUS BIGUTTATUS**
*is a squat species with very large
eyes. It is a specialist predator
of springtails, which it catches
in its strong jaws.*

bronze
sheen

long, thin
antennae

prominent
striations

▲ **CALOSOMA INQUISITOR**
*inhabits deciduous woodland.
Like other Calosoma species, it
hunts caterpillars among foliage.*

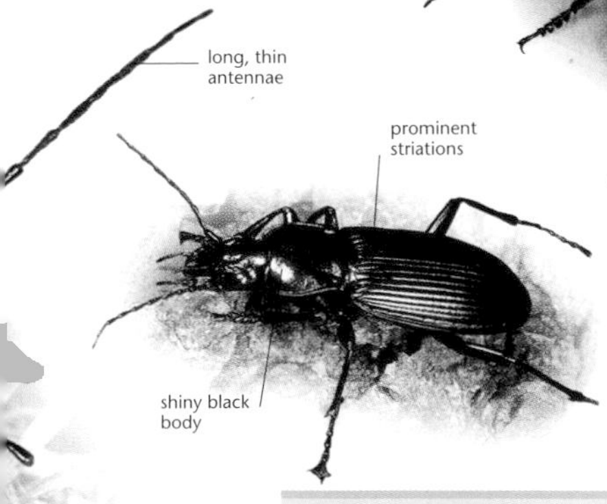

◀ **PTEROSTICHUS NIGER**
*is one of numerous similar
nocturnal species that forage on
the ground for prey or carrion.*

shiny black
body

NOTE

*The larvae of
Tiger beetles live
in vertical burrows
in sandy or gravel
soil. They seize
any passing
insects and drag
them down to
eat them.*

ORDER *Coleoptera.*
FAMILY *Carabidae.*
NUMBER OF SPECIES *29,000.*
SIZE *0.2–2.8cm.*
FEEDING *Immatures and adults: predators,
scavengers; some species partly herbivores.*
IMPACT *Many species help to control pests.*

Crawling Water Beetles

Haliplidae

These smooth-bodied, reddish- or yellowish brown beetles are oval and very rounded in side view. The head, which is much narrower than the thorax, has protruding eyes and shortish antennae. The hind legs are quite long with swimming hairs on the tarsi, while the front and middle legs are shorter with swimming hairs on the tibiae.

LIVE *along the margins of well-vegetated, silty pools, ponds, reedbeds, streams, and slow-flowing rivers.*

LARVAE

The herbivorous, aquatic larvae are elongated with well-developed legs. The body segments become gradually broader towards the rear and there is a longish tail.

dark striations on elytra

strong, reddish orange legs

NOTE
Crawling water beetles are able to store a layer of air on the underside of the body using the first segment of the hind legs, which is broad and plate-like.

HALIPLUS IMMACULATUS *is one of many very similar species that can be found in wetlands all over Europe. These beetles have a broad, convex body shape that tapers towards the rear.*

ORDER *Coleoptera.*
FAMILY *Haliplidae.*
NUMBER OF SPECIES *220.*
SIZE *3–5mm.*
FEEDING *Larvae and adults: herbivores (algae).*
IMPACT *Harmless.*

Screech Beetles

Hygrobiidae

Screech beetles are reddish brown with dark markings, smooth, and broadly oval. The upperside of the body is convex, the underside even more so. The head is fairly broad, with bulging eyes. The legs have special swimming hairs on the tibiae, femora, and tarsi; when swimming, the legs are used alternately. When disturbed, adults make a distinctive squeaking noise by rubbing the end of the abdomen against a ridged structure on the wing cases.

OCCUR *in ponds and other waterbodies with muddy bottoms.*

convex surface

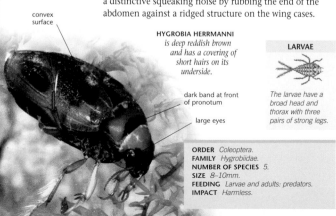

HYGROBIA HERRMANNI *is deep reddish brown and has a covering of short hairs on its underside.*

dark band at front of pronotum

large eyes

LARVAE

The larvae have a broad head and thorax with three pairs of strong legs.

ORDER *Coleoptera.*
FAMILY *Hygrobiidae.*
NUMBER OF SPECIES *5.*
SIZE *8–10mm.*
FEEDING *Larvae and adults: predators.*
IMPACT *Harmless.*

Burrowing Water Beetles

Noteridae

Yellowish brown to reddish brown, smooth-bodied, and very rounded in side view, these small beetles are recognizable by being broader at the front than the rear. The antennae are often swollen towards the tip, especially in males. The front tibiae have a comb-like structure at their ends and a single, large spur. The tibiae of the middle and hind legs have swimming hairs and when the beetles swim they use their legs together.

INHABIT *well-vegetated pools and lake edges, including stagnant or even brackish water.*

NOTE

These beetles are related to members of the Dytiscidae family (pp.86–87), but unlike them, are broader towards the front (not the rear) of the body.

LARVAE

The pale, elongated larvae live partially buried in mud and move using their short, stocky legs.

NOTERUS CLAVICORNIS *is one of a number of similar small, convex beetles that feed on small invertebrates in shallow water.*

broad, rounded head

short, thick antennae

reddish brown coloration

ORDER *Coleoptera.*
FAMILY *Noteridae.*
NUMBER OF SPECIES *160.*
SIZE *2–5mm.*
FEEDING *Larvae: predators. Adults: predators, herbivores (algae).*
IMPACT *Harmless.*

Whirligig Beetles

Gyrinidae

These oval, streamlined beetles are typically black, with a bronze or steel-blue sheen in some species. The head has short antennae and the eyes are divided into upper and lower portions for vision above and below water. The long front legs are adapted for grasping prey, while the middle and hind legs are short, flat, and paddle-like.

FOUND *on the surface of ponds, pools, slow-moving streams, and sluggish rivers.*

LARVAE

The yellowish or greenish larvae are elongated with sharp mouthparts and narrow heads.

hairy upper surface

grasping front leg

▲ **ORECTOCHILUS VILLOSUS,** *the Hairy Whirligig, has short, pale hairs on its dorsal surface. It is narrower and more elongated than other whirligig beetles.*

▶ **GYRINUS SP.** *are dark, shiny beetles that swim rapidly in circles on the water.*

smooth, dark elytra

ORDER *Coleoptera.*
FAMILY *Gyrinidae.*
NUMBER OF SPECIES *750.*
SIZE *4–8mm.*
FEEDING *Larvae and adults: predators, scavengers.*
IMPACT *Harmless.*

Predatory Diving Beetles

Dytiscidae

These voracious predators have smooth, streamlined, shiny bodies. Many species are reddish to dark brown or black, but some have extensive yellowish or reddish bands, spots, and other markings. The head appears to be partly sunk into the pronotum and the antennae are thread-like. The hind legs are flattened and paddle-like with fringes of long hairs and often are larger than the other legs. The males of some species have swollen structures on the front tarsi, used to hold the females' smooth backs during mating.

LARVAE

Due to their highly predatory nature, the larvae are often called water tigers. They are elongated with hairy legs and large, curved jaws and obtain air at the water surface.

▶ **GRAPHODERUS ZONATUS** *is recognized by the black bands at the front and rear of the pronotum, as well as the extensive mottling on the elytra.*

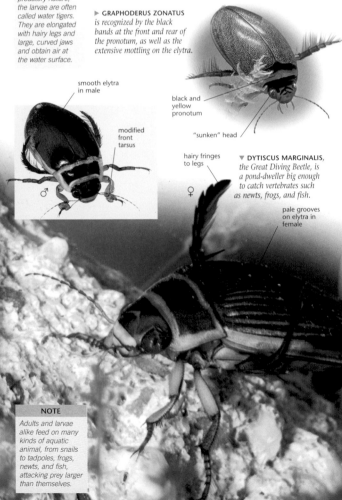

smooth elytra in male

black and yellow pronotum

modified front tarsus

"sunken" head

hairy fringes to legs

♂

♀

▼ **DYTISCUS MARGINALIS,** *the Great Diving Beetle, is a pond-dweller big enough to catch vertebrates such as newts, frogs, and fish.*

pale grooves on elytra in female

NOTE

Adults and larvae alike feed on many kinds of aquatic animal, from snails to tadpoles, frogs, newts, and fish, attacking prey larger than themselves.

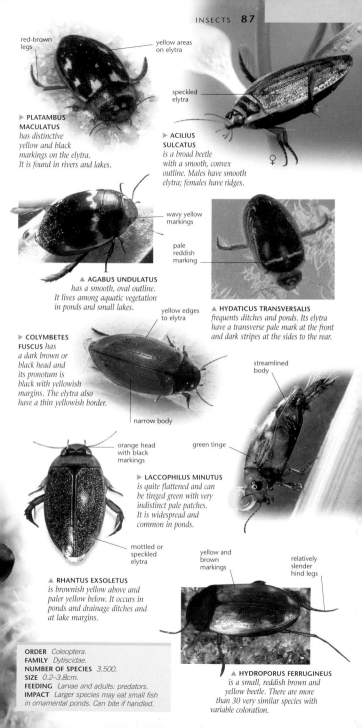

red-brown legs

yellow areas on elytra

speckled elytra

▶ **PLATAMBUS MACULATUS** *has distinctive yellow and black markings on the elytra. It is found in rivers and lakes.*

▶ **ACILIUS SULCATUS** *is a broad beetle with a smooth, convex outline. Males have smooth elytra; females have ridges.*

♀

wavy yellow markings

pale reddish marking

▲ **AGABUS UNDULATUS** *has a smooth, oval outline. It lives among aquatic vegetation in ponds and small lakes.*

yellow edges to elytra

▲ **HYDATICUS TRANSVERSALIS** *frequents ditches and ponds. Its elytra have a transverse pale mark at the front and dark stripes at the sides to the rear.*

▶ **COLYMBETES FUSCUS** *has a dark brown or black head and its pronotum is black with yellowish margins. The elytra also have a thin yellowish border.*

streamlined body

narrow body

orange head with black markings

green tinge

▶ **LACCOPHILUS MINUTUS** *is quite flattened and can be tinged green with very indistinct pale patches. It is widespread and common in ponds.*

mottled or speckled elytra

yellow and brown markings

relatively slender hind legs

▲ **RHANTUS EXSOLETUS** *is brownish yellow above and paler yellow below. It occurs in ponds and drainage ditches and at lake margins.*

ORDER *Coleoptera.*
FAMILY *Dytiscidae.*
NUMBER OF SPECIES *3,500.*
SIZE *0.2–3.8cm.*
FEEDING *Larvae and adults: predators.*
IMPACT *Larger species may eat small fish in ornamental ponds. Can bite if handled.*

▲ **HYDROPORUS FERRUGINEUS** *is a small, reddish brown and yellow beetle. There are more than 30 very similar species with variable coloration.*

Water Scavenger Beetles

Hydrophilidae

FOUND *in freshwater habitats; also occur in dung, soil, and decaying vegetation.*

Most of these beetles live in water, carrying air under their wing cases and on their body surface. Oval in shape, they are black, brown, or yellowish. The upperside of the body is convex and smooth; the underside is flat with a covering of short, velvety hairs that looks silvery underwater. The maxillary palps (a pair of sensory mouthparts) are typically longer than the short, club-ended antennae.

LARVAE

Surface-breathing or equipped with gills, the predatory larvae may have warty or hairy backs.

▶ **HYDROPHILUS PICEUS,** *the Great Silver Diving Beetle, is up to 5cm long. A sharp spine on its underside can pierce human skin.*

faint striations

long palp

smooth, rounded outline

◀ **HYDROCHARA CARABOIDES** *is quite a good swimmer and, like* Hydrophilus piceus *(above), it lays its eggs in floating cocoons. It is found in weedy, still water.*

ORDER *Coleoptera.*
FAMILY *Hydrophilidae.*
NUMBER OF SPECIES *2,000.*
SIZE *0.4–4.8cm.*
FEEDING *Larvae: predators. Adults: mainly scavengers, also predators.*
IMPACT *Harmless.*

Hister Beetles

Histeridae

LIVE *in dung, carrion, and leaf litter, under bark, and in tunnels of wood-boring insects.*

These tough-bodied beetles are oval or rounded, with a convex profile; some are flattened for living under bark. Many are shiny black or have reddish markings. The head is sunk into the prothorax. The antennae are elbowed; the front tibiae have teeth for digging.

LARVAE

The square-headed larvae are extremely long, with roughly parallel body sides.

▼ **HISTER QUADRIMACULATUS** *is compact and slightly flattened, with short elytra. It lives in horse and cow manure.*

▶ **HISTER UNICOLOR** *feeds on dung and preys on insect larvae developing in carcasses.*

red markings join at side of elytra

shiny black elytra

elytra do not cover abdomen

ORDER *Coleoptera.*
FAMILY *Histeridae.*
NUMBER OF SPECIES *3,000.*
SIZE *1–16mm.*
FEEDING *Larvae and adults: predators (mostly fly maggots and beetle grubs).*
IMPACT *Harmless.*

Carrion Beetles

Silphidae

Many of these slightly flattened, soft-bodied beetles are black or brown, often with yellow, red, or orange markings. The body surface may be dull or shiny and some have a roughened texture or ridges. The head, which is much narrower than the thorax, has round, slightly bulging eyes, strong, curved mandibles, and short, club-ended antennae. The legs of most species are strong and spiny.

OCCUR on the ground close to carcasses; also under dung and in rotting fungi in damp, shady woodland.

LARVAE

The larvae are long and flattened, with a small head and broad pronotum. In some species, they are fed on regurgitated carrion by the parents.

ridged elytra

narrow head

▶ **SILPHA ATRATA** *has a narrow, elongated head to allow it to feed on snails inside their shells. This dark, shiny species lives in dense woodland and other damp places.*

red pronotum

NOTE

Carrion beetles have an excellent sense of smell for locating corpses. Two adults are strong enough to move an animal as large as a rat in order to bury it.

▶ **OICEOPTOMA THORACICUM**, *which is identifiable by its black, ridged elytra and reddish pronotum, occurs in dung, carrion, and rotting fungi.*

wavy orange-red bands across elytra

clubbed antennae

short elytra

▲ **NICROPHORUS INVESTIGATOR** *is one of several species of burying beetle with distinctive reddish orange to yellowish bands on the elytra. It is very quickly attracted to the smell of decaying animals.*

▼ **NICROPHORUS HUMATOR** *retains the characteristic shape of a burying beetle, despite its all-black elytra.*

orange, clubbed antennae

ORDER *Coleoptera.*
FAMILY *Silphidae.*
NUMBER OF SPECIES *250.*
SIZE *0.9–3.2cm.*
FEEDING *Larvae and adults: scavengers, predators, herbivores.*
IMPACT *Major recyclers of animal corpses.*

Rove Beetles

Staphylinidae

OFTEN *found in dung and carrion, and also in soil, fungi, leaf litter, decaying plant matter, and ant nests.*

Most rove beetles are small and smooth with elongated, parallel-sided bodies and black or brown coloration. Some species have bright colours, a sculptured surface, or dense body hairs. The head is squarish with long, sharp jaws that cross over each other; the antennae are short and thread-like. All species have distinctively short elytra that expose five or six of the abdominal segments. The full-sized hind wings are folded under the elytra when not in use. The flexible abdomen may be raised in a defensive posture.

raised abdomen

matt black all over

◄ **STAPHYLINUS OLENS,** *the Devil's Coach Horse, displays alarm by raising its abdomen and opening its jaws.*

red-orange spot

broad head

▲ **STENUS BIMACULATUS** *lives in marshy places. It secretes a surface tension-reducing chemical from its rear end to move over water.*

▶ **TACHYPORUS HYPNORUM** *is one of many similar small species with tapering bodies and red elytra.*

tapering abdomen

short red elytra

▼ **EMUS HIRTUS,** *a large rove beetle of central and southern Europe, has unmistakable yellow, grey, and black hairs.*

hind wings folded beneath short elytra

large jaws

orange-red prothorax

bluish green sheen to elytra

▼ **PHILONTHUS FIMETARIUS** *eats fly maggots and beetle larvae. There are numerous very similar species.*

flexible abdomen

black end to femur

LARVAE

The larvae are dark and elongated, with short antennae and cerci. Some larvae produce odours to trick ants into taking them into their nests and feeding them.

▶ **PAEDERUS LITTORALIS** *is a flightless, orange and black species found in riverine habitats.*

NOTE

Most rove beetles can fly well. Smaller species tend to be diurnal, whereas large species are generally nocturnal. A few species are associated with ants.

ORDER Coleoptera.
FAMILY Staphylinidae.
NUMBER OF SPECIES 27,000.
SIZE 0.8–2.6cm.
FEEDING Larvae: predators, scavengers. Adults: predators, scavengers, herbivores.
IMPACT Harmless.

Stag Beetles

Lucanidae

These beetles are typically large, shiny, robust insects with black or reddish brown coloration, although some species are smaller or have a bluish sheen. The males of most species have greatly enlarged, toothed mandibles; females are often smaller and have proportionally smaller mandibles. The antennae are elbowed or bent in the middle with a terminal club of three or four expanded, flattened segments. The elytra are smooth and shiny with faint striations. Stag beetles are attracted to lights at night, when they may wander far from woodland.

OCCUR *in deciduous woodland, especially with mature trees and decaying timber.*

horn on head

▲ **SINODENDRON CYLINDRICUM** *has a very rounded shape. The male has a horn on its head and the front of its pronotum is toothed.*

▲ **DORCUS PARALLELIPIDEDUS,** *the Lesser Stag Beetle, has a relatively large head and prothorax. The male's jaws are curved but not enlarged.*

large prothorax

▶ **PLATYCERUS CARABOIDES** *is a flattened beetle with a bluish sheen in males (greenish in females). Its larvae develop in rotting beech or oak.*

clubbed antennae

bluish sheen

massive mandibles

elbowed antennae

large head

▶ **LUCANUS CERVUS,** *the Stag Beetle, is unmistakable. It has declined in recent years due to the loss of rotten wood as a breeding site for its larvae.*

smooth brown elytra

LARVAE

NOTE

During courtship, male stag beetles fight pitched battles with rivals. Their jaws have teeth that lock onto a rival's pronotum to try to flip it upside down.

The C-shaped larvae have strong legs on the thorax. They feed on decaying logs and tree stumps and may take several years to develop.

ORDER *Coleoptera.*
FAMILY *Lucanidae.*
NUMBER OF SPECIES *1,300.*
SIZE *1.4–6.4cm.*
FEEDING *Larvae: wood-feeders (decaying timber). Adults: liquid-feeders.*
IMPACT *May try to bite if handled.*

Dor Beetles

Geotrupidae

FOUND *beneath dung of all kinds and in carrion, decaying wood, and fungi.*

These stout insects are broadly oval and rounded. They are brown or black, shiny, and often have a metallic greenish, blue, or purplish sheen. In many species, males have tooth-like projections and horns on the head and thorax. The jaws are large and clearly visible; the club-ended antennae have 11 segments but are not elbowed. The elytra have obvious lengthwise grooves, while the tibiae of the broad front legs are armed with strong teeth for digging.

convex body ♂

slender horn

▲ **ODONTAEUS ARMIGER**
is a small, dark, convex-bodied beetle. The male has upturned lobes while the female is reddish brown without lobes.

three horns on thorax

spines for digging ♂

very faint grooves

iridescent body

▲ **TYPHAEUS TYPHOEUS**,
the Minotaur Beetle, digs deep into sandy soil beneath piles of sheep and rabbit droppings.

▼ **GEOTRUPES STERCORARIUS**
is often infested with parasitic mites. It is black, often with a shiny metallic blue or purplish sheen underneath.

▲ **GEOTRUPES VERNALIS**
generally has an iridescent bluish sheen and has less noticeable striations on the elytra than Geotrupes stercorarius. It is found in areas with light soil.

clubbed antennae

LARVAE

The pale C-shaped larvae is found under animal dung in burrows. Larval development can take many months. They make noises by rubbing their legs on their body.

NOTE

Adult dor beetles dig tunnels many centimetres deep below dung and carry pieces of it down to provide a food source for their larvae.

ORDER *Coleoptera.*
FAMILY *Geotrupidae.*
NUMBER OF SPECIES *600.*
SIZE *1–2.5cm.*
FEEDING *Larvae and adults: scavengers, dung-feeders.*
IMPACT *Harmless, beneficial.*

Click Beetles or Skip Jacks

Elateridae

The most remarkable feature of these elongated, narrow-bodied beetles is their ability, when lying on their backs, to click loudly as they throw themselves into the air. Most are brownish or black, although a few are greenish. The antennae are quite long and slender, but may have a comb-like appearance. The rear angles of the pronotum are sharp and often extend backwards to form an acute point that meets the rounded shoulders of the elytra.

LIVE on foliage, under bark, and in leaf litter, rotting wood, and soil.

patterns of hair on pronotum and elytra

▶ **PROSTERNON TESSELLATUM**
is black with a bronze sheen and has irregular patterns of pale hair on the pronotum.

faint circular mark

black head and pronotum

broad reddish brown band on elytra

▲ **AMPEDUS BALTEATUS**
is distinctive as the front two-thirds of the elytra are reddish brown while the rear one-third is blackish brown. The larvae develop in rotten wood.

dark central stripe

▶ **MELANOTUS VILOSUS**
is usually shiny black with a sparse covering of short grey hair. The larvae are found in rotting wood.

▲ **SERICUS BRUNNEUS**
is reddish brown with a central dark stripe running down the pronotum. The larvae live in the soil of cooler regions.

shiny black elytra with grey hair

broad head

▼ **ATHOUS HAEMORRHOIDALIS**
is one of the commonest European click beetle species and is found in a wide range of habitats. The larvae are herbivorous.

yellow-brown hairs on elytra

LARVAE

Often known as wireworms for their slender, elongated, cylindrical shape, and tough bodies, click beetle larvae are commonly found in rotten wood, under bark, or soil.

NOTE

The beetles can "flick" themselves upwards at an amazing 300 times the acceleration of gravity. The loud click and movement frightens predators.

ORDER Coleoptera.
FAMILY Elateridae.
NUMBER OF SPECIES 8,500.
SIZE 0.2–3cm.
FEEDING Larvae: scavengers, herbivores, predators. Adults: herbivores.
IMPACT May be pests of crops and pasture.

Scarab Beetles and Chafers

Scarabaeidae

OCCUR *in a huge range of places, including decaying wood, fungi, carrion, dung, flowers, vegetation, bark, and the nests of mammals and social insects.*

Scarabs and chafers comprise a very large group of beetles and there is enormous variation in shape and size between species. The body colour varies from dull brown and black through red, yellow, and orange to metallic blues and greens. Despite this variety, a single character can identify these beetles: the antennae, which have between eight and ten segments and end in a distinctive club. The club is made up of three to seven flat, moveable, plate-like flaps, which can be separated or folded together. In many species the males have horns, used to fight for mates.

LARVAE

The larvae are white grubs with strong mandibles and a C-shaped body. Many live in the soil and feed on roots; others are found in dung, rotten wood, and decaying matter.

black, convex-shaped body

curved horn

▶ **COPRIS LUNARIS,** *the Horned Dung Beetle, has a distinctive horn on the head and a large, flat-fronted pronotum. Both sexes dig brood chambers in sandy soil.*

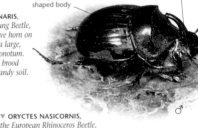

♂

dull brown elytra

small projection on head

♀

▼ **ORYCTES NASICORNIS,** *the European Rhinoceros Beetle, is a large species found in central and southern Europe, where it breeds in rotting wood and piles of mouldering sawdust.*

three blunt projections on pronotum

♂

shiny chestnut-brown elytra

◀ **POLYPHYLLA FULLO**, the Pine Chafer, is quite scarce and inhabits pine woods in central and southern Europe.

flaps on antennae

♂

shiny green

▶ **CETONIA AURATA**, the Rose Chafer, is a broad and somewhat flattened beetle that is often shiny green with white markings.

thin white markings

yellowish brown elytra

▲ **AMPHIMALLON SOLSTITIALIS** is called the Summer Chafer as it can be seen flying in swarms around the tops of trees on June evenings.

white hairs on thorax

dark brown overall

head rounded at front

▲ **APHODIUS RUFIPES** is one of many similar-looking beetles attracted to fresh cow, sheep, and horse dung. These species do not burrow or bury, but simply lay their eggs in the dung where it is.

reddish brown elytra

▲ **PHYLLOPERTHA HORTICOLA**, the Garden Chafer, can damage the leaves and buds of apple and pear trees by chewing them; its larvae eat the roots of grasses, including cereals.

5 to 7 segments in antennal club

♂

white hairs on elytra

▶ **MELOLONTHA MELOLONTHA**, the Common Cockchafer, is also known as the May Bug since the adult emerges around this time. It flies around tree tops and is attracted to lights.

huge horn

long hairs on head and thorax

bee-like markings on abdomen

NOTE

Dung beetles are extremely important recyclers in many regions. They clear away and bury vast amounts of dung, returning valuable nutrients to the soil.

ORDER Coleoptera.
FAMILY Scarabaeidae.
NUMBER OF SPECIES 20,000.
SIZE 0.2–15cm.
FEEDING Larvae: scavengers, fungi-feeders. Adults: liquid-feeders (nectar).
IMPACT A few species are serious pests.

▲ **TRICHIUS FASCIATUS**, the Bee Beetle, can be yellow or orange, but always has black markings and a very hairy body. Its larvae develop in rotting wood.

Jewel Beetles

Buprestidae

Jewel beetles are among the most beautiful of all insects and fly rapidly on sunny days. Many species are brightly coloured metallic green, blue, and red with attractive markings in the form of stripes, bands, and spots, although a few species are dull brown, or black. Jewel beetles are tough-bodied and bullet-shaped, tapering towards the rear end. The head appears bent downwards, the eyes are large, and the short antennae are slender or slightly toothed. Jewel beetles look rather like broad-bodied click beetles (p.93), but unlike that family they cannot jump.

FOUND in deciduous and coniferous woods, especially with dead trees or fallen timber, in which the larvae often develop.

black elytra with bluish purple sheen

pale yellow patches on elytra

pale stripe on pronotal margin

body tapers at rear

▲ **PTOSIMA 11-MACULATA** is easily recognized by the conspicuous orange spots on the pronotum and elytra. The larvae bore in the wood of certain fruit trees (Prunus).

▲ **BUPRESTIS NOVEMMACULATA**, the Painted Borer, seen here mating, develops as a larva inside the wood of coniferous trees such as larch, spruce, and pine.

lengthwise ridges on elytra

▶ **CHALCOPHORA MARIANA** is a fairly broad jewel beetle with noticeable ridges down the elytra. The larvae develop inside dead or fallen pine trees.

entirely green body

iridescent green elytra

rainbow stripes on pronotum

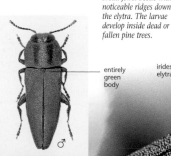

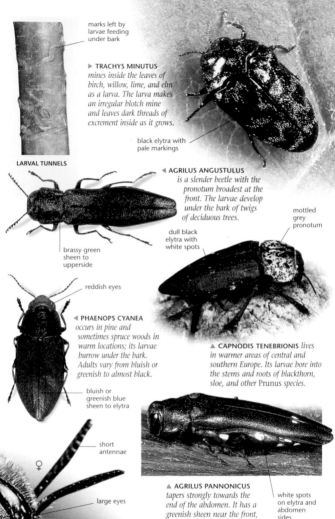

marks left by larvae feeding under bark

▶ **TRACHYS MINUTUS** *mines inside the leaves of birch, willow, lime, and elm as a larva. The larva makes an irregular blotch mine and leaves dark threads of excrement inside as it grows.*

black elytra with pale markings

LARVAL TUNNELS

◀ **AGRILUS ANGUSTULUS** *is a slender beetle with the pronotum broadest at the front. The larvae develop under the bark of twigs of deciduous trees.*

mottled grey pronotum

dull black elytra with white spots

brassy green sheen to upperside

reddish eyes

◀ **PHAENOPS CYANEA** *occurs in pine and sometimes spruce woods in warm locations; its larvae burrow under the bark. Adults vary from bluish or greenish to almost black.*

▲ **CAPNODIS TENEBRIONIS** *lives in warmer areas of central and southern Europe. Its larvae bore into the stems and roots of blackthorn, sloe, and other Prunus species.*

bluish or greenish blue sheen to elytra

short antennae

♀

large eyes

▲ **AGRILUS PANNONICUS** *tapers strongly towards the end of the abdomen. It has a greenish sheen near the front, becoming bluish at the rear.*

white spots on elytra and abdomen sides

◀ **ANTHAXIA HUNGARICA** *is small but has striking coloration, different in each sex. The male is green and the female has a multicoloured pronotum. Both sexes are purplish underneath.*

LARVAE

Known as flathead borers due to their clubbed body shape, the larvae have small heads sunk into a very broad, expanded prothorax. Their legs are short or absent.

NOTE

Jewel beetles lay their eggs in wood and the larvae chew tunnels with an oval cross section in tree roots and trunks. Weak or dying trees are usually chosen.

ORDER *Coleoptera.*
FAMILY *Buprestidae.*
NUMBER OF SPECIES *14,000.*
SIZE *0.2–3.5cm.*
FEEDING *Larvae: wood-feeders, herbivores. Adults: herbivores, nectar-feeders.*
IMPACT *Many species are pests of orchards.*

Net-winged Beetles

Lycidae

These soft-bodied, black and red or reddish brown beetles, derive their common name from the net-like pattern of cells on the wing cases of many species. They appear typically elongated and parallel-sided or slightly expanded towards the rear. The head, with conspicuous, rounded eyes, is usually hidden from above by the pronotum, which may have shallow depressed areas bounded by ridges.

INHABIT woodland and well-vegetated habitats, often in sunny areas with umbelliferous flowers.

DICTYOPTERA AURORA *has bright red elytra and segmented pronotum, which almost covers the head.*

head hidden by pronotum

sunken pits

soft, ribbed elytra

LARVAE

The larvae live under the bark of trees and eat beetle larvae, and small grubs.

ORDER *Coleoptera.*
FAMILY *Lycidae.*
NUMBER OF SPECIES *3,500.*
SIZE *0.5–1.5cm.*
FEEDING *Larvae: scavengers, predators. Adults: non-feeders, liquid-feeders (nectar).*
IMPACT *Harmless.*

Spider Beetles

Ptinidae

The common name of these small brownish beetles refers to the rounded, spider-like appearance of the females of many species. The head and prothorax are narrower than the elytra and this clear division gives them what resembles a "waist". The legs are long and quite slender. Males are more elongated and beetle-like.

FOUND in a variety of habitats, especially woodland and inside buildings.

NOTE

A few species in this family can cause damage in houses as they attack dry materials such as leather and textiles while some can be pests of stored grain.

long antennae

hood-like pronotum

patterns of white scales on elytra

ORDER *Coleoptera.*
FAMILY *Ptinidae.*
NUMBER OF SPECIES *500.*
SIZE *3–5mm.*
FEEDING *Larvae and adults: scavengers.*
IMPACT *A few species are pests in houses and of stored products.*

PTINUS SEXPUNCTATUS *has dark elytra with six irregular white spots, although some of the spots are fused together.*

LARVAE

The larvae feed on seeds and other dry plant parts. Fully grown larvae burrow into wood to pupate.

Fireflies and Glow-worms

Lampyridae

Once seen, the sight of fireflies emitting pulses of eerie greenish light as they fly through the night air is never forgotten. These slightly flattened, parallel-sided beetles are generally drab brown, but may have paler markings of red or yellow. The head, which is small with slender antennae, is concealed by the large, hood-like pronotum. Males are fully winged and the wing cases are soft and rather hairy. The females of some species look like the flattened larvae and lack wings.

FOUND *on vegetation in woods, hedgerows, meadows, and damp grassland.*

NOTE

These insects produce light by a chemical reaction in luminous organs. The flashing is used to attract a mate and is specific to each species.

dull brownish black back

pale spot on pronotum

♂

head hidden by pronotum

◀ **LAMPROHIZA SPLENDIDULA** *males look very different from the females. The females are wingless while the dull brown males are fully winged.*

wings absent

♀

LARVAE

The broad, flattened larvae are predatory and attack snails, using their narrow head and elongate, flattened body, to push inside as they feed.

light-emitting organs

▼ **LAMPYRIS NOCTILUCA**, *the Glow-worm, inhabits grassland. The female flashes to attract males.*

flattened body

dull brown elytra

pale at pronotum margins

LARVA

large eyes

ORDER *Coleoptera.*
FAMILY *Lampyridae.*
NUMBER OF SPECIES *2,000.*
SIZE *0.8–1.8cm.*
FEEDING *Larvae: predators. Adults: non-feeding, predators.*
IMPACT *Harmless.*

Soldier Beetles

Cantharidae

OCCUR *on flowers and other vegetation in grassland, woodland edges, and hedgerows.*

These beetles may have been named after the black and red coloration and contrasting markings of the commonest species, reminiscent of 18th- and 19th-century military uniforms. Soldier beetles are elongate, nearly parallel-sided, and have soft bodies. The head has curved, sharp jaws and relatively long, slender antennae. The pronotum is relatively short and squarish; the wing cases of some species are short and do not reach the abdomen's tip.

LARVAE

The larvae appear similar to those of ground beetles (pp.82–83), with flattened bodies and a fine, velvety covering of short hair.

dark elytra

black spot on pronotum

red base to antennae

◀ **CANTHARIS FUSCA** *is largely black but for the reddish pronotum with a black patch at the front.*

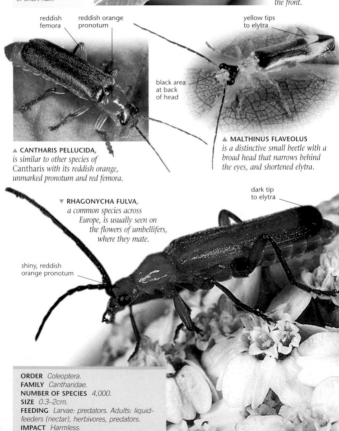

reddish femora

reddish orange pronotum

yellow tips to elytra

black area at back of head

▲ **MALTHINUS FLAVEOLUS** *is a distinctive small beetle with a broad head that narrows behind the eyes, and shortened elytra.*

▲ **CANTHARIS PELLUCIDA,** *is similar to other species of Cantharis with its reddish orange, unmarked pronotum and red femora.*

dark tip to elytra

▼ **RHAGONYCHA FULVA,** *a common species across Europe, is usually seen on the flowers of umbellifers, where they mate.*

shiny, reddish orange pronotum

ORDER *Coleoptera.*
FAMILY *Cantharidae.*
NUMBER OF SPECIES *4,000.*
SIZE *0.3–2cm.*
FEEDING *Larvae: predators. Adults: liquid-feeders (nectar), herbivores, predators.*
IMPACT *Harmless.*

Skin, Larder, and Museum Beetles

Dermestidae

Beetles in this family are small and typically broadly oval and rounded in side view. Most species are dull brown or black in colour, but others may appear variegated. They are often thickly covered with white, yellow, brown, or red scales or hair that form spots or delicate patterns. The head is mostly concealed by the pronotum, into which it fits neatly. The short, club-ended antennae can be concealed in grooves on the underside of the thorax and are often hard to see.

SCAVENGE in all kinds of places, such as bird nests, rodent burrows, fur, stored food, and museum collections.

LARVAE

The larvae are very hairy and the long hair tufts of many species produce nettle-like rashes in sensitive people. Anthrenus larvae are commonly called woolly bears.

◄ **ANTHENUS VERBASCI** is also known as the Varied Carpet Beetle. It is a small rounded beetle with distinctive patterns of white, yellow, and black scales.

variegated pattern of scales

rounded, convex body

sombre scale patterns

◄ **ANTHRENUS FUSCUS** lives mainly in sheds, outbuildings, and stone walls where the females lay eggs on dead insects.

pale front half of elytra

dark rear half of abdomen

► **DERMESTES LARDARIUS**, the Bacon or Larder Beetle is a dry carrion feeder but will also eat dried meat, fish, skins, and a large range of other stored produce.

white patches on rear of pronotum

rounded body outline

NOTE

The larvae feed on a range of organic materials, including spices and carpets. They may destroy entire museum collections of biological material.

► **ATTAGENUS PELLIO**, known as the Two-spotted Carpet Beetle or Fur Beetle, can be a serious domestic pest; it is also found outdoors.

white spots on elytra

ORDER Coleoptera.
FAMILY Dermestidae.
NUMBER OF SPECIES 800.
SIZE 2–10mm.
FEEDING Larvae: scavengers. Adults: liquid-feeders (nectar), herbivores (pollen).
IMPACT Pests of stored items and textiles.

Furniture and Drugstore Beetles

Anobiidae

NATIVE *to woodland, but thrive in all kinds of artificial wooden structures, both outside and in buildings.*

These small, hairy, light brown to black beetles are better known to many people as woodworm, although this name strictly refers to the grub-like larvae of the wood-boring species. The adults are typically elongated and cylindrical in shape, and, from the side, the head appears partly hooded by the pronotum. The antennae have eight to eleven segments, with the last three lengthened or expanded. The legs are short and can be pulled into special grooves on the underside of the body.

▼ **ANOBIUM PUNCTATUM** *is very common in trees and structural timbers alike. Its larvae are called woodworm.*

branched antennae

fine hairs on upper surface

♂

NOTE

Feeding larvae bore circular tunnels into dry or dead wood. The adults tend to emerge in May and June, leaving small exit holes and neat piles of wood dust.

exit holes

DAMAGED WOOD

◄ **PTILINUS PECTINICORNIS** *occurs all over central Europe and sometimes attacks furniture. Antennae are branched in males and more saw-like in females.*

humped pronotum

pattern of white hairs

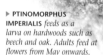

▶ **PTINOMORPHUS IMPERIALIS** *feeds as a larva on hardwoods such as beech and oak. Adults feed at flowers from May onwards.*

LARVAE

The white, soft-bodied, grub-like larvae have very small legs and antennae.

▼ **XESTOBIUM RUFOVILLOSUM**, *the Deathwatch Beetle, attacks oak as a larva. Adults make tapping noises to attract a mate.*

hood-like pronotum extends over head

ORDER *Coleoptera.*
FAMILY *Anobiidae.*
NUMBER OF SPECIES *1,500.*
SIZE *2–8mm.*
FEEDING *Larvae: scavengers, wood-feeders. Adults: scavengers, non-feeding.*
IMPACT *May damage furniture and timbers.*

Powder-post Beetles

Lyctidae

These beetles are small and slender in shape and brown in colour. The head has rounded, prominent eyes and antennae with eleven segments, of which the last two form a small club. The family's common name refers to the fine, powdery material that is all that is left after the larvae have burrowed into the sapwood of certain hardwoods.

SEEN *in dead and dying trees in woodland, and seasoned wood indoors.*

NOTE

Larvae bore in the sapwood of hardwoods such as oak or elm with high starch content and leave their tunnels packed with very fine powdery dust.

LARVAE

The larvae are white, quite hairless, and slightly curved. They bear three pairs of short legs.

LYCTUS BRUNNEUS *is very widespread. Females have long ovipositors to lay their eggs in cracks and fissures.*

elongated body

antennal club made of two segments

ORDER *Coleoptera.*
FAMILY *Lyctidae.*
NUMBER OF SPECIES *100.*
SIZE *3–7mm.*
FEEDING *Larvae and adults: wood-feeders.*
IMPACT *A few species are serious pests of wood.*

Ship-timber Beetles

Lymexylidae

These soft-bodied beetles are characteristically elongated, with parallel sides. The wing cases are shorter than the body, usually leaving the last two or three abdominal segments exposed. Males differ from the slightly larger females in that their eyes are larger and sometimes touch each other and the last segment of the maxillary palps may be enlarged and feathery.

COMMON *in parkland and old woodland, on dead wood which has usually lost its bark.*

HYLECOETUS DERMESTOIDES *is common on dead or diseased trees in central Europe. The head and thorax are brown in females and shiny black in males.*

black head and thorax

reddish brown overall

♂

darker end to elytra

♀

LARVAE

The slender larvae have a prominent prothorax and a highly distinctive, toughened spiny appendage on the last segment of the abdomen.

ORDER *Coleoptera.*
FAMILY *Lymexylidae.*
NUMBER OF SPECIES *60.*
SIZE *0.8–1.6cm.*
FEEDING *Larvae: wood-feeders, fungi-feeders. Adults: non-feeding.*
IMPACT *Lymexylon navale damages oak.*

Chequered Beetles

Cleridae

FOUND on the foliage of trees and woody plants; some live on carrion and stored animal products.

Although some species can be drab brown or yellowish brown, most chequered beetles are brightly coloured and patterned in red, yellow, blue, and black. The elongated and slightly flattened body is typically soft and very hairy. The head is large and quite elongated with prominent eyes and antennae that can be clubbed or slightly comb-like. The legs are very hairy and the second, third, and fourth segments of the tarsi are distinctively heart-shaped. Most species are predators as adults, although some feed on pollen.

irregular red bands

◀ **TRICHODES ALVEARIUS** is one of several similarly marked species that can often be seen feeding on flowers in central and southern Europe.

hairy head and pronotum

clubbed antennae

hairy legs

pale spots on elytra

LARVAE

Typically cylindrical and slender, the larvae may have bright coloration and be quite hairy. Many species prey on the larvae of jewel, bark, and longhorn beetles.

▶ **OPILO MOLLIS** is a brownish beetle found in woodland, where it and its larvae eat the grubs of bark beetles and various other wood-boring insects.

downturned head

▼ **TILLUS ELONGATUS** is found on the trunks of broad-leaved trees. The female has a red pronotum; the male is all-black. The larvae prey on beetle grubs.

black head

▼ **THANASIMUS FORMICARIUS** has very distinctive markings. It can sometimes be found on the trunks of conifers, especially pine.

pale, wavy bands

black, elongated elytra

red pronotum

♀

ORDER Coleoptera.
FAMILY Cleridae.
NUMBER OF SPECIES 3,500.
SIZE 4–16mm.
FEEDING Larvae: predators, scavengers.
Adults: predators, liquid-feeders, herbivores.
IMPACT Some species damage stored foods.

Soft-winged Flower Beetles

Melyridae

These beetles are narrow and elongated with a soft and flattened body. Many are brightly coloured in green and red and can be quite hairy. The head is typically short and broad with conspicuous eyes and slender antennae that have less than 11 segments. When disturbed, red sac-like swellings appear at the sides of the thorax and abdomen.

THRIVE *in woodland, meadows, grassland, and hedgerows.*

LARVAE

The larvae are long and slender, and may be slightly flattened or broader in the middle.

red margins and rear to elytra

▼ **MALACHIUS AENEUS** *has iridescent coloration and can often be seen feeding on flowers, especially buttercups.*

▼ **MALACHIUS BIPUSTULATUS** *is a common beetle of flower-rich grassland and meadows, where it hunts for small, soft-bodied prey.*

reddish orange tips to elytra

metallic green coloration

ORDER *Coleoptera.*
FAMILY *Melyridae.*
NUMBER OF SPECIES *1,500.*
SIZE *2–8mm.*
FEEDING *Larvae: predators. Adults: predators, herbivores (pollen).*
IMPACT *Harmless.*

Pollen or Sap Beetles

Nitidulidae

These small beetles are often oval, squarish, or rectangular in outline. The majority are smooth, shiny and either dark or black, and are often marked with reddish or yellowish irregular spots. In some species, the elytra are a little shorter than the abdomen, exposing the last two segments. The short antennae have swollen or clubbed ends. The legs are short.

FOUND *on flowers, fungi, carrion, oozing sap on trees, and decaying fruit.*

clubbed antennae

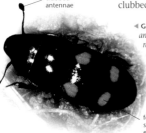

◀ **GLISCHROCHILUS HORTENSIS,** *an oval black beetle with four reddish orange spots on the elytra, can be found feeding at tree sap and the juices of ripe fruit.*

▼ **MELIGETHES AENEUS** *is often seen in large numbers in flowers where there is a good pollen supply.*

small, compact body

four orange spots on elytra

LARVAE

The larvae, which are long, pale, and slightly curved, may be pests of mustard and oilseed rape.

ORDER *Coleoptera.*
FAMILY *Nitidulidae.*
NUMBER OF SPECIES *2,800.*
SIZE *1–14mm.*
FEEDING *Larvae and adults: liquid-feeders, herbivores (pollen), predators, scavengers.*
IMPACT *Pests of crops and stored foods.*

Ladybirds or Ladybugs

Coccinellidae

FOUND *in coniferous and deciduous woodland, heather, gardens, and parks; wherever there is prey.*

These brightly marked, oval or round, sometimes almost hemispherical beetles are immediately recognizable. Ladybirds are shiny, and have a ground colour of black, red, yellow, or orange. The elytra have contrasting spots or regular markings in similar colours. The bright colouring and marking of adults warns predators of their poisonous or distasteful nature. Confusingly, many species have several colour forms. The head is nearly completely concealed from view by the pronotum, and has antennae with three to six segments, and a short, terminal club. The legs are short, and can be drawn tightly into grooves on the underside of the body. Most adults and larvae are highly predacious on soft-bodied insects. There are, however, some herbivorous species (*Epilachna*) that can be a pest on plants, such as beans and squashes.

LARVAE

Often warty or spiny with dark bodies and red or white spots, larvae moult four times before pupating. Pupae are dark coloured or look like bird droppings.

▶ **PSYLLOBORA 22-PUNCTATA** *is small with a very round outline. It lives on low vegetation, shrubs, and trees, where it feeds on mildews and moulds.*

small black spots

pale-ringed dark spots

warty bumps

PUPA

yellow background

▲ **ANATIS OCELLATA**, *the Eyed Ladybird, is quite a large predatory species, which is associated with coniferous trees.*

red elytra with seven black spots

▼ **COCCINELLA SEPTEMPUNCTATA** *is more commonly known as the Seven-spot Ladybird. It is a common species in a wide variety of habitats throughout Europe.*

white patches on pronotum

antennae

ORDER *Coleoptera.*
FAMILY *Coccinellidae.*
NUMBER OF SPECIES *5,000.*
SIZE *1–10mm.*
FEEDING *Larvae: predators, herbivores. Adults: predators, herbivores.*
IMPACT *Beneficial as predators of pests.*

NOTE

Adult ladybirds show what is known as reflex bleeding. If attacked, they can cause toxic body fluids to ooze out from the leg joints.

▶ **APHIDECTA OBLITERATA**, the Larch Ladybird, has four, dark longitudinal marks on the pronotum. The species is associated with larch and some other coniferous trees.

black and white markings on head

brown elytra

▼ **CALVIA 14-GUTTATA**, the Cream-spot Ladybird, is quite small, and has no black markings. Common on trees such as alder, hazel, and whitethorn, it has also been found on flowers of Scots Pine.

whitish yellow spots

orangish brown background

yellowish orange background

rectangular dark patches

▲ **PROPYLEA 14-PUNCTATA** is very variable in colour. Some are all yellow or all black where all the spots seem to have joined up. This species eats aphids on shrubs and trees.

one dark spot on each elytron

▶ **ADALIA BIPUNCTATA**, the Two-spot Ladybird, is a variable species, ranging from mainly black to mainly red with a large number of varieties in between.

white patches on sides of pronotum

elytra predominantly red

ADALIA BIPUNCTATA VARIANT

dark markings predominate

ADALIA BIPUNCTATA VARIANT

predominant dark markings

VARIANT

10 black spots on elytra

◀ **ADALIA DECEMPUNCTATA**, the Ten-spot Ladybird, is another variable species. Some (not pictured) are all black with two pale spots and others are black with ten yellowish orange spots.

Ant-like Beetles

Anthicidae

Named for their vaguely ant-like appearance, these small, very active beetles are brownish yellow to brownish black in colour, with reddish markings. The body is narrow and elongated and may be hairy. The head is constricted at the rear to form a neck where it joins the pronotum, which itself may be constricted near the rear. The antennae are slender, often with the last three segments expanded.

FOUND often in flowers, while the larvae are to be seen in compost and manure heaps.

LARVAE

The slender larvae are scavengers, feeding on dead insects and other rotting matter.

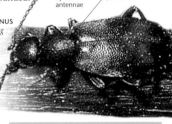

swollen tips to antennae

narrow pronotum

▶ **ANTHICUS ANTHERINUS** often lives among rotting vegetation and can look entirely dark, but usually has reddish brown elytral markings.

rounded head

▼ **NOTOXUS MONOCERUS** is unmistakable due to the forward-pointing horn extending over its head.

horn on pronotum

thin legs

ORDER Coleoptera.
FAMILY Anthicidae.
NUMBER OF SPECIES 2,500.
SIZE 2–8mm.
FEEDING Larvae: scavengers, fungi-feeders, predators. Adults: scavengers, fungi-feeders.
IMPACT Harmless.

False Oil Beetles

Oedemeridae

These beetles are soft-bodied, elongated, and parallel-sided, like soldier beetles (p.100). Many are brownish, but some are a shiny, iridescent green. The head is small and almost as wide as the pronotum, which is itself widest towards the front. The antennae are long and slender. The margins of the eyes have a small notch.

COMMON in meadows and flower-rich grassland; the adults feed at flowers.

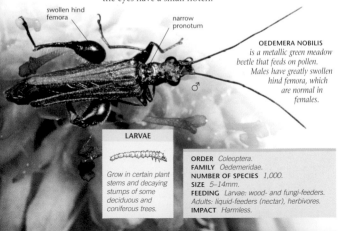

swollen hind femora

narrow pronotum

OEDEMERA NOBILIS is a metallic green meadow beetle that feeds on pollen. Males have greatly swollen hind femora, which are normal in females.

LARVAE

Grow in certain plant stems and decaying stumps of some deciduous and coniferous trees.

ORDER Coleoptera.
FAMILY Oedemeridae.
NUMBER OF SPECIES 1,000.
SIZE 5–14mm.
FEEDING Larvae: wood- and fungi-feeders. Adults: liquid-feeders (nectar), herbivores.
IMPACT Harmless.

Darkling Beetles

Tenebrionidae

Darkling beetles are mostly black or very dark brown, but some species have reddish markings. The body shape ranges from small and parallel-sided to large and broadly oval and may be smooth and shiny or dull and roughened. The antennae usually have 11 segments and can be relatively long and slender or short with clubbed ends. The eyes do not have a circular or oval outline. In many species, the hind wings are very small.

INHABIT *virtually all terrestrial habitats, including those with very dry conditions.*

LARVAE

The larvae, known as mealworms, are elongated and cylindrical, usually with very tough bodies and short legs. Some species are reared as bird and reptile food.

◀ **CTENOPIUS SULPHUREUS** *is a brightly coloured species that is often found feeding at umbelliferous flowers in sunny places.*

dense hairs on body

sulphur-yellow elytra

dark legs

◀ **BLAPS MUCRONATA**, *the Cellar or Churchyard Beetle, lives mainly in damp, dark places close to the ground.*

▲ **LAGRIA HIRTA** *favours dry localities, where its larvae feed among leaf litter. It is sometimes placed in a separate family: Lagriidae.*

distinctive striations on elytra

stout femora

elytra fused together

short antennae

▲ **TENEBRIO MOLITOR**, *the Yellow Mealworm Beetle, is found all over the world. It can be a pest of stored grain, meal, and flour.*

NOTE

Some of these species consume and breed on very dry food (bran and meal); they get all the water they need from digesting what they eat.

ORDER *Coleoptera.*
FAMILY *Tenebrionidae.*
NUMBER OF SPECIES *15,000.*
SIZE *0.2–2.5cm.*
FEEDING *Larvae and adults: scavengers.*
IMPACT *Some species are pests of stored grain, flour, meal, and dried fruit.*

Oil or Blister Beetles

Meloidae

SEEN *on the foliage and flowers of various plants, on the ground in dry grassy areas and on certain trees.*

The name "blister beetle" comes from the fact that the members of this family can produce oily defensive fluids capable of blistering skin. These beetles have a soft, leathery texture and are often bluish black, bright green, or red and black. The head is large, broadly triangular, and bent downwards, while the pronotum is often squarish and narrower than the back of the head. The elytra of ground-living species can be very short and gape to expose a large part of the swollen abdomen. In many species, the adults are herbivorous and, when present in large numbers, may completely defoliate plants.

short elytra expose abdomen

♂

▲ **MELOE PROSCARABEUS** *has short, parted elytra and (in males) antennae that look bent about halfway along their length.*

pitted upper surface

iridescent violet sheen

rounded pronotum

♂

black head and pronotum

broad head

◀ **MYLABRIS VARIABILIS,** *like several other similar species, is often found feeding on flowers in dry, sunny locations.*

▲ **MELOE VIOLACEUS** *is a parasite of solitary bees: the larvae crawl up flower stems to latch onto passing bees.*

iridescent golden-green elytra

variable black and yellow pattern on elytra

broad head on narrow "neck"

▶ **LYTTA VESICATORIA,** *called the Spanish Fly, produces a mousy defensive odour. It feeds on lilac and privet leaves in central and southern Europe.*

LARVAE

The newly hatched, predacious larvae seek out the eggs of grasshoppers or bees to eat, and becoming increasingly grub-like with each successive moult.

NOTE

In some species, the larvae attach themselves to a bee when it is visiting flowers. They travel to the bee's nest, then eat the eggs and food provisions.

ORDER *Coleoptera.*
FAMILY *Meloidae.*
NUMBER OF SPECIES *2,000.*
SIZE *0.5–3.5cm.*
FEEDING *Larvae: predators, parasites. Adults: herbivores, liquid-feeders (nectar).*
IMPACT *Many produce oily defensive fluids.*

Cardinal Beetles

Pyrochroidae

Also called fire-coloured beetles, these insects are usually
flattened and soft-bodied. The head narrows at the rear,
giving the appearance of a broad neck, and the antennae
are slender or comb-like (those of males may be feathery).
The elytra broaden noticeably
towards the rear
of the body.

OCCUR *in deciduous
woodland, where
adults are found
crawling on fallen
trees and stumps.*

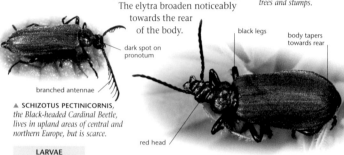

dark spot on
pronotum

branched antennae

black legs

body tapers
towards rear

red head

▲ SCHIZOTUS PECTINICORNIS,
*the Black-headed Cardinal Beetle,
lives in upland areas of central and
northern Europe, but is scarce.*

LARVAE

*The slightly flattened
larvae live under
bark and feed on
fungal threads or
smaller insects.*

ORDER *Coleoptera.*	
FAMILY *Pyrochroidae.*	
NUMBER OF SPECIES *150.*	
SIZE *0.6–1.8cm.*	
FEEDING *Larvae: predators, scavengers,
fungi-feeders. Adults: herbivores, predators.*	
IMPACT *Harmless.*	

▲ PYROCHROA
SERRATICORNIS
*can be told from
the very similar
but slightly larger
species Pyrochroa
coccinea by the
latter's black head.*

Pea and Bean Weevils

Bruchidae

These dull brownish, oval or egg-shaped beetles – which
are not true weevils (pp.116–17) – are often mottled with
patches of white or pale brown hairs or scales. The small
head has a short snout and shortish antennae, which are
comb-like or club-ended. The hind legs are often thicker
than the other legs and have strong tooth-like projections.
The elytra are typically shortened, exposing
the end of the abdomen.

FOUND *mainly near
leguminous plants or
on stored pulses, but
also on other foliage.*

mottled
pattern of
hairs on elytra

LARVAE

*The whitish, small-
headed grubs
spend their entire
larval development
inside seeds.*

head narrows
behind eyes

BRUCHUS RUFIMANUS,
*the Bean Beetle, can be a
serious pest of broad beans
and cultivated peas, but also
attacks vetches and other
wild leguminous plants.*

ORDER *Coleoptera.*	
FAMILY *Bruchidae.*	
NUMBER OF SPECIES *1,300.*	
SIZE *3–6mm.*	
FEEDING *Larvae: herbivores (in seeds).
Adults: herbivores (pollen), liquid-feeders.*	
IMPACT *Pests of stored peas and beans.*	

Longhorn Beetles

Cerambycidae

FOUND*as larvae in trees in deciduous or coniferous woodland. Adults occur mainly on flowers in a variety of habitats.*

Named for their most distinctive feature, these beetles have antennae that are always at least two-thirds as long as the body, and sometimes up to four times as long. Coloration varies from shades of brown to very brightly marked black and yellow or orange, while some species are even bluish or violet. Often large, the beetles have long bodies with parallel sides. The eyes are notched or occasionally completely divided and the antennae are usually raised on conspicuous tubercles (swellings). Adults of many species are non-feeding, but others may feed on pollen, nectar, leaves, or roots.

LARVAE

Longhorn larvae are long and cylindrical, with tiny legs or none at all. They use their powerful jaws to eat wood, creating tunnels with a circular cross-section.

greyish or greyish brown

♂

▶ **ACANTHOCINUS AEDILIS,** *the Timberman Beetle, has extremely long antennae in males. The larvae feed under the bark of dead pine trees.*

body tapers towards rear

variable yellow markings

▼ **NECYDALIS MAJOR** *is recognizable by the very short elytra from under which the hind wings protrude. Its larvae feed in the wood of mature deciduous trees.*

▲ **STRANGALIA MACULATA** *is often seen feeding on pollen at flowers. Its larvae feed in decaying tree trunks and stumps.*

very short elytra

wasp-like shape

NOTE

Longhorn beetles have been known to emerge from furniture made from attacked timber, having hidden inside the wood as developing larvae.

yellowish brown elytra

black prothorax

♂

▶ **LEPTURA RUBRA** *is bicoloured black and brown in males, whereas females are reddish brown. Its larvae feed on conifers such as pine.*

yellowish lower part of legs

ORDER Coleoptera.
FAMILY Cerambycidae.
NUMBER OF SPECIES 25,000.
SIZE 0.3–4.5cm.
FEEDING Larvae: wood-feeders. Adults: non-feeding, liquid-feeders (nectar), herbivores.
IMPACT Many species are pests of trees.

▶ **CLYTUS ARIETUS,** *commonly known as the Wasp Beetle, moves fast and has striking black and yellow coloration. The adults feed on pollen and nectar, laying their eggs on dead deciduous wood.*

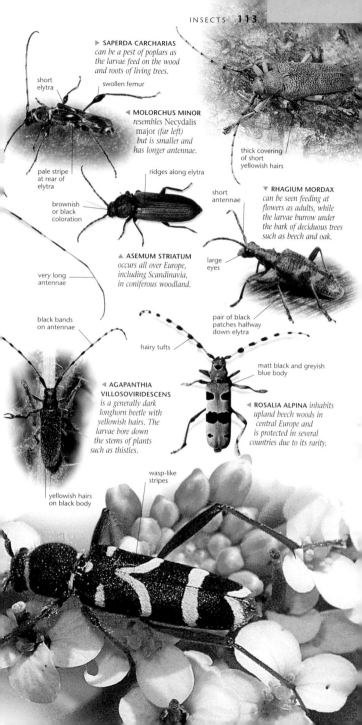

▶ **SAPERDA CARCHARIAS**
can be a pest of poplars as
the larvae feed on the wood
and roots of living trees.

short
elytra

swollen femur

thick covering
of short
yellowish hairs

◀ **MOLORCHUS MINOR**
resembles Necydalis
major (far left)
but is smaller and
has longer antennae.

pale stripe
at rear of
elytra

ridges along elytra

brownish
or black
coloration

short
antennae

▼ **RHAGIUM MORDAX**
can be seen feeding at
flowers as adults, while
the larvae burrow under
the bark of deciduous trees
such as beech and oak.

large
eyes

very long
antennae

▲ **ASEMUM STRIATUM**
occurs all over Europe,
including Scandinavia,
in coniferous woodland.

black bands
on antennae

pair of black
patches halfway
down elytra

hairy tufts

matt black and greyish
blue body

◀ **AGAPANTHIA
VILLOSOVIRIDESCENS**
is a generally dark
longhorn beetle with
yellowish hairs. The
larvae bore down
the stems of plants
such as thistles.

◀ **ROSALIA ALPINA** inhabits
upland beech woods in
central Europe and
is protected in several
countries due to its rarity.

yellowish hairs
on black body

wasp-like
stripes

Leaf Beetles

Chrysomelidae

LIFE CYCLE

Long and grub-like, leaf beetle larvae bore through plant tissues and also feed on the surface of plants. Species in the subfamily Donaciinae have aquatic larvae.

Typical leaf beetles are hairless, broadly oval when seen from above, and rounded when seen from the side. Many are brightly coloured and patterned or have a metallic sheen (such conspicuous coloration often serves to warn predators that the beetles are unpalatable). Although related to longhorn beetles (p.112), leaf beetles never have long antennae; these are usually less than half the body length. Some species look rather like ladybirds (p.106), but can be distinguished by the fact that the latter have three clearly visible tarsal segments on each leg, while leaf beetles have four.

♀ ♂

unmarked red elytra

▲ **CHRYSOMELA POPULI**, *the Poplar Leaf Beetle, feeds on the leaves of poplar and, occasionally, willow as larvae, sometimes reducing entire leaves to skeletons.*

brilliant green coloration

▲ **CHRYSOLINA MENTHASTRI** *favours hedgerows and damp waterside meadows, where it feeds on mint and related plants. Its body is extremely rounded.*

▶ **CASSIDA VIRIDIS**, *the Green Tortoise Beetle, can clamp tightly to a leaf if threatened. Like other tortoise beetles, its pronotum and elytra extend sideways around the body.*

broad pronotum

flat extensions at sides of elytra

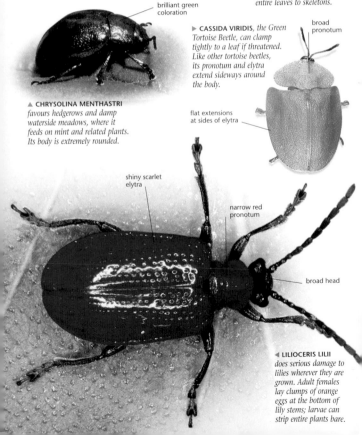

shiny scarlet elytra

narrow red pronotum

broad head

◀ **LILIOCERIS LILII** *does serious damage to lilies wherever they are grown. Adult females lay clumps of orange eggs at the bottom of lily stems; larvae can strip entire plants bare.*

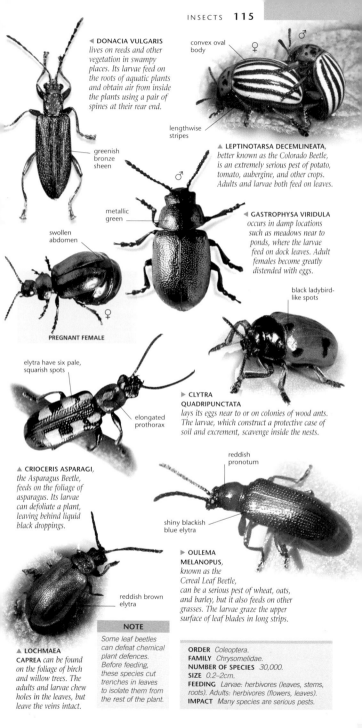

◄ **DONACIA VULGARIS** *lives on reeds and other vegetation in swampy places. Its larvae feed on the roots of aquatic plants and obtain air from inside the plants using a pair of spines at their rear end.*

convex oval body

♀ ♂

lengthwise stripes

greenish bronze sheen

▲ **LEPTINOTARSA DECEMLINEATA,** *better known as the Colorado Beetle, is an extremely serious pest of potato, tomato, aubergine, and other crops. Adults and larvae both feed on leaves.*

metallic green

♂

◄ **GASTROPHYSA VIRIDULA** *occurs in damp locations such as meadows near to ponds, where the larvae feed on dock leaves. Adult females become greatly distended with eggs.*

swollen abdomen

♀

PREGNANT FEMALE

black ladybird-like spots

elytra have six pale, squarish spots

elongated prothorax

► **CLYTRA QUADRIPUNCTATA** *lays its eggs near to or on colonies of wood ants. The larvae, which construct a protective case of soil and excrement, scavenge inside the nests.*

▲ **CRIOCERIS ASPARAGI,** *the Asparagus Beetle, feeds on the foliage of asparagus. Its larvae can defoliate a plant, leaving behind liquid black droppings.*

reddish pronotum

shiny blackish blue elytra

► **OULEMA MELANOPUS,** *known as the Cereal Leaf Beetle, can be a serious pest of wheat, oats, and barley, but it also feeds on other grasses. The larvae graze the upper surface of leaf blades in long strips.*

reddish brown elytra

▲ **LOCHMAEA CAPREA** *can be found on the foliage of birch and willow trees. The adults and larvae chew holes in the leaves, but leave the veins intact.*

NOTE

Some leaf beetles can defeat chemical plant defences. Before feeding, these species cut trenches in leaves to isolate them from the rest of the plant.

ORDER *Coleoptera.*
FAMILY *Chrysomelidae.*
NUMBER OF SPECIES *30,000.*
SIZE *0.2–2cm.*
FEEDING *Larvae: herbivores (leaves, stems, roots). Adults: herbivores (flowers, leaves).*
IMPACT *Many species are serious pests.*

Weevils

Curculionidae

WIDELY *distributed in all land habitats and associated with almost every species of plant.*

NOTE

Bark beetles carry fungal spores on the head and thorax, and thus infect trees when they lay eggs. As the fungal growth spreads, it may kill the host tree.

Weevils form the largest family in the animal world. Also known as snout beetles, they possess a snout, or rostrum, which is a prolongation of the head. It carries the jaws at its end and it may be short and broad or slender and as long as the body. The antennae, which arise from the rostrum, are normally "elbowed" and have clubbed ends. Most weevil species are covered by small scales and are cryptically coloured, although some are bright green or pinkish. This family also includes the bark beetles, which live on coniferous and deciduous trees. They are compact, either brown or black, and lack a conspicuous rostrum. Their head is usually almost hidden from view by a hood-like shield covering the thorax.

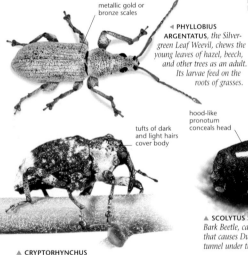

metallic gold or bronze scales

radiating larval burrows

◄ **PHYLLOBIUS ARGENTATUS**, *the Silver-green Leaf Weevil, chews the young leaves of hazel, beech, and other trees as an adult. Its larvae feed on the roots of grasses.*

BARK

hood-like pronotum conceals head

tufts of dark and light hairs cover body

▲ **SCOLYTUS SCOLYTUS**, *the Large Elm Bark Beetle, carries and spreads a fungus that causes Dutch elm disease. Females tunnel under the bark to lay their eggs.*

▲ **CRYPTORHYNCHUS LAPATHI**, *commonly known as the Poplar and Willow Borer, has effective camouflage. The larvae burrow under the bark of alders and sometimes birch.*

very long, curved snout

▶ **CURCULIO VENOSUS**, *the Acorn Nut Weevil, lays its eggs inside acorns. Larvae leave the acorn after it has fallen and then crawl into the soil to pupate.*

long snout, curved at tip

LIFE CYCLE

The pale, legless, grub-like larvae feed on roots or inside plant tissues; a few eat foliage. Bark beetle larvae hatch in brood galleries cut under bark by the adult female.

♀

▲ **CURCULIO NUCUM** *feeds on pollen and nectar. The snout is very long and curved in females, which use it to make holes in hazelnuts before they lay their eggs.*

ORDER Coleoptera.
FAMILY Curculionidae.
NUMBER OF SPECIES 50,000.
SIZE 0.3–2.4cm.
FEEDING Larvae: fungi- and wood-feeders, herbivores. Adults: fungi-feeders, herbivores.
IMPACT Many species are pests of plants.

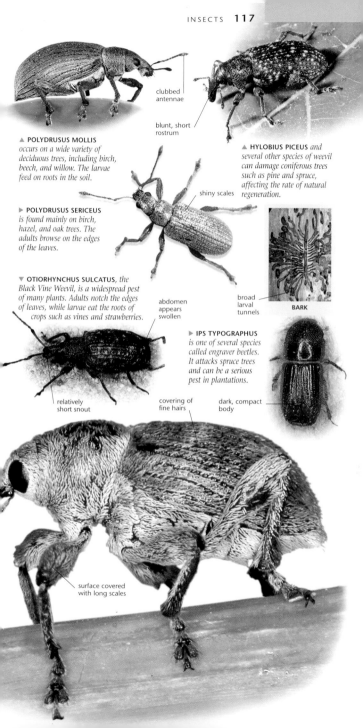

clubbed antennae

blunt, short rostrum

▲ **POLYDRUSUS MOLLIS**
*occurs on a wide variety of
deciduous trees, including birch,
beech, and willow. The larvae
feed on roots in the soil.*

▲ **HYLOBIUS PICEUS** *and
several other species of weevil
can damage coniferous trees
such as pine and spruce,
affecting the rate of natural
regeneration.*

shiny scales

▶ **POLYDRUSUS SERICEUS**
*is found mainly on birch,
hazel, and oak trees. The
adults browse on the edges
of the leaves.*

▼ **OTIORHYNCHUS SULCATUS,** *the
Black Vine Weevil, is a widespread pest
of many plants. Adults notch the edges
of leaves, while larvae eat the roots of
crops such as vines and strawberries.*

abdomen
appears
swollen

broad
larval
tunnels

BARK

▶ **IPS TYPOGRAPHUS**
*is one of several species
called engraver beetles.
It attacks spruce trees
and can be a serious
pest in plantations.*

relatively
short snout

covering of
fine hairs

dark, compact
body

surface covered
with long scales

Leaf-rolling Weevils

Attelabidae

OCCUR *on host species in scrubland, hedgerow, and woodland, especially on some coppiced species.*

These beetles are closely related to weevils (pp.106–07). They vary from oval to moderately elongated and are often bright reddish and black. The head is sometimes "pinched" at the rear to form a neck; its rostrum can be short and broad or long and narrow. The antennae are not elbowed, but the last three segments form a club.

clubbed antennae

LARVAE

Larvae feed on wilting tissue inside leaf rolls made by the female and fully grown ones drop out.

◀ **DEPORAUS BETULAE,** *the female of the Birch Leaf Roller, lays eggs on birch leaves, rolled into a tube.*

distinct "neck"

shiny black elytra

shiny red elytra

▶ **APODERUS CORYLI** *is a fairly common species. The head is tapered behind the eyes.*

red femora

ORDER Coleoptera.
FAMILY Attelabidae.
NUMBER OF SPECIES 1,800.
SIZE 3–7mm.
FEEDING Larvae and adults: herbivores.
IMPACT A few species can be serious pests of fruit trees and soft fruit.

Apionid Weevils

Apionidae

ABUNDANT *on a wide variety of habitats from wasteland to woodland margins and coasts to gardens.*

These small or very small pear-shaped weevils are usually matt black in colour but can be greenish or reddish. The head is rounded and, unlike leaf-rolling weevils (above), is not constricted behind the eyes. There is a long, narrow, curved rostrum. The antennae are usually not elbowed and end in an elongated club with three segments.

▼ **PROTAPION RYEI** *is one of several, small, yellow-legged weevils. It is thought that the larvae feed on Red Clover.*

black eyes

curved rostrum

reddish orange femora

LARVAE

reddish brown all over

Larvae bore into the stems, seed pods, and other parts of plants. Some are pests of field crops.

▲ **APION FRUMENTARIUM** *is a small weevil with a narrow, pointed front end and broad rear end.*

ORDER Coleoptera.
FAMILY Apionidae.
NUMBER OF SPECIES 2,000.
SIZE 2–5mm.
FEEDING Larvae and adults: herbivores (seeds, stems, and other plant parts).
IMPACT Many species can damage crops.

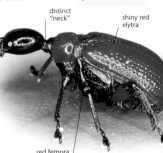

Stylopids

Stylopidae

These small insects are strange-looking parasites of other insects. The males are dark and winged with protruding, berry-like eyes, and their antennae have four to seven segments. Their front wings are very small; the hind wings are large and fan-like. The grub-like, wingless, and legless females never leave their host's body.

FOUND *mainly in sunny, flower-rich habitats where their bee and wasp hosts are plentiful.*

berry-like eyes

♂

NOTE

Male stylopids are free-flying and use scent to locate females, which live permanently inside their host insect, partly protruding from its abdomen.

fan-shaped hind wing

small number of radiating veins

STYLOPS SP. *males are strange-looking small, dark insects with large veinless hind wings. Males mate with the females inside parasitized bees.*

LARVAE

First-stage larvae (above) have six legs. They enter hosts and moult into legless parasites.

ORDER Strepsiptera.
FAMILY Stylopidae.
NUMBER OF SPECIES 260.
SIZE 0.5–4mm.
FEEDING Larvae: parasites. Adults: parasites (females), non-feeding (males).
IMPACT Harmless.

Hangingflies

Bittacidae

These insects are recognizable by their long, narrow wings, very long legs, and specially modified hind tarsi for capturing prey. The fifth tarsal segments of the hind legs are enlarged and can fold around to grip prey. Hangingflies, which can look very like crane flies (p.122), typically hang from vegetation by their front legs and trail their long hind legs to catch passing insects.

FLOURISH *in damp woodland or shady, well-vegetated places.*

LARVAE

The caterpillar-like larvae have hairy warts and stick debris to their body for camouflage.

front legs hang onto foliage

long tarsus

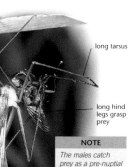

BITTACUS ITALICUS *is a pale, slender insect with long legs, and hangs from leaves by its front legs. It is found in Italy and west of the Adriatic.*

long hind legs grasp prey

NOTE

The males catch prey as a pre-nuptial gift, which the female eats as they copulate. Some males try to steal nuptial gifts from other males.

ORDER Mecoptera.
FAMILY Bittacidae.
NUMBER OF SPECIES 150.
SIZE 1–2cm (wingspan).
FEEDING Larvae: scavengers, predators. Adults: predators
IMPACT Harmless.

Snow Scorpionflies

Boreidae

These small insects are very dark brown or bronze to black in colour, so contrast strongly against a snowy background. The head, as in all scorpionflies, is extended downwards, forming an obvious beak that bears the jaws. The antennae are quite long, but the wings are very much reduced, resembling small hooks in the males or scales in females.

SEEN *in autumn and winter on the surface of snow or among mosses, mainly in cold regions or mountains.*

NOTE

Superbly adapted for life in the cold, these scorpionflies die if held in a warm hand for too long. They walk rapidly across the ground and can also jump.

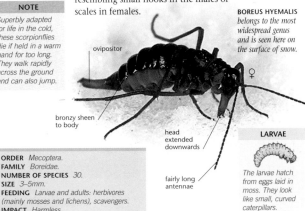

ovipositor

BOREUS HYEMALIS *belongs to the most widespread genus and is seen here on the surface of snow.*

♀

bronzy sheen to body

head extended downwards

fairly long antennae

LARVAE

The larvae hatch from eggs laid in moss. They look like small, curved caterpillars.

ORDER *Mecoptera.*
FAMILY *Boreidae.*
NUMBER OF SPECIES 30.
SIZE *3–5mm.*
FEEDING *Larvae and adults: herbivores (mainly mosses and lichens), scavengers.*
IMPACT *Harmless.*

Common Scorpionflies

Panorpidae

The head of these brownish yellow and black insects is elongated downwards to form a beak that carries biting mouthparts. The wings often have dark markings. Males have an upturned abdomen with bulbous genitalia; the abdomen of females tapers towards the rear.

FOUND *in low-growing vegetation in shady places such as woods.*

LARVAE

The larvae look like caterpillars, with eight pairs of short abdominal feet and (often) spines.

♂

▶ **PANORPA COMMUNIS** *lives in cool, moist places and feeds on dead or dying insects. The enlarged genitalia of this male are clearly visible.*

spotted wings

♀

elongated head

▼ **PANORPA MERIDIONALIS** *is a pale, heavily spotted species from the southern regions of Europe.*

pale yellow body

♀

pointed abdomen

ORDER *Mecoptera.*
FAMILY *Panorpidae.*
NUMBER OF SPECIES 360.
SIZE *0.9–2.5cm.*
FEEDING *Larvae: scavengers. Adults: liquid-feeders (nectar, honeydew), scavengers.*
IMPACT *Harmless.*

Common Fleas

Pulicidae

Fleas are immediately recognizable by their small size, dark brown or black coloration, winglessness, laterally flattened bodies, and – above all – remarkable jumping ability. The head is fused to a small thorax and carries short antennae concealed in grooves at the side. The simple lateral eyes are quite well developed and the mouthparts are modified for piercing skin and sucking blood. On many fleas there is a comb of stout bristles at the back of the pronotum and at the sides of the head. Fleas are prolific breeders; owners of untreated pets risk having flea eggs and larvae in their home.

PARASITES *on a range of mammals, such as dogs, cats, hedgehogs, rabbits, and humans.*

NOTE

In general, fleas avoid light and are attracted to a variety of hosts. Hungry fleas may jump hundreds of times an hour for several days to find a host.

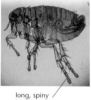

◀ **PULEX IRRITANS** *is called the Human Flea but is more often found attacking pigs and goats. People are more likely to be bitten by cat and dog fleas.*

long, spiny hind legs

▶ **SPILOPSYLLUS CUNICULI**, *the Rabbit Flea, is a major vector of the rabbit disease myxomatosis.*

"comb" on pronotum

piercing mouthparts

"comb" on pronotum

flat, shiny abdomen

LARVAE

Flea larvae are tiny and elongated. They feed on detritus in the host's nest, the faeces of adult fleas, and dried blood. When fully grown, they each spin a silken cocoon.

▼ **CTENOCEPHALIDES FELIS**, *the Cat Flea, is capable of a high jump of 34cm at up to 130 times the acceleration of gravity.*

◀ **CTENOCEPHALIDES CANIS**, *the Dog Flea, also lives on wolves. It is the intermediate host for the tapeworm* Dipylidium caninum, *which also infects cats.*

ORDER *Siphonaptera.*
FAMILY *Pulicidae.*
NUMBER OF SPECIES *200.*
SIZE *1–8mm.*
FEEDING *Larvae: scavengers (dried blood and faeces). Adults: blood-feeders.*
IMPACT *Bites may cause allergic reactions.*

Crane Flies

Tipulidae

Also known as daddy-long-legs, crane flies are easy to identify due to their slender, fragile bodies, elongated wings, and long, thread-like legs. A highly characteristic feature of these flies is that their legs are shed very easily if they are trapped or handled. The body is brown, black, or grey, often with yellow, orange, or pale brown markings, and there is a distinctive V-shaped groove on top of the thorax.

ADULTS *live near water and lush vegetation; larvae occur in diverse places such as rotting wood, soil, and water.*

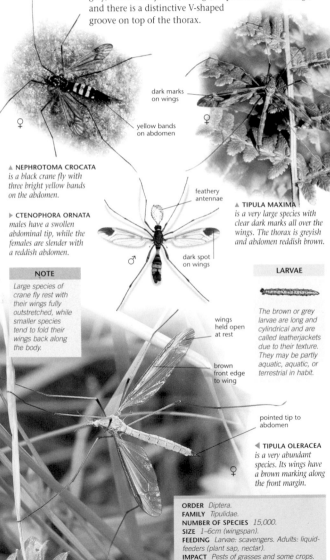

dark marks on wings

yellow bands on abdomen

▲ **NEPHROTOMA CROCATA** *is a black crane fly with three bright yellow bands on the abdomen.*

feathery antennae

▶ **CTENOPHORA ORNATA** *males have a swollen abdominal tip, while the females are slender with a reddish abdomen.*

dark spot on wings

▲ **TIPULA MAXIMA** *is a very large species with clear dark marks all over the wings. The thorax is greyish and abdomen reddish brown.*

NOTE

Large species of crane fly rest with their wings fully outstretched, while smaller species tend to fold their wings back along the body.

LARVAE

The brown or grey larvae are long and cylindrical and are called leatherjackets due to their texture. They may be partly aquatic, aquatic, or terrestrial in habit.

wings held open at rest

brown front edge to wing

pointed tip to abdomen

◀ **TIPULA OLERACEA** *is a very abundant species. Its wings have a brown marking along the front margin.*

ORDER *Diptera.*
FAMILY *Tipulidae.*
NUMBER OF SPECIES 15,000.
SIZE *1–6cm (wingspan).*
FEEDING *Larvae: scavengers. Adults: liquid-feeders (plant sap, nectar).*
IMPACT *Pests of grasses and some crops.*

Winter Gnats

Trichoceridae

Sometimes called winter crane flies, these delicate, long-legged flies are often seen in breeding swarms on sunny days during the colder months. They have a similar V-shaped groove on the thorax to that in crane flies (left), but their legs are not shed nearly so easily. The antennae are elongated and slender with 16 segments.

FLOURISH in damp, cool places such as woodland and even mines and caves.

LARVAE

The larvae are scavengers and develop in a wide range of rotting matter including leaf mould, decaying fungal fruiting bodies, and animal dung.

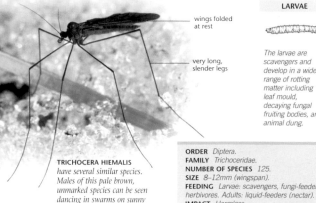

wings folded at rest

very long, slender legs

TRICHOCERA HIEMALIS have several similar species. Males of this pale brown, unmarked species can be seen dancing in swarms on sunny autumn and winter days.

ORDER Diptera.
FAMILY Trichoceridae.
NUMBER OF SPECIES 125.
SIZE 8–12mm (wingspan).
FEEDING Larvae: scavengers, fungi-feeders, herbivores. Adults: liquid-feeders (nectar).
IMPACT Harmless.

Phantom Midges

Chaoboridae

These brownish or greyish flies look a bit like mosquitoes (p.124), but do not bite. The head has well-separated eyes and antennae: the latter are slender in females and feathery in males, with a large, globular basal segment. The rear margins of the wings and many of the wing veins are covered by narrow, scale-like hair.

FOUND often in large swarms flying over ponds and lakes in all but the coldest months.

LARVAE

The larvae have an enlarged thorax and use tiny gas bubbles inside the body to regulate their depth.

adult fly emerging from pupa

♂

feathery antennae

CHAOBORUS SP. adults emerge from their pupae at the water's surface. Females have normal wings and males have short wings.

ORDER Diptera.
FAMILY Chaoboridae.
NUMBER OF SPECIES 100.
SIZE 2–8mm.
FEEDING Larvae: predators (small prey such as mosquito larvae). Adults: liquid-feeders.
IMPACT Harmless.

Mosquitoes

Culicidae

REMAIN near to the larval breeding grounds in a range of aquatic habitats, from puddles to ponds and lakes.

It might not be easy to spot these very slender, delicate flies, but they produce a high-pitched whine in flight that is a sure sign of their presence. The head is small and rounded with very long and slender, forward-facing sucking mouthparts. The body and legs are covered with tiny scales and appear pale brown to reddish brown, although some species have bright markings. The wings are long and narrow with scales along the veins and margins. The antennae are feathery in males and slightly hairy in females. Females suck blood from vertebrate hosts; males feed on nectar or honeydew.

REMAIN near to the larval breeding grounds in a range of aquatic habitats, from puddles to ponds and lakes.

LARVAE

The larvae, known as "wrigglers" after the way in which they thrash about in water, are mainly scavengers, but a few are predators. Most obtain air at the surface.

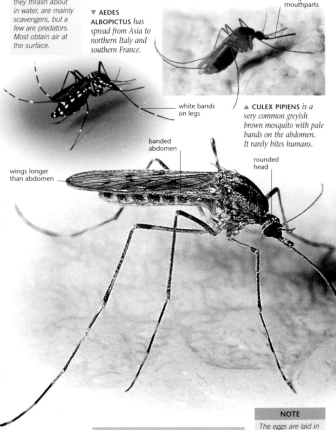

▼ **AEDES ALBOPICTUS** has spread from Asia to northern Italy and southern France.

biting mouthparts

white bands on legs

▲ **CULEX PIPIENS** is a very common greyish brown mosquito with pale bands on the abdomen. It rarely bites humans.

banded abdomen

rounded head

wings longer than abdomen

▲ **CULISETA ANNULATA**, a large species, has spotted wings and banded legs. It can breed in quite polluted water and often enters houses.

ORDER Diptera.
FAMILY Culicidae.
NUMBER OF SPECIES 3,100.
SIZE 3–9mm.
FEEDING Larvae: scavengers. Adults: blood-feeders (females), liquid-feeders (males).
IMPACT Bites are painful; transmit diseases.

NOTE

The eggs are laid in almost any standing water. Although they tend to remain near water, the adults may be common in shady woodland and forest at dusk.

Non-biting Midges

Chironomidae

These pale green, brown, or grey flies are delicate and look a bit like mosquitoes (left), but lack scales on the wings and their mouthparts are very short or absent. Males have very feathery antennae and a slender body, while females have hairy antennae and a stoutish body.

SWARMS *at dusk near to ponds, lakes, and streams. Larvae occur in all aquatic habitats.*

LARVAE

The long, slender larvae occasionally have gills at the rear of the body. Their coloration varies.

humped thorax

♂

feathery antennae

greenish tinge

▲ CHIRONOMUS RIPARIUS *is common in streams and rivers. It forms mating swarms at certain times of year.*

▼ CHIRONOMUS PLUMOSUS *may be greenish in colour. Its mud-dwelling larvae, known as bloodworms, contain haemoglobin.*

ORDER *Diptera.*
FAMILY *Chironomidae.*
NUMBER OF SPECIES *5,000.*
SIZE *1–9mm.*
FEEDING *Larvae: scavengers, predators. Adults: liquid-feeders.*
IMPACT *May be a nuisance, but do not bite.*

Biting Midges

Ceratopogonidae

These small flies are similar to but somewhat smaller than non-biting midges (above), with shorter front legs. They often have dark patterns on their wings. The rounded head is not concealed from above by the thorax and the antennae of males are feathery. The mouthparts, especially those of the females, are short and piercing for sucking up fluids.

PLENTIFUL *near the margins of ponds, lakes, and rivers, and in boggy areas.*

humped thorax

shortish front legs

wings folded flat over body

LARVAE

The minute, slender, worm-like larvae can be aquatic or may live in damp soil or under tree bark.

ORDER *Diptera.*
FAMILY *Ceratopogonidae.*
NUMBER OF SPECIES *2,000.*
SIZE *1–6mm.*
FEEDING *Larvae: predators. Adults: blood-feeders (females), predators, liquid-feeders.*
IMPACT *Several species bite humans.*

CULICOIDES IMPUNCTATUS, *an abundant insect of northern and upland areas, is notorious as a frequent, painful biter of humans.*

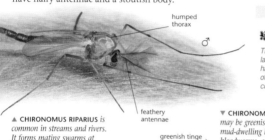

THRIVE *around rivers and other fast-flowing bodies of water.*

Black Flies

Simuliidae

Black flies have stout bodies, short legs, and a distinctively humped thorax. The head is relatively large and rounded with short, thick mouthparts, which, in the females of most species, are used for cutting skin and sucking blood. The antennae are short with no more than nine segments. The wings are broad at the base and narrow towards the end with distinct veins at the leading edge.

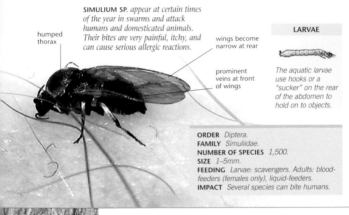

SIMULIUM SP. appear at certain times of the year in swarms and attack humans and domesticated animals. Their bites are very painful, itchy, and can cause serious allergic reactions.

humped thorax

wings become narrow at rear

prominent veins at front of wings

LARVAE

The aquatic larvae use hooks or a "sucker" on the rear of the abdomen to hold on to objects.

ORDER *Diptera.*
FAMILY *Simuliidae.*
NUMBER OF SPECIES *1,500.*
SIZE *1–5mm.*
FEEDING *Larvae: scavengers. Adults: blood-feeders (females only), liquid-feeders.*
IMPACT *Several species can bite humans.*

Owl Midges

Psychodidae

Also called moth flies due to the long hairs or scales covering their bodies, wings, and legs, these small flies are greyish or brownish. The eyes are large and the antennae are made up of 10 to 14 bead-like segments. The wings are usually broad with pointed tips and have few, if any, cross-veins. Like night-flying moths, owl midges are largely nocturnal and are often attracted to lights after dark.

FOUND *in damp and shady places such as woods and bogs; often rest in cracks, crevices, or burrows by day.*

LARVAE

Owl midge larvae are elongated and cylindrical. They live in decaying matter, often in sewers.

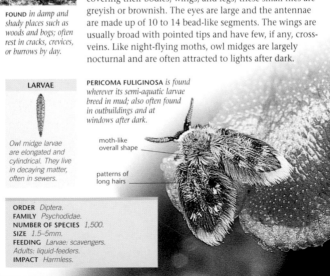

PERICOMA FULIGINOSA is found wherever its semi-aquatic larvae breed in mud; also often found in outbuildings and at windows after dark.

moth-like overall shape

patterns of long hairs

ORDER *Diptera.*
FAMILY *Psychodidae.*
NUMBER OF SPECIES *1,500.*
SIZE *1.5–5mm.*
FEEDING *Larvae: scavengers. Adults: liquid-feeders.*
IMPACT *Harmless.*

Wood Gnats

Anisopodidae

Wood gnats are small to medium-sized, gnat-like flies with long legs and a slightly flattened head. The eyes are quite large and may touch in males; the antennae are about as long as the head and thorax together. The wings are large and lie flat on the abdomen at rest. Some species are known as window flies because they are common inside houses and can often be seen at windows.

OCCUR *in damp or wooded areas, often near larval habitats of sewage and decaying organic matter.*

LARVAE

slightly flattened head

long legs

relatively large wings

The larvae are slender and elongate with a smooth body and a small head.

SYLVICOLA SP. *often form mating swarms in the late afternoon or around dusk. Some species are known as window flies and are sometimes confused with mosquitoes.*

ORDER *Diptera.*
FAMILY *Anisopodidae.*
NUMBER OF SPECIES *100.*
SIZE *2–10mm.*
FEEDING *Larvae: scavengers. Adults: liquid-feeders.*
IMPACT *Harmless.*

March Flies

Bibionidae

These flies are stout-bodied, black or dark brown insects, often with very hairy bodies and shortish legs. The heads of males and females are differently shaped: the former are larger and have large compound eyes that meet on top of the head; females have narrower heads, and eyes which do not meet. March flies are common in spring, when males can swarm in large numbers.

PLENTIFUL *on flowers in pastures, meadows, gardens, and other similar habitats.*

hairy black thorax

clear wings

BIBIO MARCI *is distinctively hairy and slow-flying; males are often found in numbers flying over short grasses in spring.*

shortish legs

♀

LARVAE

The larvae are large, elongated, slightly flattened, and large-headed, with strong mouthparts.

ORDER *Diptera.*
FAMILY *Bibionidae.*
NUMBER OF SPECIES *800.*
SIZE *5–11mm.*
FEEDING *Larvae: scavengers, herbivores. Adults: non-feeding.*
IMPACT *Some damage seedlings of cereals.*

Gall Midges

Cecidomyiidae

THRIVE *in almost all habitats, around fungi, the larval host plants, and decaying organic matter.*

Gall midges are tiny, delicate, pale or sombre flies with slender legs. The antennae are long and slender, with each bead-like segment bearing a whorl of fine hairs. The wings can be hairy and, characteristically, have only a few unbranched veins. The eyes of both sexes touch or nearly touch on top of the head and in some species are divided in two. Most species induce galls on plants; a few are free-living.

no more than four veins reach wing margin

pointed tip

GALLS

smooth surface

thread- or bead-like antennae

each gall contains several larvae

▲ **MIKIOLA FAGI** *induces egg-shaped galls on the leaves of beech trees. The galls each contain a single fly larva and can be very numerous.*

▲ **CECIDOMYIA SP.** *are gall midges with adults, such as the one pictured, that all look very similar: they can be separated only by examination under a micrope.*

long, slender legs

GALLS

▲ **WACHTLIELLA ROSARUM** *makes galls on wild and cultivated roses, whose affected leaves thicken and fold into a pouch-like gall.*

▼ **JAAPIELLA VERONICAE** *lays eggs in the buds of Germander Speedwell, causing hairy galls.*

white, hairy gall

LARVAE

The larvae are red, yellow, or orangish and they lack any clear distinguishing feature, except for a structure called the sternal spatula, or breast plate.

▼ **DIDYMOMYIA TILIACEA** *galls are commonly clustered on lime leaves. The pale, yellowish green galls stick out on both sides of the leaf.*

pale greenish coloration

GALLS

GALLS

galls packed together

ORDER Diptera.
FAMILY Cecidomyiidae.
NUMBER OF SPECIES 4,600.
SIZE 1–5mm.
FEEDING Larvae: herbivores, fungi-feeders, predators. Adults: liquid-feeders.
IMPACT Damage plants, including crops.

Fungus Gnats

Mycetophilidae

The best recognition features for these mosquito-like flies are the thorax, which is very humped in side view, and the long legs, which have two strong spurs at the end of the bristly tibiae. Most species of fungus gnat are dull black, brown, or yellow, but some have brighter markings. The head is flattened from front to back and the antennae are generally long, although the females of some species may have short antennae. In many species, the larvae live gregariously in fungi and can be serious pests of cultivated mushroom beds; pupation occurs inside the host fungus or in a loose cocoon made of soil particles and silk. Other larvae damage the roots of wheat seedlings, cucumber, and potted plants.

ATTRACTED *to moist, dark places, often in woodland, where found on fungi, under bark, and in dead wood, and bird nests.*

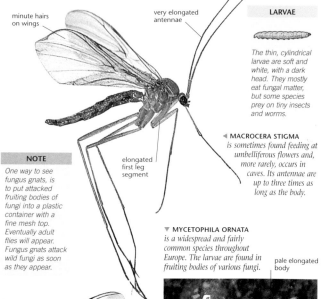

minute hairs on wings

very elongated antennae

LARVAE

The thin, cylindrical larvae are soft and white, with a dark head. They mostly eat fungal matter, but some species prey on tiny insects and worms.

◄ **MACROCERA STIGMA** *is sometimes found feeding at umbelliferous flowers and, more rarely, occurs in caves. Its antennae are up to three times as long as the body.*

elongated first leg segment

NOTE

One way to see fungus gnats, is to put attacked fruiting bodies of fungi into a plastic container with a fine mesh top. Eventually adult flies will appear. Fungus gnats attack wild fungi as soon as they appear.

▼ **MYCETOPHILA ORNATA** *is a widespread and fairly common species throughout Europe. The larvae are found in fruiting bodies of various fungi.*

pale elongated body

humped thorax

dark, slender abdomen

yellowish legs

spines on tibia

▲ **PLATYURA MARGINATA** *is a fairly large, dark species found in western Europe. Its larvae live under rotting wood and prey on insects.*

ORDER *Diptera.*
FAMILY *Mycetophilidae.*
NUMBER OF SPECIES *3,000.*
SIZE *2–13mm.*
FEEDING *Larvae: herbivores, fungi-feeders, scavengers, predators. Adults: liquid-feeders.*
IMPACT *Pests of mushrooms.*

Snipe Flies

Rhagionidae

FOUND *in wooded areas, where adults often rest head-down on tree trunks.*

Snipe flies are small to medium-sized and quite slender, with longish legs and a long abdomen that tapers to the rear end. Most species are brown or grey, but some have brighter markings. The head is generally hemispherical with large eyes that nearly touch each other in males. The antennae are short.

LARVAE

Elongate and maggot-like, the rough "welts" on their undersides help the larvae to move.

large green eyes

♂

ORDER *Diptera.*
FAMILY *Rhagionidae.*
NUMBER OF SPECIES *350.*
SIZE *0.6–1.5cm.*
FEEDING *Larvae and adults: predators.*
IMPACT *Harmless.*

ATHERIX IBIS, *known as the Water Snipe Fly, is found near fresh water. Females are grey with more prominent stripes.*

smoky patches on wings

Small-headed Flies

Acroceridae

LIVE *in grassland and flower-rich meadows where their spider hosts occur.*

There is no mistaking these oddly-shaped flies. The large thorax can appear very humped in side view and the abdomen is typically rounded and swollen. The head is small but covered almost entirely by the eyes, which touch each other in both sexes, unlike snipe flies (above). The short antennae sometimes look as if they have only two segments because the basal segment is concealed.

small head hidden by thorax

very rounded thorax

ACROCERA SP. *are small flies, with a large thorax and a globular abdomen, which may be marked black and yellow.*

LARVAE

Inside a spider, the larvae wait till it is about to moult for the last time, before emerging to pupate.

ORDER *Diptera.*
FAMILY *Acroceridae.*
NUMBER OF SPECIES *500.*
SIZE *4–8mm.*
FEEDING *Larvae: parasites (spiders). Adults: liquid-feeders (nectar).*
IMPACT *Harmless.*

Horse Flies

Tabanidae

Also called deer flies, clegs, or gad flies, these insects are stout-bodied, hairless, and fast-flying. They are black, grey, or brown and often have bright yellow or orange bands or other markings. The head is large, hemispherical, and flattened; the short antennae are the most typical feature. The large eyes, which occupy most of the head, are green or purple with iridescent bands and spots. The females' mouthparts are adapted to cut skin and lap blood.

SEEN *near mammals, often far from larval breeding grounds in marshy areas or near water.*

NOTE

Female horse flies approach victims with great stealth and feed in hard-to-reach places. Their bites are painful and may cause allergic reactions.

mottled wings

bands on legs

hairy, striped thorax

▲ **HAEMATOPOTA PULVIALIS**, *known as the Cleg, is a silent and notorious biter of humans. It is found close to water in woodland.*

LARVAE

The larvae are predacious on small worms, crustaceans, and insect larvae and may be aquatic or live in very damp soil, litter, or rotting wood.

▶ **CHRYSOPS RELICTUS** *has broad brown marks on its wings and shiny green eyes. It is very common near water, especially in upland areas and on heathland.*

iridescent, "spotty" eyes

blade-like mouthparts

▶ **TABANUS SUDETICUS** *is a large horse fly with a bee-like abdomen with distinctive pale, triangular marks in a line down the middle.*

pale tibiae

pale triangle on each abdominal segment

▼ **TABANUS BOVINUS** *is found in meadows and light woodland near flowing water. Females attack cattle and horses. The larvae develop in wet soil.*

stripes on abdomen

hairy thorax

ORDER *Diptera.*
FAMILY *Tabanidae.*
NUMBER OF SPECIES *4,100.*
SIZE *0.6–2.8cm.*
FEEDING *Larvae: predators. Adults: blood-feeders (females), liquid-feeders (males).*
IMPACT *Severe nuisance with painful bite.*

Soldier Flies

Stratiomyidae

FOUND *mainly in damp areas on the flowers of willow, hawthorn, irises, and umbellifers.*

These robust, rather flattened flies sometimes have yellow, green, or pale abdominal markings. Some large species resemble wasps, while others are smaller, and coloured brown, green, or metallic bluish black. The eyes cover a large area of the broad, hemispherical or very rounded head, especially in males. The short antennae are distinctive, with the third segment bent outwards from the basal segments. The wings are folded flat over the body at rest. Although they are not particularly strong fliers, some can hover.

green thorax

LARVAE

The larvae of the soldier flies are elongate and flattened; their tough and leathery bodies are impregnated with calcareous deposits.

smoky-tinged wings

◄ **CHLOROMYIA FORMOSA** *has a rather blunt-ended, broad abdomen. It is bronze coloured in males and bluish in females.*

yellow scutellum

yellow stripes on head

◄ **OXYCERA RARA** *is a stout-bodied species with strong yellow on black markings. It favours sunny clearings in wet areas, such as fenland.*

pale tibia

broad abdomen

elbowed antennae

◄ **STRATIOMYS CHAMELEON** *has a broad black abdomen with yellow patches on the sides. The scutellum has two long spines.*

black central stripe

▲ **ODONTOMYIA VIRIDULA** *has a black, hairy thorax and a broad, flattened abdomen. It is found in wet meadows.*

lime green sides to abdomen

ORDER *Diptera.*
FAMILY *Stratiomyidae.*
NUMBER OF SPECIES *1,800.*
SIZE *2–17mm.*
FEEDING *Larvae: scavengers, predators, herbivores. Adults: liquid-feeders (nectar).*
IMPACT *Harmless.*

Stiletto Flies

Therevidae

Elongate, yellowish brown to black, and often very hairy flies, therevids are similar in shape to small robber flies, but lack the groove between the eyes and tuft of facial hair. The large eyes touch each other in males. Antennae have three segments, and the proboscis is short, soft, and fleshy.

OCCUR *mainly in well-vegetated habitats; also in coastal sand dunes.*

LARVAE

The larvae are white and slender with a dark head. They usually feed on small insects.

pointed abdomen

♂

slender legs

hairy thorax

▲ **THEREVA NOBILITATA** *is a dark brown species with a thick covering of yellowish hairs, especially at the front of the head, around the thorax, and at the sides of the abdomen.*

ORDER *Diptera.*
FAMILY *Therevidae.*
NUMBER OF SPECIES *550.*
SIZE *4–15mm.*
FEEDING *Larvae: predacious. Adults: liquid-feeders.*
IMPACT *Harmless.*

♂

▲ **ACROSATHE ANNULATA** *is a hairy species. The males are silver in appearance, whereas the females have greyish silver abdomens with light brown markings.*

Bee Flies

Bombyliidae

As the name implies, bee flies can look very similar to bees. Some are stout-bodied and very hairy. Their body colour is usually brown, red, and yellow. The wings may be clear or have dark bands or patterned markings, particularly at the leading edge. The head is often rounded, and the proboscis can be very long for sucking nectar from deep flowers.

SEEN *feeding or flying in open, sunny locations or resting on bare sandy ground.*

hairy, bee-like body

▶ **VILLA MODESTA** *looks quite bee-like. It has a rounded head, short proboscis, and a furry body.*

head pale at sides

clear wings

dark area on front of clear wing

LARVAE

Most larvae are parasitic on other insect larvae. Some eat eggs of grass–hoppers in the soil.

▲ **BOMBYLIUS MAJOR** *looks like a bee and hovers like a hover fly. It has a long proboscis that projects in front of the head.*

ORDER *Diptera.*
FAMILY *Bombyliidae.*
NUMBER OF SPECIES *5,000.*
SIZE *2–18mm.*
FEEDING *Larvae: parasitic, predators. Adults: liquid-feeders (nectar).*
IMPACT *Harmless.*

Robber or Assassin Flies

Asilidae

Robber flies are aerial or ambush hunters with excellent eyesight. Most are brownish or black with reddish orange or yellow markings and the body varies from slender and relatively hairless to stout and hairy. The head has a groove between the separated, bulging eyes and the face has a tuft of long hairs, called the beard. The forward-pointing proboscis is stiff and sharp for stabbing and sucking. The legs are strong and bristly for catching insect prey in flight.

OCCUR *in a variety of habitats, but prefer sunny sites in open or lightly wooded areas.*

LARVAE

The ground-living larvae are cryptically coloured, elongated, and tapered at both ends. They are scavengers or prey on the eggs, larvae, and pupae of other insects.

◀ **PHILONICUS ALBICEPS** *inhabits sandy areas, including coastal sand dunes. It is pale yellowish grey, with a "dusty" appearance.*

widely separated eyes

long, cylindrical abdomen

yellowish bristles on abdomen sides

dusky wings

▲ **LEPTOGASTER CYLINDRICA** *flies holding its front and middle legs forward, ready to catch prey. It hunts aphids, small flies, and bugs.*

four yellow abdomen segments

▲ **ASILUS CRABRONIFORMIS** *is a very large, wasp-like fly that makes short, darting flights to seize large prey such as crane flies (as here).*

bee-like abdomen

facial tuft

NOTE

Most species perch on an exposed twig or stone to spot passing prey, then give chase. They quickly stab victims and inject a protein-dissolving saliva.

▼ **DIOCTRIA BAUMHAUERI** *has a less-developed facial hair tuft than in other genera of robber flies. It occurs in cool, deciduous woodland.*

◀ **LAPHRIA SP.** *can seem very bee-like due to their large size and hairy bodies. Their larvae burrow inside wood and eat wood-boring beetle larvae.*

very hairy legs

dark, slender wasp-like body

ORDER *Diptera.*
FAMILY *Asilidae.*
NUMBER OF SPECIES *5,000.*
SIZE *0.3–2.8cm.*
FEEDING *Larvae: predators, scavengers. Adults: predators.*
IMPACT *Harmless.*

Long-legged Flies

Dolichopodidae

These flies are small or very small, bristly-bodied, and have very shiny green or yellow coloration. The head is rounded and bears a short, fleshy proboscis. The wings are oval and about as long as the body. In males, the genitalia are large and held curved forward under the abdomen; in females the abdomen ends in a sharp point. Males may have hairy tufts on the tarsi, antennae, and other parts of the body, used as sexual signals to females during mating.

COMMON *in damp habitats such as hedgerows, woodland, meadows, and lake and stream margins.*

NOTE

Long-legged flies are mostly predators of small, soft-bodied insects, which they squeeze and chew with their fleshy mouthparts before sucking the juices.

LARVAE

spines on front femur

These fly larvae are white, cylindrical, and taper towards the front end, where there is a retractable head. The body has tiny pseudopods (leg-like structures) to aid movement.

▲ **SCELLUS NOTATUS** *lives in grassy habitats. Males have a pair of yellow structures near the end of the abdomen and spines on the front femur.*

metallic green body

bristly tibia

large genitalia

▲ **POECILOBOTHRUS NOBILITATUS** *has bright green males that are often found on sunny patches of bare soil, displaying to females by wing-waving.*

dark, triangular head

silvery grey thorax

greenish tinge to body

▲ **MEDETERA STRIATA** *runs in all directions to catch prey and walks about on tree trunks. The larvae of this genus are beneficial as they eat bark beetle larvae.*

pale bands on abdomen

▲ **LIANCALUS VIRENS** *is commonly found near small streams, where fresh water runs down rock surfaces.*

ORDER *Diptera.*
FAMILY *Dolichopodidae.*
NUMBER OF SPECIES *5,500.*
SIZE *1–7mm.*
FEEDING *Larvae: predators. Adults: mostly predators, also liquid-feeders (nectar).*
IMPACT *Harmless.*

Dance Flies

Empididae

These flies' common name refers to the mating swarms in which the males fly up and down as if dancing. Most are small with a stout thorax and a slender, tapering abdomen. The coloration varies from dark brown and black to yellow or light brown. The rounded head has large eyes, antennae with three segments, and a long, downward-pointing proboscis. Dance flies are all predators, but may drink nectar as well.

FOUND on vegetation in moist locations, often resting on tree trunks or branches and sometimes on water.

LARVAE

The spindle-shaped larvae can retract their head and live in leaf litter, humus, wood, and water.

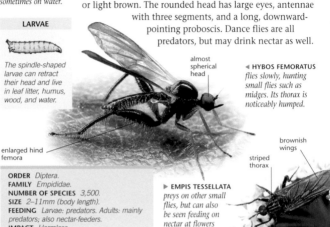

almost spherical head

enlarged hind femora

◄ **HYBOS FEMORATUS** flies slowly, hunting small flies such as midges. Its thorax is noticeably humped.

brownish wings

striped thorax

ORDER Diptera.
FAMILY Empididae.
NUMBER OF SPECIES 3,500.
SIZE 2–11mm (body length).
FEEDING Larvae: predators. Adults: mainly predators; also nectar-feeders.
IMPACT Harmless.

▶ **EMPIS TESSELLATA** preys on other small flies, but can also be seen feeding on nectar at flowers such as hawthorn.

Scuttle Flies

Phoridae

Scuttle flies are named for the adults' fast, jerky running movements. Their alternative name of hump-backed flies refers to their distinctive, well-developed thorax. They are small in size and dark brown, black, or yellowish. The fairly large wings are clear or light brown, and only have obvious veins near the front edge. The hind legs are often enlarged and flattened.

ATTRACTED to rotting fungi, compost heaps, and carcasses in many habitats. Also seen at flowers, dung, and the nests of social insects.

LARVAE

The larvae are fattest in the middle and feed on a wide variety of plant and animal foods.

▼ **PHORA ATRA**, shown here mating, feeds on flowers and honeydew. Males often form mating swarms in sunny spots.

strong hind legs

humped thorax

small head angled downwards

prominent bristles on head

◄ **ANEVRINA THORACICA** is a widespread species whose larvae live in soil, in the corpses of small mammals, and the nests of moles.

ORDER Diptera.
FAMILY Phoridae.
NUMBER OF SPECIES 2,800.
SIZE 0.5–5mm (body length).
FEEDING Larvae: scavengers, predators. Adults: predators, liquid-feeders.
IMPACT May feed on cultivated mushrooms.

Thick-headed Flies

Conopidae

Many of these species resemble bees or wasps, some having
yellow and black stripes on the abdomen and others being
reddish brown or black. The head is often the broadest part
of these flies and carries short, erect antennae with three

*OCCUR in a variety
of mainly open
habitats, usually
feeding at flowers.*

constricted
abdomen

segments and (usually) a long proboscis.
The abdomen is narrow where it joins
the thorax and is swollen and bent
down at the rear. Females lay
eggs on a variety of hosts.

wasp-like
markings

broad
head

long
proboscis

▲ PHYSOCEPHALA RUFIPES
*is a parasite of bumble bees and
honey bees. It closely resembles
some digger wasps (p.173).*

LARVAE

> **ORDER** *Diptera.*
> **FAMILY** *Conopidae.*
> **NUMBER OF SPECIES** *1,000.*
> **SIZE** *0.4–2cm (body length).*
> **FEEDING** *Larvae: parasites. Adults: liquid-
> feeders (nectar).*
> **IMPACT** *Harmless.*

**▲ CONOPS
QUADRIFASCIATA**
*grabs wasps and bees
in flight and lays an
egg on them. Its larvae
are internal parasites,
finally killing the host.*

*Much narrower at
the front, the larvae
suck the body fluids
of wasps, bees, and
other hosts.*

Black Scavenger or
Ensign Flies

Sepsidae

In summer these slender flies may form large swarms on
plants. They have a shiny black, purplish, or reddish body,
narrow wings, a rounded head, and slender legs. The wings
of most species are clear, with a noticeable, dark spot at the
ends. Adult males gather on vegetation and display their
wing tips by walking back and forth,
flicking their wings.

*LIVE in many different
types of habitat, on
dung and decaying
matter or at flowers.*

LARVAE

black shiny
body

rounded head

*The somewhat slim
and tapering larvae
may occur in huge
numbers in ideal
conditions.*

► SEPSIS FULGENS
*can be seen in groups
on plants and cow
dung. The base of
the abdomen often
has an orange tinge.*

> **ORDER** *Diptera.*
> **FAMILY** *Sepsidae.*
> **NUMBER OF SPECIES** *250.*
> **SIZE** *2–6mm (body length).*
> **FEEDING** *Larvae: scavengers, dung-feeders.
> Adults: liquid-feeders (nectar).*
> **IMPACT** *Harmless.*

Hover Flies or Flower Flies

Syrphidae

Hover flies are the most easily recognizable of all the flies due to their often wasp-like or bee-like appearance and their ability to hover. These superb aerial acrobats can move in all directions, including backwards, and can hold a fixed position in the air even in gusty conditions. The adults are typically slender-bodied with black and yellow or white stripes; some are stout and hairy. The eyes are large and in males meet on top of the head. The wings have a characteristic false vein running down the middle and a false margin at the edge (the joining together of the outer wing veins).

FOUND in a range of habitats, particularly localities with plenty of umbelliferous (flat-topped) flowers.

NOTE

Most hover flies are important as plant pollinators and pest controllers. Often it is possible to find four or five different species feeding on a single flowerhead.

pointed beak

▶ **RHINGIA CAMPESTRIS**, although not very brightly coloured, can be identified by its odd pointed beak. The larvae are found mainly in cow dung.

orange body with black stripes

♀

◀ **EPISYRPHUS BALTEATUS** is common in any habitat with suitable nectar-rich flowers. The larvae prey on aphids; the adults often migrate south in swarms.

▼ **SYRPHUS VITRIPENNIS** lives in a wide variety of habitats, preferring woodland. This species is very hard to distinguish from S. ribesii, but the female's hind femora are dark.

broad yellow bands

♀

LARVAE

Some larvae are aquatic or live in liquid manure, and possess a breathing tube (above). Many others are slug-like and fierce predators of aphids and other soft-bodied pests.

♀

all legs yellow

dark hind legs

false margin

◀ **SYRPHUS RIBESII** commonly occurs in gardens, where its larvae are major aphid predators. The adults feed on nectar, so planting suitable flowers will improve pest control.

DARK FORM

◀ **VOLUCELLA BOMBYLANS** *may have a reddish or a whitish tail and mimics the red- and buff-tailed bumble bees, but can be distinguished by its large eyes and single pair of wings.*

large, stout, hairy body

separated eyes

black posterior of abdomen

▲ **VOLUCELLA PELLUCENS** *is often to be seen feeding at bramble blossom. Its larvae live inside the nests of wasps and bees, where they are scavengers.*

♀

▶ **VOLUCELLA ZONARIA,** *a very big hover fly, resembles a large wasp or hornet. Its larvae develop in wasps' nests, while the adults feed on nectar in sheltered habitats.*

very broad abdomen

▶ **XYLOTA SEGNIS** *is recognized by the broad orange band on its slender abdomen. The adults feed on honeydew and sap, while the larvae live in rotten wood.*

furry, bee-like thorax

♂

orange band

♀

▼ **HELOPHILUS PENDULUS,** *also called the Sun Fly as it likes to bask, favours damp habitats. The larvae inhabit rotting matter such as liquid manure.*

three black stripes on thorax

♀

orange-brown body

▲ **ERISTALIS TENAX** *is known as the Drone Fly for its resemblance to male honey bees. Its larvae, called rat-tailed maggots, live in shallow, nutient-rich or stagnant water.*

yellow face

white patches

shiny black thorax

♂

brownish veins on wings

▼ **MYATHROPA FLOREA** *looks like a paler version of the Drone Fly (above left). Like rat-tailed maggots, the larvae have a breathing siphon at their rear end, but live in water-filled tree holes.*

◀ **SERICOMYIA SILENTIS** *occurs on acid heathland. The larvae of this species live in boggy pools, such as those that form after cutting peat.*

ORDER *Diptera.*
FAMILY *Syrphidae.*
NUMBER OF SPECIES *6,000.*
SIZE *0.4–2.8cm (body length).*
FEEDING *Larvae: predators and scavengers. Adults: liquid-feeders, herbivores.*
IMPACT *Beneficial as predators of aphids.*

orange hairs

♀

Rust Flies

Psilidae

OCCUR *in damp or moist areas near their host plants.*

Rust flies are slender or moderately robust, and reddish brown to black in colour. The body does not have strong bristles and may be virtually bare. The head is rounded or slightly triangular in outline, and the antennae may be relatively long. The wings are generally clear, but may be smoky or yellowish in some species. Some species induce galls on their host plants.

LARVAE

Larvae are usually smooth, slender herbivores. Some species induce galls on their hosts.

smooth surface
(without bristles)

shiny body

rounded head

PSILA ROSAE, *the Carrot Root Fly, is shiny black with a reddish yellow head and yellow legs. Larvae damage the roots of umbelliferous plants.*

ORDER *Diptera.*
FAMILY *Psilidae.*
NUMBER OF SPECIES *250.*
SIZE *3–7mm.*
FEEDING *Larvae: herbivores. Adults: liquid-feeders.*
IMPACT *Psilia rosae can be a serious pest.*

Leaf-mining Flies

Agromyzidae

FOUND *in a variety of habitats wherever their host trees, shrubs, or herbaceous plants grow.*

These small to medium-sized grey, black, or greenish yellow flies have moderately hairy heads and thoraxes. The wings are relatively large and usually clear. The abdomen is distinctly tapered, and females have a rigid, pointed ovipositor for laying eggs. The distinct feeding trails or mines made in leaves by the larvae are easy to see.

clear wings

◀ **PHYTOMYZA ILICIS** *lays its eggs on holly leaves. The feeding larva makes a mine between the upper and lower leaf surfaces.*

irregular blotch mine

▶ **LIRIOMYZA SP.** *are typically black, but some species have yellow markings. The genus has more than 140 European species.*

yellow scutellum

mine

LARVAE

Larvae pupate inside their mine or gall, or drop to the ground and pupate in the soil.

ORDER *Diptera.*
FAMILY *Agromyzidae.*
NUMBER OF SPECIES *2,500.*
SIZE *1–6mm.*
FEEDING *Larvae: herbivores. Adults: liquid-feeders.*
IMPACT *Many species are pests.*

▶ **AGROMYZA ALNIBETULAE** *lays eggs on birch or alder leaves. As the larvae feeds, the width of the mine becomes larger.*

Fruit Flies

Tephritidae

Sometimes called picture-winged flies, these small to medium-sized species are immediately recognizable by their wing markings. The patterning, which can be present in the form of transverse bands, patches, zigzag stripes, or spotting, can help to identify species. The females' abdomen tapers and ends in a pointed, rigid ovipositor, while in males, it is blunt or round-ended and does not taper. The larvae often feed inside galls that develop on the host plants. During courtship, the males of many species show a high degree of territoriality. They display by walking about slowly, waving one patterned wing while holding the other upright.

OCCUR *in many habitats, wherever their host plants are found.*

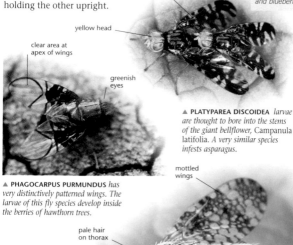

patterned wings

yellow head

clear area at apex of wings

greenish eyes

▲ **PLATYPAREA DISCOIDEA** *larvae are thought to bore into the stems of the giant bellflower,* Campanula latifolia. *A very similar species infests asparagus.*

▲ **PHAGOCARPUS PURMUNDUS** *has very distinctively patterned wings. The larvae of this fly species develop inside the berries of hawthorn trees.*

mottled wings

pale hair on thorax

yellowish orange head

LARVAE

The yellowish, pale brown, or whitish larvae live inside soft fruit, and in the flowerheads of daisies and related plants, either as stem or leaf miners or as gall formers.

▲ **OXYNA PARIETINA** *has wings with dark areas, large clear patches, and smaller semi-clear spots. The larvae bore into the stems of mugwort,* Artemisia vulgaris.

swollen gall

▶ **UROPHORA CARDUI** *lays eggs on stems of creeping thistle,* Cirsium arvense. *This causes the growth of a gall inside which several larvae develop.*

ORDER Diptera.
FAMILY Tephritidae.
NUMBER OF SPECIES 4,500.
SIZE 4–14mm.
FEEDING Larvae: herbivores. Adults: liquid-feeders (nectar, sap).
IMPACT Several species are serious pests.

Shore Flies

Ephydridae

OCCUR in ditches, bogs, marshes, and seashores; also found around stagnant water, cesspits, and drains.

Many shore flies are dark grey, brownish, or black, without any clear identification features. The wings are usually clear but can be patterned in some species. The face can appear somewhat bulging, with reddish eyes. Some species swarm in large numbers over salt marshes. The larvae generally feed by filtering micro-organisms from the water; others feed on decaying plant matter or are predators.

LARVAE

The larvae are pointed towards the front, with many small hairs all over their surface.

large red eyes

clear wings

enlarged front legs

ORDER Diptera.
FAMILY Ephydridae.
NUMBER OF SPECIES 1,400.
SIZE 2–9mm.
FEEDING Larvae and adults: scavengers, herbivores (algae only in adults), predators.
IMPACT Some are pests of cereals.

insect prey

OCHTHERA MANTIS preys on small insects, while its aquatic larvae eat the larvae of chironomid midges (p.125) and other flies.

Lesser Fruit Flies

Drosophilidae

FOUND in a variety of habitats and buildings where there is a supply of rotting plant matter.

If you want to see these small flies, which are also known as vinegar flies, simply leave out some wine, cider, or rotting fruit. Most species are light yellow or brown with clear or lightly marked wings and pale or bright red eyes. The thorax (and sometimes the abdomen) has spots or stripes. These insects are often used as laboratory insects in studies of genetics.

red eyes

reddish coloration

▶ **DROSOPHILA MELANOGASTER** is often used for genetics studies as it breeds quickly and has large, easily observable chromosomes.

LARVAE

banded abdomen

The pale, maggot-like larvae, which can develop rapidly, have hooked spines on each segment.

▲ **DROSOPHILA SP.** are quickly attracted to rotting fruit of all kinds and to the smell of cider or vinegar, both in buildings and outdoors. One species breeds in leftover milk.

ORDER Diptera.
FAMILY Drosophilidae.
NUMBER OF SPECIES 2,900.
SIZE 1–6mm.
FEEDING Larvae: scavengers, herbivores. Adults: liquid-feeders.
IMPACT May be pests in orchards.

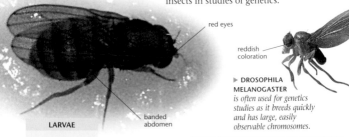

Stem, Grass, or Fruit Flies

Chloropidae

Species in this large and common group of flies are grey, green, or black with bright yellow markings, especially on the thorax. The body has very few obvious hairs or bristles, but a good recognition feature is a clear, shiny triangular mark on top of the head between the eyes. The abdomen is usually broad and tapers towards the rear.

LIVE *in cereal crops, grassland, reedbeds, and hedgerows.*

LARVAE

Usually the larvae are slender and cylindrical, tapering at the head and with a blunt rear.

elongated abdomen

iridescent green eyes

striped thorax

MEROMYZA PRATORUM *occurs in coastal sand dunes, where its larvae burrow and feed inside the stems of marram grasses.*

ORDER *Diptera.*
FAMILY *Chloropidae.*
NUMBER OF SPECIES *2,000.*
SIZE *2–7mm.*
FEEDING *Larvae: scavengers, herbivores, predators. Adults: liquid-feeders.*
IMPACT *Some are pests of cereals.*

Dung Flies

Scathophagidae

Dung flies are black, yellow, grey, or brown and sometimes show two of these colours in striking contrast. These flies may look superficially like house flies (p.146), but the commonest species are very hairy or bristly, some looking almost furry. The wings are usually clear but may have darkish tinges or spots. The abdomen is slender, but, in males, is enlarged at the rear end.

FOUND *in a variety of habitats, often on dung or in boggy areas.*

hairy body

LARVAE

The pale-coloured larvae are cylindrical and taper sharply to a point at the head end.

strong bristles on legs

♀

flies gathered to breed

ON DUNG

SCATHOPHAGA STERCORARIA, *the Yellow Dung Fly, is abundant on sheep and cow dung, where its larvae develop. It also breeds in the faeces of poultry, horses, and humans.*

ORDER *Diptera.*
FAMILY *Scathophagidae.*
NUMBER OF SPECIES *250.*
SIZE *3–11mm.*
FEEDING *Larvae: herbivores, dung-feeders, predators. Adults: predators.*
IMPACT *Generally harmless.*

Anthomyiid Flies

Anthomyiidae

These rather ordinary-looking flies are very similar in general appearance to house flies (p.146), although some may be larger or smaller. The body colour may be dull yellowish brown, grey, brown, or black, and the slender, bristly legs are yellowish brown or black. The wings may be clear or have a light smoky tinge. The adults of many species feed on pollen and nectar at umbelliferous and other flowers, while some species are predators of small insects. The larvae can be terrestrial or semiaquatic and show a wide range of feeding types.

OCCUR *in a very wide range of habitats from cultivated land and grassland to woodland and gardens; widespread and ubiquitous.*

LARVAE

Herbivorous white larvae are found as stem borers, gall formers, and leaf miners in the roots, stems, flower heads, and leaves of a huge range of host plants.

grey bands on abdomen

black patches on thorax

♂

♀

▲ **ANTHOMYIA PROCELLARIS** *is a common species, which is distinctively marked grey and black and is quite bristly. Its larvae develop in rotting plant matter.*

black legs

bristly thorax

smoky tinge to wings

slender, bristly abdomen

◄ **DELIA RADICUM**, *the Cabbage Root Fly, is a widespread pest in Europe. Females lay their eggs on soil close to cabbages and other brassica crops.*

♂

NOTE

Many anthomyiids are associated with cultivated plants, and are pests of crops, such as onion, cabbage, spinach, wheat, and raspberries.

ORDER Diptera.
FAMILY Anthomyiidae.
NUMBER OF SPECIES 1,500.
SIZE 2–12mm.
FEEDING Larvae: herbivores, scavengers.
Adults: liquid-feeders, herbivores, predators.
IMPACT Many species are serious pests.

Lesser House Flies

Fanniidae

Like smaller and more slender house flies (p.146), these flies are generally dark, although the legs or abdomen may be wholly or partly yellowish. The eyes of the males can be large and may even touch each other, while those of the females are smaller and separated. Males swarm in the shade of branches or overhangs and will fly indoors, where they dart about and land on the underside of ceiling lights.

COMMON *near decaying matter, in sheltered, well-vegetated locations, and under trees at woodland margins, parkland, or gardens.*

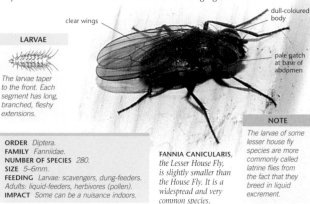

clear wings

dull-coloured body

pale patch at base of abdomen

LARVAE

The larvae taper to the front. Each segment has long, branched, fleshy extensions.

ORDER *Diptera.*
FAMILY *Fanniidae.*
NUMBER OF SPECIES *280.*
SIZE *5–6mm.*
FEEDING *Larvae: scavengers, dung-feeders. Adults: liquid-feeders, herbivores (pollen).*
IMPACT *Some can be a nuisance indoors.*

FANNIA CANICULARIS, *the Lesser House Fly, is slightly smaller than the House Fly. It is a widespread and very common species.*

NOTE

The larvae of some lesser house fly species are more commonly called latrine flies from the fact that they breed in liquid excrement.

Flesh Flies

Sarcophagidae

These stout-bodied, non-metallic flies are mostly dull grey or black with yellowish body hair. The most distinctive features are the longitudinally striped thorax, and the chequered or marbled abdominal patterns, which change from light to dark depending on the viewing angle. Adults are frequently seen feeding on nectar, sap, and honeydew. The females lay larvae, not eggs, often in carrion.

FOUND *in a variety of habitats, wherever there is decaying matter or carrion. Often associated with human habitations.*

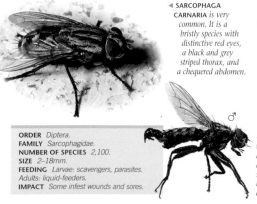

◀ **SARCOPHAGA CARNARIA** *is very common. It is a bristly species with distinctive red eyes, a black and grey striped thorax, and a chequered abdomen.*

LARVAE

The larvae taper to the front and hatch inside the female, which lays them in a suitable place.

ORDER *Diptera.*
FAMILY *Sarcophagidae.*
NUMBER OF SPECIES *2,100.*
SIZE *2–18mm.*
FEEDING *Larvae: scavengers, parasites. Adults: liquid-feeders.*
IMPACT *Some infest wounds and sores.*

◀ **SARCOPHAGA MELANEURA** *is very difficult to identify as there are numerous similar species; however, males have distinctive genitalia.*

House Flies and their relatives

Muscidae

The House Fly is a typical member of this family. These flies can be slender or stoutish, dull black, grey, or yellowish in colour, with clear wings. All parts of the body usually have strong, dark bristles. The legs are slender and quite long. The mouthparts act like a sponge and draw in liquid foods, except in blood-feeding species, which have piercing mouthparts. Identification of species relies on bristle patterns and structure of the genitalia. Muscids are found on flowers, excrement, and decaying organic matter. Blood-feeding species are associated with their hosts.

LARVAE

The larvae are typically maggot-shaped, tapering towards the front and blunt at the rear. They develop quickly in rotting material, and pupate in just over a week.

▼ **STOMOXYS CALCITRANS**, *the Stable Fly, looks like a House Fly with a striped thorax, and lightly chequered abdomen.*

yellowish orange at base of wings

sharp proboscis

grey patches on abdomen

▲ **MESEMBRINA MERIDIANA** *is an unmistakable large, shiny, dark fly, identified by the yellowish orange patches at the wing bases.*

▼ **POLIETES LARDARIUS** *is grey with a bluish tinge, a longitudinally striped thorax, and a dark-marked abdomen.*

clear wings

abdomen with orange patches

silvery stripes on thorax

reddish eyes

▲ **MUSCA DOMESTICA**, *the House Fly, is dark grey with lighter, longitudinal stripes down its thorax.*

NOTE

Many of these flies transmit harmful micro-organisms via their mouthparts and feet, which cause diseases such as dysentery and typhoid.

ORDER Diptera.
FAMILY Muscidae.
NUMBER OF SPECIES 3,000.
SIZE 2–12mm.
FEEDING Larvae: scavengers, herbivores. Adults: predators, scavengers, herbivores.
IMPACT Some bite, others transfer disease.

Blow Flies

Calliphoridae

Typical species, often called blue bottles or green bottles, are stout-bodied, medium to large, metallic green or blue flies that are attracted to carrion, as well as fresh and cooked meat and fish. Some species are shiny black or drab coloured. Most are usually the same size or bigger than a house fly. The tips of the antennae are distinctively feathered, and the proboscis is short. In some species, the sexes are different colours.

OCCUR *on all habitats, with the larvae on soil, dung, and carcasses.*

LARVAE

The larvae are typical white maggots that taper at the front end and are blunt ended at the rear. The head is narrow with dark, hook-like mouthparts.

metallic green coloration

▶ LUCILIA CAESAR *is a cosmopolitan, shiny, metallic green species that breeds on rotting carcasses and dung.*

shiny blue abdomen

◀ CALLIPHORA VOMITORIA *is a common "bluebottle". The dark thorax has faint longitudinal stripes and the abdomen has a metallic blue sheen.*

yellowish hairs

▶ POLLENIA RUDIS, *also known as the Cluster Fly, has distinctive, golden-yellow hair on its thorax.*

dark red eyes

bristly rear of abdomen

◀ CALLIPHORA VICINA *is very similar to C.* vomitoria, *but can be separated from it by the "cheeks" of the head below the eyes, which are red, not black, in colour.*

NOTE

Many species in this family are of medical and veterinary importance. Besides flesh-eating larvae, some calliphorids carry diseases such as dysentery.

hair

wings

CALLIPHORA VICINA

ORDER *Diptera.*
FAMILY *Calliphoridae.*
NUMBER OF SPECIES *1,200.*
SIZE *4–16mm.*
FEEDING *Larvae: scavengers, parasites. Adults: scavengers, liquid-feeders, herbivores.*
IMPACT *Can infest livestock and humans.*

Parasitic Flies

Tachinidae

Although parasitic flies show a wide range of body colour and patterns, most of them are dark-coloured, and stout-bodied. Some are like very bristly house flies, others are much larger, very hairy, and almost bee-like. The wings are usually clear, but some species have dark markings.

FOUND *in a wide variety of habitats, often at flowers or sap oozing from plants.*

LARVAE

Larvae are white or yellowish and may have spines or hairs. They are rarely seen.

mottled, angular wings

♂

▶ **ALOPHORA HEMIPTERA** *males are slightly larger than the females, and have dark wing markings.*

▶ **TACHINA GROSSA** *looks like a bumble bee. The front margins of the wings are yellowish towards the base.*

large, dark bristly body

wings yellowish at base

ORDER *Diptera.*
FAMILY *Tachinidae.*
NUMBER OF SPECIES *7,800.*
SIZE *0.5–2cm.*
FEEDING *Larvae: parasites. Adults: liquid-feeders.*
IMPACT *Beneficial control agents of pests.*

▶ **TACHINA FERA** *has a distinct dark stripe on the abdomen.*

Horse Bot Flies

Gasterophilidae

These flies, which are stout-bodied, resemble honey bees in colour and hairiness. They have strong legs, and non-functional mouthparts. Typically, the females lay their eggs on the shoulders and legs of horses. When licked off, the larvae burrow into the gums and tongue of the horse before completing their development in the stomach or intestines. When mature, the larvae pass out with the excrement, and pupate in the soil.

FOUND *in association with horses, wherever they are found.*

dark patches on wings

broad head

short antennae

LARVAE

Lavae are stout with distinct bands of backward-pointing spines encircling the body. The spines help the larvae to burrow through the host's tissues.

hairy bee-like body

GASTEROPHILUS INTESTINALIS *is short-lived and does not feed. Adults survive long enough to lay their eggs.*

ORDER *Diptera.*
FAMILY *Gasterophilidae.*
NUMBER OF SPECIES *50.*
SIZE *1–2cm.*
FEEDING *Larvae: parasites. Adults: non-feeding.*
IMPACT *Serious veterinary pest species.*

Bot Flies and Warble Flies

Oestridae

These hairy flies often resemble honey or bumble bees. The head is large, broad, and flattened from front to back, the antennae are small, and mouthparts are small or absent. The males of some species congregate on hilltops for mating purposes. Females are rarely encountered. Species are host-specific.

OCCUR *anywhere that their host animals are found, often on fields and pasture.*

antenna hidden in groove

wrinkled surface

mottled abdomen

▲ HYPODERMA BOVIS, *the Ox Warble Fly, is a widespread bee-like fly that attacks cattle.*

LARVAE

Larvae are broad, stout-bodied, and circled with bands of backward-pointing spines.

ORDER *Diptera.*
FAMILY *Oestridae.*
NUMBER OF SPECIES *80.*
SIZE *0.8–1.8cm.*
FEEDING *Larvae: parasites. Adults: non-feeding.*
IMPACT *Serious veterinary pest.*

▲ OESTRUS OVIS, *the Sheep Nostril Fly, has a characteristically wrinkled-looking body surface, and a broad blunt head.*

Louse Flies or Flat Flies

Hippoboscidae

There can be no mistaking these odd, flattened, parasitic flies. The head has a short, piercing proboscis, short antennae, and rounded or oval eyes. Many species have reduced wings or are wingless. The fully-winged species lose their wings once a bird or mammalian host is found. They have strong claws to hold onto feathers or hair.

LIVE *mainly in wooded areas where their host animals occur.*

small abdomen   strong legs

LARVAE

Females produce fat, rounded larvae, which pupate almost immediately on the host.

◀ LIPOPTENA CERVI, *the reddish brown Deer Fly, has a short, broad head that appears to be partly sunk into the thorax.*

broad, flat thorax

▶ HIPPOBOSCA EQUINA *is known as the Forest Fly. It is reddish brown with dark markings on the head and thorax.*

fully winged in both sexes

ORDER *Diptera.*
FAMILY *Hippoboscidae.*
NUMBER OF SPECIES *200.*
SIZE *2–8mm.*
FEEDING *Larvae: parasites. Adults: blood-feeders.*
IMPACT *Some species are considered pests.*

Rhyacophilid Caddisflies

Rhyacophilidae

OCCUR *near rivers, ponds, and lakes, in mating swarms at certain times of year.*

The wings of these caddisflies are brownish or yellowish and are sometimes lightly mottled. The antennae are about as long as the body. The front, middle, and hind tibiae have three, four, and four spurs respectively. Unlike other caddisflies, the aquatic larvae live without a case. When fully grown, they spin a case of small stone fragments in which to pupate. Most adult caddisflies do not feed and at certain times of the year, large mating swarms can be seen.

LARVAE

The larvae have conspicuous tufts of abdominal gills and strong legs with sharp claws.

▼ **RHYACOPHILA DORSALIS** *is one of many similar species with broad, yellowish, slightly hairy wings. It lives in upland or mountain streams.*

prominent dark eye

antennae same length as body

broad, yellowish wings

ORDER *Trichoptera.*
FAMILY *Rhyacophilidae.*
NUMBER OF SPECIES *500.*
SIZE *6–14mm.*
FEEDING *Larvae: herbivores (algae), predators. Adults: non-feeding.*
IMPACT *Harmless.*

Net-spinning Caddisflies

Hydropsychidae

COMMON *along streams, rivers, and other watercourses.*

These insects are named after the cup-shaped nets spun by their aquatic larvae to gather floating organisms and debris to eat. The drab adults have hairy or clear wings. The antennae are shorter or longer than the wings; the basal segment is short and bulbous. The middle and hind tibiae usually have four spurs; the front tibiae may have two.

yellowish hairs on head and thorax

variably mottled wings

LARVAE

The immobile larvae inhabit a tube-like retreat made from stones and other fragments of debris.

ORDER *Trichoptera.*
FAMILY *Hydropsychidae.*
NUMBER OF SPECIES *1,000.*
SIZE *5–14mm.*
FEEDING *Larvae: predators, scavengers. Adults: non-feeding.*
IMPACT *Harmless.*

▲ **HYDROPSYCHE SP.** *are very common in all kinds of flowing water. The wings are often mottled with patches of dark grey and light brown hairs.*

scattered patches of light hairs

Finger-net Caddisflies

Philopotamidae

Named after the tube-like silk nets that their larvae make on the underside of rocks, these caddisflies are often dull greyish brown, although some species have distinctly mottled front wings in shades of yellow and brown. The antennae are usually shorter than the body length, unlike Rhyacophilid caddisflies (left); another difference is that the front tibiae usually have two spurs, not three. There are four on the middle and hind tibiae.

FOUND *near moderate to fast-flowing streams and springs.*

pattern of yellowish spots and bands

shortish, dark antennae

long palps

LARVAE

The flattened, yellowish larvae live in slender silk tubes that filter very fine food particles, such as diatoms, from the water current.

▲ **PHILOPOTAMUS MONTANUS** *has a very distinctive dark greyish brown and yellow pattern on the front wings.*

ORDER *Trichoptera.*
FAMILY *Philopotamidae.*
NUMBER OF SPECIES 400.
SIZE *6–12mm.*
FEEDING *Larvae: scavengers (detritus, algae). Adults: non-feeding.*
IMPACT *Harmless.*

Giant Casemakers or Large Caddisflies

Phryganeidae

These insects are light brown or grey, often mottled, and their wings can be quite brightly marked with black and yellow-orange or have dark margins and stripes. The antennae are quite short: in some cases about as long as the front wings. The front, middle, and hind tibiae bear two, four, and four spurs respectively.

LIVE *near slow-moving rivers and streams and around ponds, lakes, and marshes.*

LARVAE

The larvae move around in beautifully regular cases made of plant fibres and lined with silk.

▼ **PHRYGANIA GRANDIS**, *a common species, lays its eggs in jelly-like masses on aquatic plants.*

smoky brown wings

shortish antennae

▼ **PHRYGANEA VARIA** *is attractively mottled and well camouflaged at rest. It flies at dusk.*

ORDER *Trichoptera.*
FAMILY *Phryganeidae.*
NUMBER OF SPECIES 500.
SIZE *1–2.8cm.*
FEEDING *Larvae: predators, scavengers. Adults: non-feeding.*
IMPACT *Harmless.*

mottled upperside

Northern Caddisflies

Limnephilidae

Abundant at northern latitudes and in hills or mountains, these caddisflies are quite large with a pale reddish, yellowish, or dark brownish coloration, often with dark wing markings. The front wings are fairly narrow, paper-like, and have few hairs. The antennae have a bulbous basal segment and are as long as the front wings.

WIDESPREAD around pools, lakes, streams, ditches, rivers, and marshes of all sizes.

mottled front wings

LARVAE

The larvae make a diverse variety of elegant cases from sand, stones, sticks, shells, or plants.

▶ **ANABOLIA NERVOSA** *varies in size as an adult. Its larvae attach sticks to their cases as defence against fish.*

▼ **GLYPHOTAELIUS PELLUCIDUS** *has a distinctive notch at the end of its wings. It is grey or brown and mottled all over.*

yellowish brown wings

notch on wing margin

ORDER *Trichoptera.*
FAMILY *Limnephilidae.*
NUMBER OF SPECIES *1,500.*
SIZE *0.8–3cm.*
FEEDING *Larvae: scavengers, herbivores, predators. Adults: non-feeding.*
IMPACT *Harmless.*

Brachycentrid Caddisflies

Brachycentridae

These greyish brown caddisflies have quite broad wings which are not very hairy, and can be elongate and pointed in females. The head is short and wide and the antennae are slender with the stout basal segment being about as long as the head. The front, middle, and hind tibiae have two, three, and three spurs, respectively

OCCUR in rivers, canals, and other slow- to fast-moving bodies of clean water.

antennae shorter than wings

yellowish grey hairs on thorax

yellowish patches at wing margins

LARVAE

Brachycentrid larvae differ from other families by making four-sided cases, from plant material.

ORDER *Trichoptera.*
FAMILY *Brachycentridae.*
NUMBER OF SPECIES *150.*
SIZE *5–14mm.*
FEEDING *Larvae: scavengers. Adults: non-feeding.*
IMPACT *Harmless.*

BRACHYCENTRUS SUBNUBILIS *has yellowish grey hair on its head and thorax. Its greyish wings have yellow patches.*

Goerid Caddisflies

Goeridae

The wings of these caddisflies are blackish, brownish, or yellowish in colour and are typically short, broad, and very hairy. The basal segment of the antennae is stout, hairy, and about twice the length of the head. The front tibiae have two spurs, while the middle and hind tibiae have four. In some species, sexes are different: males are black while females are brown.

FOUND *around lakes as well as moderately fast-flowing streams and rivers.*

SILO NIGRICORNIS *has very dark, almost black, males and light brown females.*

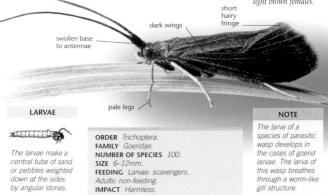

dark wings

short hairy fringe

swollen base to antennae

pale legs

LARVAE

The larvae make a central tube of sand or pebbles weighted down at the sides by angular stones.

ORDER *Trichoptera.*
FAMILY *Goeridae.*
NUMBER OF SPECIES *100.*
SIZE *6–12mm.*
FEEDING *Larvae: scavengers. Adults: non-feeding.*
IMPACT *Harmless.*

NOTE

The larva of a species of parasitic wasp develops in the cases of goerid larvae. The larva of this wasp breathes through a worm-like gill structure.

Long-horned Caddisflies

Leptoceridae

As their common name implies, these caddisflies have slender antennae that are typically two to three times longer than the front wings. The basal segment of the antenna is bulbous and about as long as the head. The front wings are long, narrow, and very hairy, often with dark cross bands. The front tibiae may have one or two spurs or none; the middle and hind tibiae always have two spurs.

ABUNDANT *around lakes, large ponds, and medium to large rivers.*

LARVAE

The larval cases are mostly made of sand grains, small stones, and plant material.

extremely long antennae

OECETIS OCHRACEA *is widely distributed and has very long antennae typical of its family.*

ORDER *Trichoptera.*
FAMILY *Leptoceridae.*
NUMBER OF SPECIES *850.*
SIZE *0.6–1.6cm.*
FEEDING *Larvae: scavengers, herbivores, predators. Adults: non-feeding.*
IMPACT *Harmless.*

Leaf-rolling Sawflies

Pamphilidae

Also known as web-spinning sawflies, these robust, fast-flying insects have a broad head and are flattened from top to bottom. Most species are black or dark with yellow markings. The antennae are slender and tapered. The larvae, which do not have prolegs on the abdomen, feed in groups under silken webs or in the rolled up foliage of deciduous trees such as hawthorn, birch, and aspen.

FAVOUR *woodland scrub and hedgegrow where host trees grow, in a variety of habitats.*

ACANTHOLYDA ERYTHROCEPHALA *has a broad red head in females; males have a narrower head with a yellow patch at the front.*

dark, smoky wings

broad red head

♀

LARVAE

The larvae are greyish green with brown spots and live in groups in silken webs on pine trees.

ORDER *Hymenoptera.*
FAMILY *Pamphilidae.*
NUMBER OF SPECIES *200.*
SIZE *1–1.6cm.*
FEEDING *Larvae: herbivores. Adults: herbivores, liquid-feeders (nectar).*
IMPACT *One species damages pear trees.*

Stem Sawflies

Cephidae

Stem sawflies are cylindrical, slender-bodied, slow-flying insects with a large prothorax, clear or smoky-tinged wings, and a slightly flattened abdomen. Although the basic coloration is dark, many species have yellow thorax markings and abdominal bands. The antennae are quite long and slender and may be slightly clubbed at the ends. Species in the genera *Cephus* and *Trachelus* attack a variety of cereals.

FOUND *among cereal crops and in meadows and grassland; adults often at yellow flowers.*

slightly clubbed antennae

CEPHUS NIGRINUS *is an all-black sawfly with a slim body. There are two very similar species both with yellow markings.*

very slender body

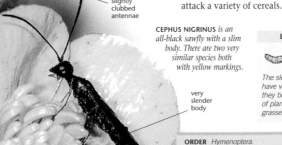

LARVAE

The slender larvae have vestigial legs; they bore into stems of plants such as grasses and willows.

ORDER *Hymenoptera.*
FAMILY *Cephidae.*
NUMBER OF SPECIES *100.*
SIZE *4–12mm.*
FEEDING *Larvae: herbivores. Adults: herbivores, liquid-feeders (nectar).*
IMPACT *Some species attack cereal crops.*

Horntails or Woodwasps

Siricidae

The common names for these large, stout-bodied sawflies refer to a spine-like structure at the end of their abdomen, which is short and triangular in males and long and spear-like in females. In addition, females have an even longer ovipositor, with which they drill into wood to lay a single egg. Despite their large size and (sometimes) wasp-like appearance, these insects do not sting. The head is quite large, broadest behind the eyes, and usually has long and slender antennae. The wings are generally clear, but may be dark or tinged yellowish.

OCCUR in coniferous or deciduous forests, where females attack diseased, weakened, or fallen trees.

▼ **UROCERUS GIGAS**, the Horntail, has strikingly wasp-like females with long ovipositors; males are smaller and less wasp-like.

reddish orange antennae

yellow spot behind eye

yellow antennae

♂

♀

reddish abdomen

long ovipositor

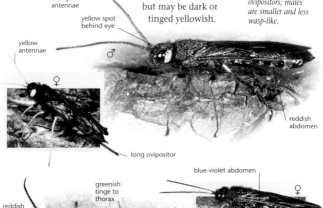

blue-violet abdomen

greenish tinge to thorax

reddish base to antennae

♀

reddish brown end to abdomen

LARVAE

Woodwasp larvae have a stout spine at their rear end, with which they push themselves through tunnels in heartwood. Their development takes up to two years.

NOTE

Despite their large size and alarmingly long ovipositors, which are often mistaken for stings, these insects are entirely harmless to humans.

▲ **SIREX JUVENCUS** lays its eggs in spruce and pine. The abdomen is bluish in females and reddish brown in males.

ORDER Hymenoptera.
FAMILY Siricidae.
NUMBER OF SPECIES 100.
SIZE 2–4cm.
FEEDING Larvae: wood-feeders, fungi-feeders. Adults: liquid-feeders.
IMPACT Many species are pests of trees.

Common Sawflies

Tenthredinidae

LIVE *in nearly all land habitats, especially gardens, pastures, and woodland, as far north as the Arctic.*

Common sawflies vary a great deal and may be quite narrow-bodied and wasp-like or broader and more robust. The body colour is typically brown, black, or green but many are brightly marked with yellow or red. The slender antennae can be made up of anything between 7 and 13 segments, but usually have 9 segments. The tibiae of the front legs have two apical (near the tip) spurs, and in many species the sexes have different coloration.

vivid red swelling

GALL

◄ **PONTANIA VESICATOR** *is one of several similar sawflies in its genus that make bright red galls on willow leaves.*

transparent "blotch" mine

thick yellow antennae

wasp-like markings

▶ **TENTHREDO SCROPHULARIAE**, is called the Figwort Sawfly because its larvae feed on this plant (Scrophularia) in boggy habitats, woodland, and hedgerows.

LARVAL MINE

▲ **SCOLIONEURA NIGRICANS** *is common in central and northern Europe. Its larvae tunnel inside birch tree leaves, making a transparent mine before emerging.*

distinctive black markings

black wing veins

broad head

▶ **RHOGOGASTER VIRIDIS**, *seen here resting on a bracken frond, is a large and distinctive sawfly of woodland and scrub. It preys on small insects.*

green legs

LARVAE

NOTE

Females use their ovipositor to cut egg-laying slits in the leaves, twigs, and shoots of host plants. Most larvae browse on foliage; some produce galls.

The caterpillar-like larvae may have warning coloration or be cryptically coloured. Some are smooth, while others have spines, hairs, and bumps.

ORDER Hymenoptera.
FAMILY Tenthredinidae.
NUMBER OF SPECIES 4,000.
SIZE 4–15mm (body length).
FEEDING Larvae: herbivores (leaves). Adults: predators, liquid-feeders.
IMPACT Many species are pests of crops.

Cimbicid Sawflies

Cimbicidae

Many of these large, broad-bodied sawflies can look superficially like hairless bees and even make a buzzing noise when they fly. Most species are black or yellowish and black, but some are metallic green. The antennae have less than seven segments, with the last one or two segments greatly swollen to form a club. The larvae eat the foliage of specific hosts, such as birch and hawthorn trees.

FOUND *wherever their host plants – usually trees – grow.*

▼ **CIMBEX LUTEUS** *feeds on willow and sometimes poplar foliage as a larva. The adult has a largely yellow abdomen.*

club

metallic green sheen

▲ **ABIA SERICEA** *has a fat body. Its larvae feed on Devil's Bit Scabious (Succisa pratensis), and Field Scabious (Knautia arvensis).*

clouded brown wings

bronze sheen

▶ **ZARAEA LONICERA** *feeds on Dwarf or Fly Honeysuckle (Lonicera xylosteum), during its larval stage.*

LARVAE

Slightly curved in shape, the larvae have several legs on the thorax and numerous prolegs (unsegmented legs) on the abdomen. They pupate inside a tough cocoon.

stout body

brownish wings

◀ **TRICHIOSOMA LUCORUM** *is a stout-bodied sawfly whose larvae feed on hawthorn foliage in scrub and hedgerows. When fully grown, the larvae pupate inside a tough cocoon attached to twigs.*

NOTE

The population of some of these species are declining due to the disappearance of hedgegrows, and efficient methods of hedge trimming.

very hairy

ORDER *Hymenoptera.*
FAMILY *Cimbicidae.*
NUMBER OF SPECIES *150.*
SIZE *2–2.6cm (body length).*
FEEDING *Larvae: herbivores (leaves). Adults: liquid-feeders.*
IMPACT *Harmless.*

Argid Sawflies

Argidae

These stout-bodied sawflies are sometimes known as rose sawflies. They are normally black and red or black and yellow but some species are metallic blue or green. The antennae characteristically have only three segments; the last segment is very long and, in males, is divided into a "Y" or "V". The larvae feed externally on the foliage of trees and shrubs, often in groups, although some are leaf-miners.

DISTRIBUTION *matches that of host trees and plants, with most species found in warmer regions.*

▼ **ARGE ROSAE** *has social larvae that feed gregariously. Females lay their eggs in slits in the shoots of roses.*

LARVAE

Larvae are generally caterpillar-like and some have bright warning coloration.

dark patch and wing edges

▼ **ARGE USTULATA** *occurs in scrubby habitats, where the larvae feed on the foliage of hawthorn, willow, and birch.*

smoky yellow wings

ORDER Hymenoptera.
FAMILY Argidae.
NUMBER OF SPECIES 600.
SIZE 4–16mm (body length).
FEEDING Larvae: herbivores (mainly leaves). Adults: liquid-feeders.
IMPACT A few species are pests of trees.

Conifer Sawflies

Diprionidae

These very stout-bodied, slow-flying sawflies are mainly dull brown or black in colour, although some may have yellowish or reddish thorax markings and abdominal bands. The antennae of males are very broad and feathery; those of females are narrow and slightly toothed. The abdomen is widest across the middle and slightly flattened.

CONFINED *to areas of coniferous woodland, including plantations.*

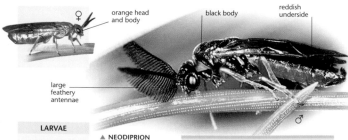

orange head and body

black body

reddish underside

large feathery antennae

♀

♂

LARVAE

The larvae are either solitary with cryptic coloration or social and vividly coloured.

▲ **NEODIPRION SERTIFER**, *the Pine Sawfly, can be a major pest in plantations of pine and occasionally spruce. The males are active, but the larger females rarely fly.*

ORDER Hymenoptera.
FAMILY Diprionidae.
NUMBER OF SPECIES 100.
SIZE 6–12mm (body length).
FEEDING Larvae: herbivores (pine needles). Adults: liquid-feeders.
IMPACT Some species damage host trees.

Ichneumon Wasps

Ichneumonidae

Ichneumons are generally slender-bodied with antennae at
least half as long as the body and composed of a minimum
of 16 segments. Many species are uniformly coloured pale
yellowish- or reddish brown to black, while others are
brightly patterned with yellow and black. The slender,
sometimes laterally flattened abdomen is joined
to the thorax by a slender stalk of variable length. Most
species are fully winged with a prominent pterostigma
on the leading edge of the front wings.

COMMON *almost
everywhere, above
all in damp habitats.
Strongly attracted to
umbelliferous (flat-
topped) flowers
and lights.*

♀ — ovipositor sheath

ovipositor in use

red legs

yellowish brown all over

▲ **NETELIA SP.** *parasitize the
caterpillars of moths. If handled,
females will try to "sting"
fingers with their ovipositors.*

► **LISSONOTA SP.**
*parasitize wood-
feeding moth larvae,
which females drill
down to reach.*

► **PROTICHNEUMON
PISORIUS** *can be seen
at flowers; females lay
their eggs inside hawk
moth caterpillars.*

pale bands on antennae

► **DIPLAZON LAETATORIUS**
*is extremely widespread.
Females lay their eggs
inside the eggs of
hover flies.*

banded hind femura

very long ovipositor

► **RHYSSA
PERSUASSORIA,** *the
Sabre Wasp, drills into
the trunks of pine trees
to locate the larvae
of wood wasps deep
within the wood.*

black and white body

♀

reddish legs

LARVAE

*Pale and maggot-
like, the larvae may
have a tail that
gets shorter with
age. Most are
internal parasites
that eventually kill
the host organism.*

ORDER *Hymenoptera.*
FAMILY *Ichneumonidae.*
NUMBER OF SPECIES *20,000.*
SIZE *0.3–4.2cm (body length).*
FEEDING *Larvae: parasites. Adults: liquid-
feeders.*
IMPACT *Many species control other pests.*

NOTE

*Females use their
long ovipositors to
lay eggs on or inside
the larvae or pupae
of insects such as
beetles, flies, moths,
butterflies, sawflies,
and other wasps.*

Braconid Wasps

Braconidae

The majority of braconid wasps are brownish, reddish brown, or black, and none are brightly coloured. Nearly all are small and inconspicuous, and the slender antennae may have anything from 10 to more than 50 segments. The abdomen – which is never particularly long – is slender, laterally flattened, or stalked. The ovipositor may be long and thin, or short and inconspicuous.

FOUND *almost everywhere there are insect pests to parasitize.*

yellowish cocoons

host caterpillar

▲ **APANTELES GLOMERATUS** *is an internal parasite of certain white butterflies, such as the Cabbage White.*

orangish abdomen

rounded head

ovipositor

LARVAE

The pale larvae live inside host insects. Minute differences in the mouthparts distinguish species.

ORDER Hymenoptera.
FAMILY Braconidae.
NUMBER OF SPECIES 15,000.
SIZE 2–8mm.
FEEDING Larvae: parasites. Adults: liquid-feeders.
IMPACT Many help to control insect pests.

▲ **COELOIDES BOSTRICHORUM** *parasitizes certain bark beetles. Females use their ovipositor to lay eggs on grubs in wood.*

Scelionid Wasps

Scelionidae

These very small, black or rarely brownish wasps vary in body shape from quite slender to stout with a flattened abdomen. The antennae normally have 11 or 12 segments and in females may have a distinct terminal club. The antennae, which are elbowed, arise from low on the head. When not in use, the ovipositor is concealed within the female's body.

OCCUR *in a wide variety of habitats in association with their hosts.*

antennae swollen at tip

antennae join head low down

shiny body

TRIMORUS PEDESTRIS *is a widespread species that parasitizes the eggs of ground-living beetles. Both sexes lack wings.*

flattened abdomen

LARVAE

The larvae are pale and grub-like, with a flattened rear. The head often appears to be "withdrawn".

ORDER Hymenoptera.
FAMILY Scelionidae.
NUMBER OF SPECIES 1,250.
SIZE 1–4mm.
FEEDING Larvae: parasites. Adults: liquid-feeders.
IMPACT Some help to control insect pests.

Chalcid Wasps

Chalcididae

Most species of chalcid wasp are dark brown, black, red, or yellow. Although the tough body may have pitting or sculpturing, it never has a metallic sheen. A distinguishing feature of these tiny insects is that the first two segments of each hind leg – the coxa and femur – are greatly enlarged. The hind femora are also toothed underneath. Females have a short, inconspicuous ovipositor.

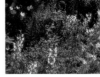

FOUND in a variety of well-vegetated habitats wherever there are host insects.

▼ **CHALCIS SISPES** is a parasite of soldier fly larvae in coastal marshes and fenland.

▼ **BRACHYMERA MINUTA** parasitizes moth pupae and fly puparia. Adults vary considerably in size and can be up to 6mm long.

stout antennae

pitted surface

stout antennae

LARVAE

The white, grub-like larvae have small heads and few other obvious features. They develop inside their hosts' bodies.

ORDER Hymenoptera.
FAMILY Chalcididae.
NUMBER OF SPECIES 1,500.
SIZE 2–8mm.
FEEDING Larvae: parasites. Adults: liquid-feeders.
IMPACT Many help to control insect pests.

Eurytomids

Eurytomidae

These wasps are yellow, reddish, or dull black. A few have a metallic sheen, while others can be shiny and dimpled. Eurytomids look similar to chalcid wasps, but the hind coxae are never very enlarged and the femora do not have tooth-like projections. The antennae, which are elbowed low down, have 6 to 13 segments. The larvae of many species develop inside seeds and are called seed chalcids.

LIVE in habitats where there are suitable seeds and stem-mining or other insect larvae or galls to attack.

LARVAE

The tiny larvae are white and grub-like, with a few long hairs. Many develop inside seeds; others parasitize insect larvae or eggs.

EURYTOMA BRUNNIVENTRIS is a parasite of the larvae of gall-forming wasps. This adult is visiting a gall.

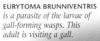

dimpled thorax

elbowed antennae

shiny black abdomen

ORDER Hymenoptera.
FAMILY Eurytomidae.
NUMBER OF SPECIES 1,400.
SIZE 3–6mm.
FEEDING Larvae: parasites, herbivores. Adults: liquid-feeders.
IMPACT Many help to control insect pests.

Gall Wasps

Cynipidae

THRIVE *in a range of habitats, wherever suitable host trees or plants grow.*

Gall wasps are tiny and have shiny black or blackish brown bodies. The thorax has a characteristic humped appearance in side view. Most species are fully winged, with much reduced vein patterns; some are short-winged or wingless. Males are typically smaller than females, which have an oval abdomen flattened from side to side. The galls that these wasps induce on their host plants are unique to each species and much easier to identify than the wasps themselves as they vary greatly in size, colour, texture, and location. Gall wasps have complex life cycles, often involving sexual and asexual (no males involved) generations that occur at different times of year.

hairy surface

GALLS

▲ **LIPOSTHENES GLECHOMAE** *makes small, globular, hairy galls on ground ivy (Glechoma species). Inside each gall is a single developing larva.*

▶ **DIPLOLEPIS EGLANTERIAE** *causes rounded, green or red galls on the underside of wild and cultivated roses. A single larva feeds inside each gall.*

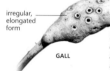

GALLS

pea-like shape

irregular, elongated form

GALL

◀ **DIASTROPHUS RUBI** *induces swollen galls on the shoots and young stems of Rubus species such as raspberry, dewberry, and bramble. Each contains many larvae.*

▶ **BIORHIZA PALLIDA** *has a unisexual generation (shown right) that develops in galls on oak tree roots. This emerges to lay eggs on oak buds, producing Oak Apple Galls (below). These in turn give rise to a bisexual generation.*

reddish and spongy

GALL

smooth, shiny abdomen

♀

large thorax

GALL

hard and knobbly gall

spherical, woody galls

green first, then brown when mature

GALLS

▲ **ANDRICUS QUERCUSCALICIS** *induces knobbly galls to grow from the base of acorns of the English Oak. Each houses a larva of the unisexual generation.*

▲ **ANDRICUS KOLLARI** *causes Marble Galls on oak trees. These were once collected as their high tannin content was important in ink-making.*

"crown" of points at apex

▶ **ANDRICUS QUERCUSTOZAE** *triggers the appearance of very large galls on several oak tree species. A single larva lives inside each gall.*

▼ **DIPLOLEPIS ROSAE** *causes the Rose Bedeguar Gall, or Robin's Pincushion, on wild roses and sometimes on cultivated varieties. The gall contains many larvae.*

GALL

hard, scaly orange galls

GALLS

▲ **NEUROTERUS QUERCUSBACCARUM** *is one of several species to produce Spangle Galls on the underside of oak leaves. Some leaves may be completely covered with galls.*

extensive "mossy" growth

GALL

green at first, then turn red

GALLS

▼ **CYNIPS QUERCUSFOLII** *has two generations. The second, bisexual generation lays eggs on the lower surface of oak leaves, creating Cherry Galls (left).*

♀

humped thorax

shiny abdomen

LARVAE

The pale, smooth, grub-like larvae hatch from eggs laid inside plant tissues, inducing the plant to produce galls that both protect and nourish the developing larvae.

ORDER *Hymenoptera.*
FAMILY *Cynipidae.*
NUMBER OF SPECIES *1,250.*
SIZE *1–8mm.*
FEEDING *Larvae: herbivores, parasites. Adults: liquid-feeders.*
IMPACT *High infestations weaken host plants.*

Torymid Wasps

Torymidae

The body of these small wasps is typically elongated and usually metallic blue or green. The thorax is sculptured with dimples and the abdomen is normally smooth, with a very long ovipositor in females. The first segment (coxa) of the hind legs is much larger than the coxa of the front legs and the femora of the hind legs may have one or more tooth-like projections.

OCCUR *in a range of habitats, wherever suitable host insects can be found.*

long ovipositor

long ovipositor

♀

▲ **TORYMUS NITENS** *is a parasite of the gall wasp* Andricus kollari. *The female has a long ovipositor to reach host larvae inside their gall.*

♀

▲ **MEGASTIGMUS DORSALIS** *has a long ovipositor and is able to drill deep into oak galls such as the oak apple to parasitize the occupant. It also attacks marble galls.*

LARVAE

The larvae are pale, grub-like, and often hairy, with indistinct segments on the abdomen.

ORDER *Hymenoptera.*
FAMILY *Torymidae.*
NUMBER OF SPECIES *1,500.*
SIZE *1–6mm.*
FEEDING *Larvae: parasites, herbivores. Adults: liquid-feeders.*
IMPACT *Some species help to control pests.*

Pteromalid Wasps

Pteromalidae

Most pteromalids are black or metallic blue or green, although some are brown or yellowish. The body shape ranges from elongated and slender to moderately robust and the antennae have 8 to 13 segments. The thorax is usually large and covered with dimples; the small, smooth abdomen is triangular in females and oblong in males.

LIVE *in many habitats where insect hosts are plentiful.*

♀

few veins on wings

MESOPOLOBUS TYPOGRAPHI *attacks* Ips typographus *and other bark beetles. It may be attracted to the aggregation pheromone produced by its beetle hosts.*

pointed abdomen

LARVAE

The pale larvae are grub-like and have small heads. Some species have small bumps on the body.

NOTE

Pteromalids attack the larvae or pupae of many insects, including butterflies, moths, and beetles. In most cases, the host is paralyzed and eggs laid on it.

ORDER *Hymenoptera.*
FAMILY *Pteromalidae.*
NUMBER OF SPECIES *3,100.*
SIZE *1–6mm.*
FEEDING *Larvae: parasites. Adults: liquid-feeders.*
IMPACT *Many species help to control pests.*

Trichogrammatid Wasps

Trichogrammatidae

Due to their small size, these wasps are often overlooked. Nevertheless, most species are stout-bodied and have fully developed wings with characteristic lines of small hairs in radiating patterns. The front wings are fairly broad with a single vein, while the hind wings are much smaller and narrower with a fringe of hairs. Unlike other wasps, the tarsi have only three segments.

FOUND *in a wide variety of habitats where there are insect eggs (usually exposed on foliage) to parasitize.*

LARVAE

The pale, minute larvae have few obvious features and live inside the eggs of host insects.

NOTE

Females lay their eggs inside those of other insects, so the best way to see these tiny wasps is to collect insect eggs and wait to see what emerges.

TRICHOGRAMMA SEMBLIDIS *is widespread but rarely seen due to its small size, and has been used in the biological control of certain species of moth pests.*

broad head

ORDER *Hymenoptera.*
FAMILY *Trichogrammatidae.*
NUMBER OF SPECIES *530.*
SIZE *0.3–1.2mm.*
FEEDING *Larvae: parasites. Adults: liquid-feeders.*
IMPACT *Many species help to control pests.*

fine hairs at wing margin

veinless wings

♀

Fairyflies

Mymaridae

This family includes the world's smallest flying insects. Fairyflies are very small or minute wasps with non-metallic yellow, dark brown, or black coloration broken with pale or dark markings. The narrow front wings have no obvious venation and are fringed with fine hairs, while the hind wings – which are very narrow or even stalk-like – are fringed with long hairs. Fairyflies are mostly parasites of the eggs of leaf hoppers and various bugs.

INHABIT *any well-vegetated location with insect eggs to parasitize.*

LARVAE

During their early development, the larvae are tiny and have tails; later, they are more grub-like.

ANAGRUS SP. *are small, delicate wasps, which are usually parasites of leafhopper eggs.*

stalk-like wing bases

thick base to antennae

♀

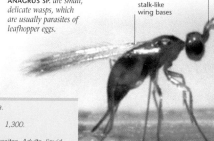

ORDER *Hymenoptera.*
FAMILY *Mymaridae.*
NUMBER OF SPECIES *1,300.*
SIZE *0.2–1mm.*
FEEDING *Larvae: parasites. Adults: liquid-feeders.*
IMPACT *Many species help to control pests.*

Ruby-tailed Wasps or Jewel Wasps

Chrysididae

Rather like miniature gems, these shiny, metallic insects are unmistakable. The body can be blue, green, red, or combinations of these colours, the commonest species having a red abdomen. The armour-like body surface, which offers protection from bee and wasp stings, is sculptured with coarse pits and dimples. The eyes are large and the antennae normally have 13 segments. A distinctive feature is that the underside of the abdomen is nearly always flattened or concave, enabling the wasps to curl into a ball if attacked.

NOTE

These species are also called cuckoo wasps because in many cases their larvae steal the host larvae's provisions; sometimes, the host is eaten as well.

▶ **PSEUDOMALUS AURATUS** *is one of several species in Europe that parasitize digger wasps, such as* Pemphredon *species.*

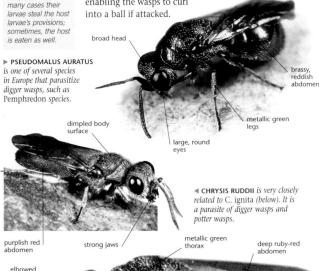

broad head

brassy, reddish abdomen

metallic green legs

large, round eyes

dimpled body surface

◀ **CHRYSIS RUDDII** *is very closely related to* C. ignita *(below). It is a parasite of digger wasps and potter wasps.*

purplish red abdomen

strong jaws

metallic green thorax

deep ruby-red abdomen

elbowed antennae

LARVAE

The larvae are stout, smooth, and the middle of their body is the broadest part. Most species eat the larval food supply of solitary bees and wasps; others target butterflies or moths.

ORDER Hymenoptera.
FAMILY Chrysididae.
NUMBER OF SPECIES 3,000.
SIZE 3–12mm.
FEEDING Larvae: parasites. Adults: liquid-feeders (nectar).
IMPACT Harmless; do not sting.

▲ **CHRYSIS IGNITA** *lays its eggs in the nests of a wide variety of solitary wasps and bees.*

Spider-hunting Wasps

Pompilidae

These slender-bodied wasps are generally dark in colour with yellowish or orange bands or other markings on the abdomen and yellowish or smoky wings. The pronotum is quite large and extends back towards the wing bases. The legs, especially the hind legs, are long and spiny. Pompilids rarely fly but are highly active: they can be seen running quickly, flicking and jerking their wings, as they look for spiders. When found, the spider is swiftly paralyzed and the female then digs a burrow. She buries the spider and lays an egg on it before sealing the burrow.

FOUND *at flowers or on the ground, often in open, sandy habitats.*

LARVAE

The larvae are pale and grub-like. Like those of ruby-tailed or jewel wasps (left), they are widest in the middle. They are rarely seen as they live in burrows dug by the females.

◀ **ANOPLIUS VIATICUS** *is a widespread dark species with distinctive reddish orange patches on the abdomen.*

NOTE

The venom of these wasps is strong enough to overcome even the largest spiders. Before a wasp stings, it must grapple with its prey and avoid its fangs.

overall dark coloration

strong front legs

orange patches on abdomen

large, oval eyes

greyish bands of hairs

ORDER Hymenoptera.	
FAMILY Pompilidae.	
NUMBER OF SPECIES 4,200.	
SIZE 0.5–2.5cm.	
FEEDING Larvae: parasites. Adults: liquid-feeders (nectar).	
IMPACT The stings can be extremely painful.	

▲ **POMPILIUS CINEREUS** *has a grey appearance, with bands of hairs across the abdomen. Females have strong combs on their front legs for digging in sandy soil and mainly hunt for wolf spiders.*

Common Wasps, Paper Wasps, and Potter Wasps

Vespidae

The commonest species in this family are yellow-jackets, which live in colonies inside rounded paper nests and catch insects, often caterpillars, to feed to their larvae. Most species are black or brown with yellow or white markings. Vespid's eyes are notched on the internal margins and may look crescent-shaped. At rest, the wings are folded in longitudinal pleats along the sides of the body. Paper wasps make nests of combs that are never enclosed by an outer carton. The solitary potter wasps make small mud nests on stems and in natural cavities.

FOUND *practically wherever there is suitable prey, including woodland, parkland, and gardens.*

LARVAE

The wrinkled body is broadest about a third of the way from the head. The larvae are fed by workers which live in colonies inside individual nest cells.

NOTE

Nest shape, colour, and location help to identify social wasps, which may look very similar. Wasps remove many garden pests to feed their larvae.

eyes

antennae

longitudinally pleated wings

yellow tibia

▶ **VESPULA GERMANICA**, *the German Wasp, has three small black spots on its face. This species makes greyish coloured nests underground, in hollow trees, or inside sheds and attics.*

antennae

yellow stripes on thorax

▶ **VESPULA VULGARIS**, *the Common Wasp, has a small anchor-shaped mark on its face. This worker (right) is scraping wood fibres from a tree to make paper for its nest.*

large nest on roof timbers

NEST

ORDER *Hymenoptera.*
FAMILY *Vespidae.*
NUMBER OF SPECIES *4,000.*
SIZE *8–26mm.*
FEEDING *Larvae: carnivorous. Adults: predators, liquid-feeders (nectar).*
IMPACT *Very beneficial but can sting.*

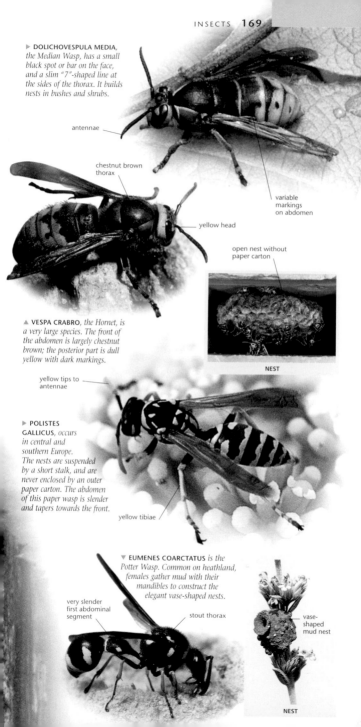

▶ **DOLICHOVESPULA MEDIA**, the Median Wasp, has a small black spot or bar on the face, and a slim "7"-shaped line at the sides of the thorax. It builds nests in bushes and shrubs.

antennae

chestnut brown thorax

yellow head

variable markings on abdomen

open nest without paper carton

NEST

▲ **VESPA CRABRO**, the Hornet, is a very large species. The front of the abdomen is largely chestnut brown; the posterior part is dull yellow with dark markings.

yellow tips to antennae

▶ **POLISTES GALLICUS**, occurs in central and southern Europe. The nests are suspended by a short stalk, and are never enclosed by an outer paper carton. The abdomen of this paper wasp is slender and tapers towards the front.

yellow tibiae

▼ **EUMENES COARCTATUS** is the Potter Wasp. Common on heathland, females gather mud with their mandibles to construct the elegant vase-shaped nests.

very slender first abdominal segment

stout thorax

vase-shaped mud nest

NEST

Ants

Formicidae

Ants are familiar and ubiquitous social insects, and may be pale yellow, reddish to brown, or black. The individuals commonly seen are the wingless workers, but the reproductive males and females that appear at from time to time are fully winged. The second, or second and third segments of the abdomen are constricted to form a waist, called the pedicel, which may have bumps or spine-like processes. The head carries strong jaws, and the antennae are elbowed immediately after the long first segment.

NOTE

Ants are essential elements of all terrestrial habitats, and they are often the most abundant and significant carnivorous group of insects present.

reddish thorax of worker

▼ **FORMICA RUFA**, *the Wood Ant, is an active predator, but also likes honeydew. The ants shown below are tending a colony of aphids.*

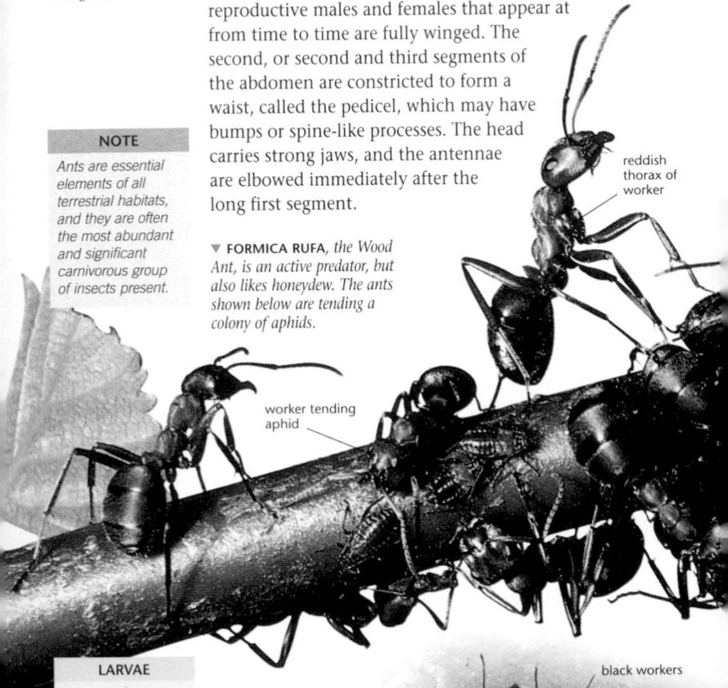

worker tending aphid

black workers

LARVAE

The white larvae are grub-like, slightly curved, and may have fine body hairs. They are fed by worker ants and moved to a new site if the nest is disturbed.

▶ **LASIUS NIGER**, *the common Black Garden Ant, occurs in soil under stones and pavements. In late summer, large mating swarms of winged ants are produced.*

▼ **CREMATOGASTER SCUTELLARIS** *is a small ant with the habit of raising its abdomen in a defensive posture if disturbed. It is found throughout southern Europe.*

reddish brown head

ORDER *Hymenoptera.*
FAMILY *Formicidae.*
NUMBER OF SPECIES *8,800.*
SIZE *1–12mm.*
FEEDING *Larvae and adults: predators, herbivores, liquid-feeders.*
IMPACT *May sting, bite, or spray formic acid.*

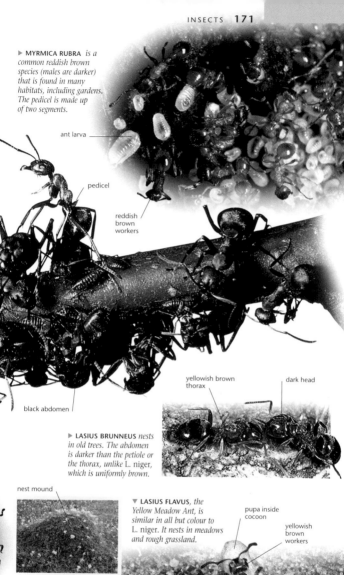

▶ **MYRMICA RUBRA** *is a common reddish brown species (males are darker) that is found in many habitats, including gardens. The pedicel is made up of two segments.*

ant larva

pedicel

reddish brown workers

black abdomen

yellowish brown thorax

dark head

▶ **LASIUS BRUNNEUS** *nests in old trees. The abdomen is darker than the petiole or the thorax, unlike L. niger, which is uniformly brown.*

nest mound

ANT NEST

▼ **LASIUS FLAVUS**, *the Yellow Meadow Ant, is similar in all but colour to L. niger. It nests in meadows and rough grassland.*

pupa inside cocoon

yellowish brown workers

Velvet Ants

Mutillidae

Velvet ants are stout-bodied and black or reddish brown in colour, with abdominal spots or bands of red, yellow, or silver hairs. The sexes often have different markings, but the body is always sculptured with coarse dimples. The males are fully winged; the wingless females are more strongly built, with a powerful sting.

FEMALES run over the ground in dry, shady or open locations; males often visit flowers.

box-like thorax

large head

◄ **MYRMILLA CALVA** *parasitizes solitary bees. The female lays her eggs on the host's fully developed larvae or freshly formed pupae.*

LARVAE

Females lay their eggs in the larval cells of bees or wasps. Their larvae eat the host grubs.

yellow-tinged wings

▶ **MUTILLA EUROPEA** *females have pale abdominal hair patches and parasitize bumble bees. Males have two yellow abdominal bands.*

pale patches

ORDER *Hymenoptera.*
FAMILY *Mutillidae.*
NUMBER OF SPECIES *5,000.*
SIZE *3–15mm.*
FEEDING *Larvae: parasites (bee and wasp larvae and pupae). Adults: liquid-feeders.*
IMPACT *Females have very powerful stings.*

Tiphiid Wasps

Tiphiidae

These wasps are quite slender, shiny, and either black or reddish brown and black. The body is slightly hairy, the legs are short and spiny, and the waist may be very strongly constricted. The males of all species are fully winged and usually have a short upturned spine at the end of the abdomen. Females can be fully winged or wingless. The larvae are parasitic on the larvae of various beetles, bees, and wasps.

OCCUR in open, sunny, flower-rich habitats; females often run over the bare ground.

shiny black abdomen

rounded black head

LARVAE

Elongate, smooth, and white, the larvae attack beetle larvae in soil or decayed wood.

red thorax

METHOCHA ICHNEUMONIDES *has sexes of different sizes: males are larger to be able to carry females during the nuptial flight. The wingless females lay their eggs on tiger beetle larvae.*

ORDER *Hymenoptera.*
FAMILY *Tiphiidae.*
NUMBER OF SPECIES *1,500.*
SIZE *0.4–3cm.*
FEEDING *Larvae: parasites (larvae of beetles, bees, and wasps). Adults: liquid-feeders.*
IMPACT *Help to control certain pests.*

Solitary Hunting, Digger, and Sand Wasps

Sphecidae

These wasps paralyze insects as food for their larvae. Some species are stocky; in others the abdomen is elongated and thread-like where it joins the thorax. The body is typically black with yellow or reddish markings. The head is fairly broad and the pronotum is narrow, collar-like, and does not extend back towards the wing bases. Both sexes are fully winged. Females often have a comb-like, digging structure on their front legs.

ACTIVE *in sandy, open localities, especially in bright sunshine, and often visit flowers.*

LARVAE

The carnivorous larvae are pale creamy white and have dark mouthparts. The body is tapered slightly at both ends and is usually slightly curved.

black and yellow bands ♀

slender body ♀

▲ **BEMBIX ROSTRATA** *makes a cluster of nests in shady places, and the females catch flies to stock their larval cells.*

▲ **PEMPHREDON LUGUBRIS** *is a small wasp that nests in rotting wood. Females stock their larval cells with paralyzed aphids.*

▶ **PHILANTHUS TRIANGULUM,** *the Bee Killer or Bee Wolf, fills its nests with paralyzed honey bees, with up to six bees in each larval cell.*

broad head ♀   yellow legs

slender abdomen, narrow at front

large jaws for carrying prey

♀

▶ **AMMOPHILA SABULOSA** *is a species of sand wasp that hunts for large caterpillars to stock its nests. Females deposit one paralyzed victim in each nest, sealing it with sand.*

OXYBELUS UNIGLUMIS *nests in sandy ground. Remarkably, females carry flies back to their nests by spearing them on their sting.*

large, patterned eyes

yellow spots on head

▶ **CERCERIS ARENARIA** *is shown stinging a weevil, with which to stock her nest. The female pushes soil out of her burrow backwards, using her abdomen.*

♀

ORDER *Hymenoptera.*
FAMILY *Sphecidae.*
NUMBER OF SPECIES *8,000.*
SIZE *0.6–2.4cm.*
FEEDING *Larvae: carnivorous (paralyzed prey provided by adults). Adults: liquid-feeders.*
IMPACT *Help to control certain pests.*

Mammoth Wasps

Scoliidae

OCCUR *in a range of habitats, where their scarab beetle hosts live.*

These large, very stout-bodied wasps are dark bluish black with yellow abdominal markings. The ends of the wings, which may be smoky, orangish, or violet-tinged, appear finely wrinkled. The body is densely covered with dark or golden hair. The males are smaller and slimmer than the females, with noticeably longer and thicker antennae.

LARVAE

Each fat larva feeds on a paralyzed scarab beetle larva provided by the adult female wasp.

▼ **SCOLIA FLAVIFRONS** *is a parasite of Rhinoceros Beetle larvae. Females are larger with reddish heads.*

bluish purple tinge to wings

broad head

♀

▲ **SCOLIA HIRTA** *has a bluish purple tinge to the wings and two broad yellow bands on the abdomen.*

ORDER *Hymenoptera.*
FAMILY *Scoliidae.*
NUMBER OF SPECIES *350.*
SIZE *1–3cm.*
FEEDING *Larvae: predators. Adults: herbivores (pollen), liquid-feeders (nectar).*
IMPACT *May deliver a sting.*

Plasterer and Yellow-faced Bees

Colletidae

FOUND *at flowers in many habitats, nesting in areas of sandy, well-drained soil.*

Generally slender to moderately robust, these solitary bees are very dark or black with no distinct markings, and have sparse light golden or whitish body hairs (those on the abdomen are often arranged in conspicuous bands). Some species also have yellow facial markings. The mouthparts are short and broad.

reddish hairs on thorax

bands of pale hair

▶ **HYLAEUS COMMUNIS** *is rather wasp-like and can often be found foraging at bramble flowers.*

hairless body

◀ **COLLETES SUCCINTUS** *digs nesting tunnels in dry, sandy soil. It sometimes nests in quite dense groups.*

LARVAE

The larvae are curved, maggot-like, and feed on a runny mixture of pollen and honey.

ORDER *Hymenoptera.*
FAMILY *Colletidae.*
NUMBER OF SPECIES *3,000.*
SIZE *3–13mm.*
FEEDING *Larvae and adults: herbivores (pollen), liquid-feeders (nectar).*
IMPACT *Essential plant pollinators.*

Sweat Bees

Halictidae

Most of these small to medium-sized, ground-nesting bees are brownish or black, but some have a metallic blue or green appearance or are entirely shiny, bluish green. The surface of the body is not generally very hairy and may have sculpturing in the form of pits or dimples. Sweat bees have a single groove under the socket of each antenna; the similar-looking mining bees (below) have two.

WIDELY *distributed, mainly in flower-rich meadows, woodland edges, and areas of waste ground.*

bands of pale hair

single groove under socket of antenna

LARVAE

The larvae may have bumps on the upper surface, as well as a covering of tiny spines.

LASIOGLOSSUM MALACHURUS *makes vertical nests in the ground, with clusters of cells.*

ORDER *Hymenoptera.*
FAMILY *Halictidae.*
NUMBER OF SPECIES *5,000.*
SIZE *4–10mm.*
FEEDING *Larvae and adults: herbivores (pollen), liquid-feeders (nectar).*
IMPACT *Essential plant pollinators.*

Mining or Andrenid Bees

Andrenidae

Superficially resembling honey bees, mining bees can be reddish brown, brown, or brownish black, although some species are yellow and a few are white. The thorax may be covered with white, yellow, or golden hairs and the abdomen, which is often rather flattened, may have crosswise bands of hairs.

INHABIT *virtually every flower-rich habitat; particularly common at flowers in spring.*

reddish front to abdomen

◀ **ANDRENA FLOREA** *has variable reddish brown coloration. The males are paler.*

LARVAE

The larvae can be slender or relatively stout. There are small swellings on the abdomen.

reddish brown hairs on thorax

dark bands on abdomen

◀ **ANDRENA FULVA,** *the Tawny Mining Bee, appears in early spring and nests in the soil of lawns and short turf.*

ORDER *Hymenoptera.*
FAMILY *Andrenidae.*
NUMBER OF SPECIES *4,000.*
SIZE *0.4–2cm.*
FEEDING *Larvae and adults: herbivores (pollen), liquid-feeders (nectar).*
IMPACT *Essential plant pollinators.*

Leaf-cutter and Mason Bees

Megachilidae

Most of these bees are solitary. Leaf-cutter bees cut circular pieces of leaves to line their nests' brood cells, while mason bees make mud cells under stones and in burrows. The former are typically stout-bodied and many species are dark brown to black, often with yellow or pale markings. Mason bees are short, broad, and metallic blue or green. The mouthparts are long and pointed and the wings may be clear or smoky.

OCCUR *in many habitats, especially where dead wood and pithy plant stems provide nest sites.*

LARVAE

The larvae of these bees are rather fat, especially near the rear of the body. Most feed on pollen or honey provided by the female, but a few are parasites in other bees' nests.

▶ **ANTHIDIUM MANICATUM**, *known as the Common Carder Bee, nests in old beetle or moth larvae burrows.*

♀

bright yellow hairs

wide-set mandibles

◀ **HOPLITIS SPINULOSA** *nests inside empty snail shells and uses sheep or rabbit dung to make the walls between adjacent cells.*

yellow edging to black abdomen

densely hairy abdomen

▲ **OSMIA RUFA**, *the Red Mason Bee, nests in natural cavities and holes in walls. It can be encouraged to nest using bundles of dry bamboo.*

pollen carried in a brush of hairs below abdomen

stout body

NOTE

A group of species known as carder bees use their jaws to strip the hairs from woolly-leaved plants, which they then tease out to make cell linings.

◀ **MEGACHILE CENTUNCULARIS** *is a common leaf-cutter bee. Leaves with semicircular holes along the edges are evidence that a nest is nearby.*

pieces cut by female leaf-cutter

DAMAGED LEAF

ORDER Hymenoptera.
FAMILY Megachilidae.
NUMBER OF SPECIES 3,000.
SIZE 0.7–2.1cm.
FEEDING Larvae: pollen- and honey-feeders. Adults: pollen- and nectar-feeders.
IMPACT Essential plant pollinators.

Cuckoo, Digger, and Carpenter Bees

Anthophoridae

Cuckoo bees are black and yellow or brown and white, lack pollen baskets on their hind legs, are relatively hairless, and can look extremely wasp-like. Digger bees are typically bumble bee-like and hairy. Carpenter bees can be divided into two main groups: very large, hairy, blackish or bluish species; and small, relatively bare, dark bluish green species. Female digger and carpenter bees have densely hairy pollen baskets on their hind legs.

THRIVE in a variety of flower-rich habitats, especially in sunny, open localities.

golden, hairy body

long antennae in male

purplish blue wings

huge, robust body

▲ **EUCERA LONGICORNIS** nests on the ground, often in groups. Males are attracted to the Bee Orchid and attempt to mate with it, thus serving as the flower's pollinators.

▼ **ANTHOPHORA PLUMIPES** has distinct sexes: males are yellowish brown, while females are blackish. Nests are excavated in soil or the soft mortar of old walls.

resembles small bumble bee

entirely black

▲ **XYLOCOPA VIOLACEA,** the Violet Carpenter Bee, is a very large, noisy-flying species found mainly in southern Europe. It nests in old wood.

short, straight antennae

pinched "wasp-like" waist

black and yellow markings

▲ **NOMADA FLAVA,** a very wasp-like cuckoo bee, does not make a nest of its own but is a parasite of various mining bees, in whose nests it lays its eggs.

LARVAE

These bees' larvae may be fat-bodied or slender and pale or yellow. Cuckoo bee larvae develop in the nests of other bees, killing the resident larvae and eating their food.

ORDER Hymenoptera.
FAMILY Anthophoridae.
NUMBER OF SPECIES 4,200.
SIZE 0.5–2.2cm.
FEEDING Larvae: pollen- and honey-feeders. Adults: pollen- and nectar-feeders.
IMPACT Essential plant pollinators.

NOTE

Also known as the long-tongued bees, this family is notable for its members' long tongues, which in some cases may exceed the length of the body itself.

Bumble Bees and Honey Bees

Apidae

These familiar social bees live in complex and often very large colonies with a queen, males, and sterile worker females. Bumble bees are very hairy, stout-bodied, and brownish or orange to black with yellow markings. Their body hairs are typically yellow, orange, or black. Honey bees are smaller, more slender, and golden brown with pale hairs. The females of most species have a specialized pollen-carrying structure called the corbiculum on the outer surface of the hind tibiae.

SEEN *in almost any flower-rich habitat. Bumble bees are particularly common in northern regions and in mountains.*

yellow scutellum

white tail

♂

▲ **PSITHYRUS BARBUTELLUS** *does not collect pollen and is a "cuckoo" that lays its eggs in the nests of* Bombus hortorum *(right), which it resembles.*

▼ **APIS MELLIFERA,** *the Western Honey Bee, nests in cavities in trees. Widely domesticated, it also lives in artificial hives, providing honey, wax, and other products.*

enlarged abdomen

thousands of workers

QUEEN

WORKER

DRONE

SWARM

NOTE

Western Honey bees have been spread by commerce all over the world. The value of the crops that they pollinate exceeds that of their honey and wax.

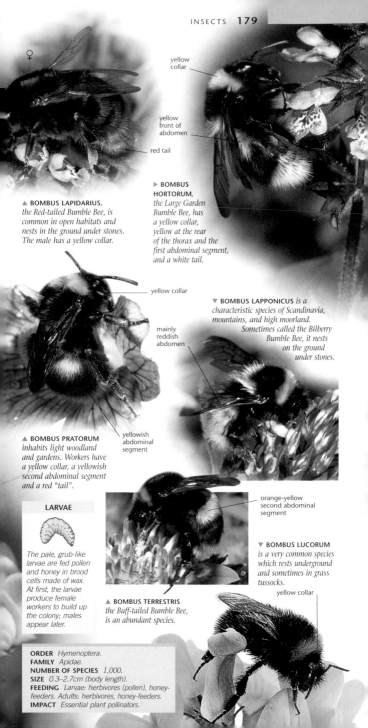

yellow collar

yellow front of abdomen

red tail

▲ **BOMBUS LAPIDARIUS,** *the Red-tailed Bumble Bee, is common in open habitats and nests in the ground under stones. The male has a yellow collar.*

▶ **BOMBUS HORTORUM,** *the Large Garden Bumble Bee, has a yellow collar, yellow at the rear of the thorax and the first abdominal segment, and a white tail.*

yellow collar

▼ **BOMBUS LAPPONICUS** *is a characteristic species of Scandinavia, mountains, and high moorland. Sometimes called the Bilberry Bumble Bee, it nests on the ground under stones.*

mainly reddish abdomen

▲ **BOMBUS PRATORUM** *inhabits light woodland and gardens. Workers have a yellow collar, a yellowish second abdominal segment and a red "tail".*

yellowish abdominal segment

orange-yellow second abdominal segment

LARVAE

The pale, grub-like larvae are fed pollen and honey in brood cells made of wax. At first, the larvae produce female workers to build up the colony; males appear later.

▲ **BOMBUS TERRESTRIS** *the Buff-tailed Bumble Bee, is an abundant species.*

▼ **BOMBUS LUCORUM** *is a very common species which rests underground and sometimes in grass tussocks.*

yellow collar

ORDER *Hymenoptera.*
FAMILY *Apidae.*
NUMBER OF SPECIES *1,000.*
SIZE *0.3–2.7cm (body length).*
FEEDING *Larvae: herbivores (pollen), honey-feeders. Adults: herbivores, honey-feeders.*
IMPACT *Essential plant pollinators.*

Arachnids

Arachnids occur in virtually every terrestrial habitat and there are even some aquatic species. All arachnids are wingless with four pairs of legs and two body regions – the cephalothorax and abdomen – but individual groups are extremely diverse in appearance. Perhaps the most familiar group are the spiders (*Argiope lobata*, below), which possess silk-spinning organs. Scorpions have powerful pincers and a sting on the end of a long tail, while pseudoscorpions look like miniature tailless scorpions. Ticks and mites are tiny and distinctively rounded.

CRAB SPIDERS   TICKS   PSEUDOSCORPIONS   HARVESTMEN

Buthids

Buthidae

Close examination of live scorpions is best avoided, but a good identifying feature for this family is that the sternum on the underside of the cephalothorax has a roughly triangular outline and the legs have spurs on the tibiae. These scorpions are strictly nocturnal, only hunting for food after dark.

LIVE in dry, stony habitats, crawling into crevices and under stones, logs, and bark during the day.

BUTHUS OCCITANUS, *common across the Mediterranean, lives on the ground under rocks and logs. Its sting can be very painful.*

NOTE

Fat-tailed scorpions with thin pincers are generally far more venomous than thin-tailed species with broad pincers. The latter rely on strength to kill prey.

sting

fat tail

orange limbs

spines on tibiae

thin pincers

ridged cephalothorax

ORDER *Scorpiones.*
FAMILY *Buthidae.*
NUMBER OF SPECIES *520.*
SIZE *6–8cm (body length, including tail).*
FEEDING *Nymphs and adults: predators.*
IMPACT *Can deliver a very painful sting if disturbed or handled.*

Euscorpiids

Euscorpiidae

These scorpions pose no real danger to healthy humans, and the effect of the sting in most people is comparable to that of bee or wasp stings. They include the only species of scorpion found in Britain, which was introduced accidentally from mainland Europe.

COMMON across the Mediterranean. They are found on the ground under rocks and logs.

thin tail

pale legs

strong pincers

◀ **EUSCORPIUS FLAVICAUDIS,** *common in central and southern Europe, is the only scorpion found in the UK. It lives in cracks in walls in areas of London.*

dark, shiny body

ORDER *Scorpiones.*
FAMILY *Euscorpiidae.*
NUMBER OF SPECIES *6.*
SIZE *2–4.5cm (body length, including tail).*
FEEDING *Nymphs and adults: predators.*
IMPACT *May sting, and can be very painful in humans.*

▶ **EUSCORPIUS CARPATHICUS** *lives in southern and western Europe and occurs in a variety of habitats, from gardens to woodland.*

Neobisiids

Neobisiidae

FOUND *mainly in leaf litter and soil, with some species in caves.*

The back of the thorax of these widely distributed pseudoscorpions is quite angular or square and the chelicerae are quite large. In all the pairs of walking legs, the tarsi are made up of two segments. There are usually four eyes, although there may be fewer or none at all in cave-living species. Overall coloration varies from olive to brown and the legs are often slightly green in colour.

red-brown pedipalps

olive-green legs

ORDER *Pseudoscorpiones.*
FAMILY *Neobisiidae.*
NUMBER OF SPECIES *500.*
SIZE *1–5mm.*
FEEDING *Immatures and adults: predators.*
IMPACT *Harmless.*

NEOBISIUM MARITIMUM *is native to coastal regions of the British Isles and France. It is found in cracks in rocks and under stones from the upper shore to the splash zone.*

Chernetids

Chernetidae

OCCUR *under the bark of dead or very old deciduous trees, and in soil and leaf litter.*

In these brown or greenish brown pseudoscorpions, the abdomen is typically much longer than the thorax and often has parallel sides. Most species have four eyes and the tarsi of the first two pairs of legs have a single segment, while those of the third and fourth pair have two segments.

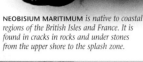

brown pedipalp

pinkish brown tibia

pale central stripe down abdomen

ORDER *Pseudoscorpiones.*
FAMILY *Chernetidae.*
NUMBER OF SPECIES *570.*
SIZE *1–2mm.*
FEEDING *Immatures and adults: predators.*
IMPACT *Harmless.*

CHERNES CIMICOIDES *occurs throughout most of Europe. It lacks eyes and the body is covered with numerous tiny club-ended hairs.*

Phalangiids

Phalangiidae

These harvestmen usually have soft bodies and may have many spiny projections. Typical species are brownish or greyish with a dark area on the upper surface known as the saddle. On the front edge of the carapace there is often a cluster of three closely grouped spines, called the trident. Leg segments may have longitudinal ridges, which are sometimes spined. Males and females can look different, especially in the shape of the chelicerae, which are enlarged in males.

LIVE under stones and among leaf litter in wooded and grassy areas; some also found in buildings.

> **NOTE**
>
> Harvestmen in this family are mainly nocturnal: look for them after dark, when they wander about searching for food or mates. Some species are active during the day as well, and a few are adapted to life in buildings.

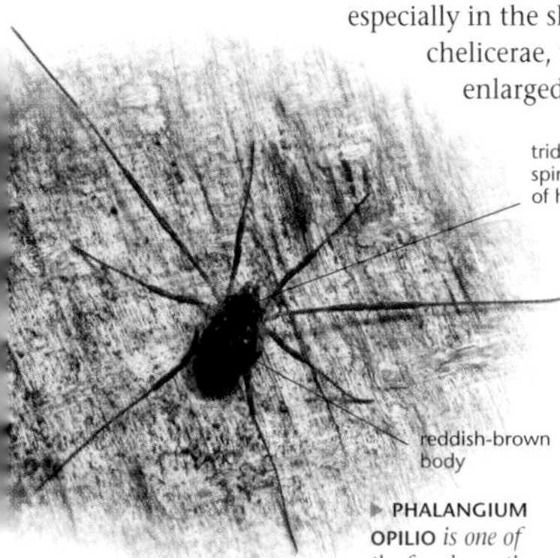

trident of short spines at front of head

second leg is up to 1.8cm long

reddish-brown body

▲ **OLIGOLOPHUS TRIDENS** has a brown body with a black central mark, which is broad at the front and more parallel-sided towards the rear.

▶ **PHALANGIUM OPILIO** is one of the few day-active species in gardens. Males (shown here) have horn-like extensions on the chelicerae.

horned chelicerae in male

pale sides

second leg up to 4cm long

▲ **MITOPUS MORIO** is variable in general body colour, but always has a very broad, saddle-shaped dark band running down its back. It lives among low-growing vegetation and bushes.

ORDER Opiliones.
FAMILY Phalangiidae.
NUMBER OF SPECIES 200.
SIZE 1–12mm.
FEEDING Immatures and adults: predators, scavengers.
IMPACT Harmless.

Hard Ticks

Ixodidae

These flattened, yellowish red to dark brown or almost black ticks have a very tough (sometimes patterned) plate on the back of the body. In males, this plate covers the whole body, but in females and immatures it covers only the front half. Some species are distinctively marked. The abdomen is soft and flexible to allow large blood meals to be taken from the animal hosts on which these ticks are found. Hard ticks transmit disease and may carry viral diseases that affect humans, such as encephalitis.

flattened abdomen

tough dorsal shield

sucking mouthparts

IXODES RICINUS, the Sheep Tick, actually sucks blood from a wide range of hosts. It is greyish to reddish brown with a dark dorsal plate and head.

> **NOTE**
>
> Females gorge on blood after mating, then drop off to lay their eggs. There are two immature stages: a six-legged larva and an eight-legged nymph.

ORDER Acari.
FAMILY Ixodidae.
NUMBER OF SPECIES 650.
SIZE 2–10mm.
FEEDING Immatures and adults: blood-feeders (mammals and birds).
IMPACT Serious pests of domestic animals.

Soft Ticks

Argasidae

Soft ticks generally have a rounded, berry-like body, although some species can be flattened. The body surface, which is tough and leathery, may appear wrinkled or roughened. The strong mouthparts are adapted for cutting through the skin of their hosts, including mammals such as bats, birds, and snakes. Feeding mostly takes place at night. Many species are significant vectors of disease and they may be commercially important pests of poultry.

> **NOTE**
>
> Female soft ticks usually lay their eggs in the nests of birds or the burrows of mammals. Argas persicus transmits a disease known as fowl relapsing fever.

leathery body

pale, curved legs

ARGAS PERSICUS, the Chicken or Fowl Tick, has a distinct rim separating its upper and lower surfaces.

ORDER Acari.
FAMILY Argasidae.
NUMBER OF SPECIES 150.
SIZE 2–10mm.
FEEDING Immatures and adults: blood-feeders (mammals and birds).
IMPACT Serious pests of domestic animals.

Spider Mites

Tetranychidae

These tiny, soft-bodied mites are orange, red, greenish, or yellow in colour and have a spider-like appearance. Large numbers infest and feed on plants, which may then develop pale blotches and wither or die. Spider mites produce silk from glands in the front part of the body and often cover affected plant parts with a fine webbing. The plants attacked include a number of commercially important crops such as wheat, citrus and other fruit trees, cotton, and coffee; yields may suffer dramatically.

OCCUR *in a variety of habitats on shrubs, trees, and herbaceous plants.*

▼ **TETRANYCHUS URTICAE** *feeds on a wide range of host plants. It hibernates deep in leaf litter in winter.*

NOTE

The eggs of spider mites are reddish, rounded, and quite large. They are laid on the bark of host plants. Immatures – and adults – live under the leaves.

orange-red coloration

pale, fine body hairs

ORDER *Acari.*
FAMILY *Tetranychidae.*
NUMBER OF SPECIES *650.*
SIZE *0.2–0.8mm.*
FEEDING *Immatures and adults: herbivores.*
IMPACT *Several species are important pests of grasses, clovers, and crops.*

Varroa Mites

Varroidae

Typically, varroa mites are tan in colour, broader than they are long, and have smooth, convex bodies. These mites are parasites of bees. Their eggs are laid inside bees' nests in the brood cells and the varroa mite nymphs feed on the bee larvae. The adult mites attach themselves to adult bees both to feed off them and as an efficient means of dispersal.

LIVE *in association with both wild and domesticated honey bees.*

▶ **VARROA SP.** *larvae feed on bee pupae; the pupae in this image have been removed from their brood cells to show this.*

smooth, oval outline

mite nymph feeding on bee pupa

◀ **VARROA PERSICUS** *attaches itself to the body of a honey bee to suck its body fluids.*

sucking mouthparts

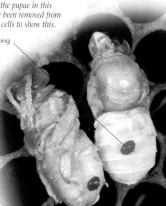

ORDER *Acari.*
FAMILY *Varroidae.*
NUMBER OF SPECIES *5.*
SIZE *1–1.75mm.*
FEEDING *Immatures and adults: parasites (bee adults and larvae).*
IMPACT *Serious pests of bees.*

Gall Mites

Eriophyidae

FOUND *in woodland, parkland, gardens, hedgerows, and wherever their host species grow.*

NOTE

Female gall mites lay their eggs on plants in spring, giving rise to a gall. Once fully developed, the mite leaves the gall to find a crevice in which to overwinter.

It is extremely difficult indeed to see these tiny mites, but very easy to recognize the galls that they make on the leaves of their host plants and inside which they develop. Each species of mite produces a uniquely shaped gall, often on a specific host plant. Gall mites range from white to yellowish, pinkish, or transparent and are widest just behind the head, giving them a distinctive, carrot-like shape. The thorax and abdomen are completely fused and, unlike any other mites, which have four pairs of legs, gall mites have only two pairs of legs. Many species are parthenogenetic.

GALLS

◄ **ACERIA MACROCHELUS** *galls found on the surface of Field Maple leaves, are green and hairy. They grow up to 5mm across, and occur in groups of up to 4.*

silver-white hair

GALLS

▶ **PHYTOPUS AVELLANAE** *occurs on the buds of hazel. This causes the buds to swell and open, making them more conspicuous than normal buds.*

▶ **ACERIA FRAXINIVORUS** *inhabits the flower buds of ash trees. Growing up to 2cm, the galls are green but darken as they mature.*

swollen hazel bud

irregular shape

GALLS

two pairs of legs

pale tapered body

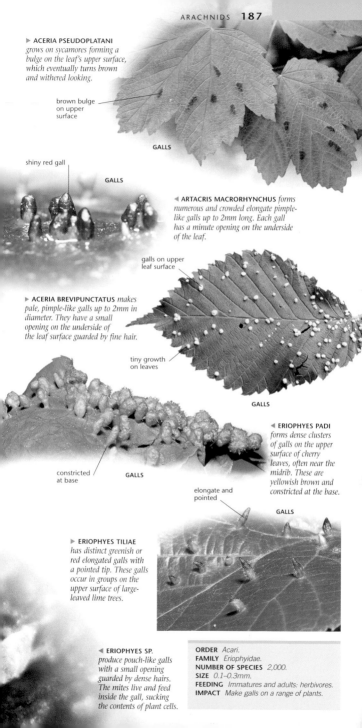

► **ACERIA PSEUDOPLATANI** *grows on sycamores forming a bulge on the leaf's upper surface, which eventually turns brown and withered looking.*

brown bulge on upper surface

GALLS

shiny red gall

GALLS

◄ **ARTACRIS MACRORHYNCHUS** *forms numerous and crowded elongate pimple-like galls up to 2mm long. Each gall has a minute opening on the underside of the leaf.*

galls on upper leaf surface

► **ACERIA BREVIPUNCTATUS** *makes pale, pimple-like galls up to 2mm in diameter. They have a small opening on the underside of the leaf surface guarded by fine hair.*

tiny growth on leaves

GALLS

constricted at base

GALLS

◄ **ERIOPHYES PADI** *forms dense clusters of galls on the upper surface of cherry leaves, often near the midrib. These are yellowish brown and constricted at the base.*

elongate and pointed

GALLS

► **ERIOPHYES TILIAE** *has distinct greenish or red elongated galls with a pointed tip. These galls occur in groups on the upper surface of large-leaved lime trees.*

◄ **ERIOPHYES SP.** *produce pouch-like galls with a small opening guarded by dense hairs. The mites live and feed inside the gall, sucking the contents of plant cells.*

ORDER *Acari.*
FAMILY *Eriophyidae.*
NUMBER OF SPECIES *2,000.*
SIZE *0.1–0.3mm.*
FEEDING *Immatures and adults: herbivores.*
IMPACT *Make galls on a range of plants.*

Velvet Mites

Trombidiidae

FOUND in a range of habitats, mainly in or on the soil.

Many of these soft-bodied mites have bright red or orange bodies that are extremely hairy, giving them a dense, velvety appearance. The legs are relatively long and the body, which does not appear pinched in the middle, is often broader towards the front than the rear. At certain times of year, usually after rain, adults emerge from the soil to mate and lay eggs.

▼ **TROMBIDIUM HOLOSERICEUM** is a fairly large, red mite. It can be seen crawling about on tree trunks in early spring.

> **NOTE**
>
> Females produce tens of thousands of eggs. The larvae are parasites on insects such as grasshoppers and on other arthropods, such as spiders.

dense covering of hairs

long front legs

wrinkled surface

▶ **EUTROMBIDIUM ROSTRATUS** feeds as an immature by attaching itself to an insect, sucking its blood for 1–2 days. It then detaches and burrows into soil.

ORDER Acari.
FAMILY Trombidiidae.
NUMBER OF SPECIES 250.
SIZE 2–5mm (body length).
FEEDING Immatures and adults: parasites, predators, scavengers.
IMPACT Harmless.

Parasitid Mites

Parasitidae

COMMONLY found in leaf litter and decaying wood in wooded areas.

Most of these mites are slightly pear-shaped and yellowish brown with one or two visible plates on the upper surface of the body. In the male, the second pair of legs may be stouter than the others in order to grasp the female during mating. Female parasitid mites lay their eggs in organic debris. The immatures are often found on the bodies of insects and many feed on small insects, their larvae, and other mites.

> **NOTE**
>
> The immatures of parasitid mites may be located in dung, wood and plant debris, stored produce, and the nests of mammals, bees, and wasps.

cluster of mites

underside of host insect

PARASITUS SP. feed on haemolymph as immatures. Their mouthparts penetrate the soft parts of the host.

ORDER Acari.
FAMILY Parasitidae.
NUMBER OF SPECIES 375.
SIZE 0.75–2mm (body length).
FEEDING Immatures and adults: parasites.
IMPACT Harmless.

Purse-web Spiders

Atypidae

These unmistakable reddish brown
spiders make distinctive silk tube
nests in burrows, with part of the silk
extending outwards over the ground.
They have massive, forward-facing
chelicerae that look almost as large
as the cephalothorax. Unlike most
spiders, in which the fangs act like a
pair of pincers, the fangs are parallel
and stab downwards. There are eight,
closely grouped eyes: two middle eyes
with two groups of three either side.

FANGS

LIVE *inside silk-lined
burrows in sandy or
chalky soil in south-
facing spots with low
vegetation.*

downward-
stabbing fangs

ATYPUS AFFINIS *makes very
distinctive finger-like silk
tubes. Prey walking over the
silk is impaled from below
and dragged inside.*

huge
chelicerae

large, broad
cephalothorax

ORDER *Araneae.*
FAMILY *Atypidae.*
NUMBER OF SPECIES *30.*
SIZE *0.7–1.8cm (body length).*
FEEDING *Immatures and adults: predators.*
IMPACT *Beneficial and harmless.*

Lace-webbed Spiders

Amaurobiidae

Named for their distinctive webs, these small spiders make
irregular or tangled webs with a tube-shaped retreat in
dark or concealed places. The silk produced by these spiders
has a bluish appearance when fresh. The spiders have a
dark reddish brown cephalothorax
with eight eyes in two rows at the
front. The abdomen is dark or greyish
brown with lighter, sometimes
chevron-shaped, markings.

WEBS *of these spiders
can be found in holes
in walls and bark,
underneath stones,
and in leaf litter.*

WEB

funnel-like
retreat

abdominal
pattern similar
in both sexes

AMAUROBIUS FENESTRALIS
*spins its webs under the bark of
old trees or stumps but is most
commonly found in the
crevices of stone walls.*

dark head

NOTE

*A vibrating tuning
fork held to the web
of a lace-webbed
spider will lure it out
of its retreat. The
webs are produced
at night under the
cover of darkness.*

ORDER *Araneae.*
FAMILY *Amaurobiidae.*
NUMBER OF SPECIES *350.*
SIZE *4–14mm (body length).*
FEEDING *Immatures and adults: predators.*
IMPACT *Beneficial and harmless.*

Orb Web Spiders

Araneidae

The most distinctive feature of these spiders is their vertical and circular webs, which have a central hub with radiating lines and spirals of sticky and non-sticky silk. The spider usually sits at the hub of the web, awaiting the arrival of prey. These species often have very large, egg-shaped abdomens, which can be brightly coloured and patterned with all manner of bands, spots, and irregular markings. There are eight eyes, the middle four often forming a square, with two pairs further out towards the side of the head.

extra silk, called the stabilimentum, may protect the web

lobes on abdomen

▲ **ARGIOPE LOBATA** *is recognized by the three or four lobes on each side of the abdomen. Found only in southern Europe, it spins orb webs in thick vegetation.*

striped abdomen

NOTE

Orb web designs differ between species. The spider usually sits at the hub of the web while others hide close by, to wait for prey.

▶ **ARGIOPE BRUENNICHI** *has distinctive yellow or cream and black bands on the abdomen. Males are much smaller than females.*

grey hairs

▼ **AGALENATEA REDII** *is a variably marked, reddish brown spider with a very broad abdomen. It spins webs with close-woven silk at the hub on shrubs, and low vegetation.*

▶ **ARANIELLA CUCURBITINA** *is very small and has a small red patch just above the spinners. Females have a bright green abdomen and are larger than males.*

yellow abdomen

white patches on abdomen

green and reddish brown bands

♂

▼ **CYCLOSA CONICA** *is seen resting at the centre of the web with its legs drawn up over the cephalothorax. It has a mottled abdomen.*

prey

pointed abdomen

ORDER *Araneae.*
FAMILY *Araneidae.*
NUMBER OF SPECIES *4,000.*
SIZE *3–16mm.*
FEEDING *Immatures and adults: predatory.*
IMPACT *Beneficial and harmless, although some larger species may bite in defence.*

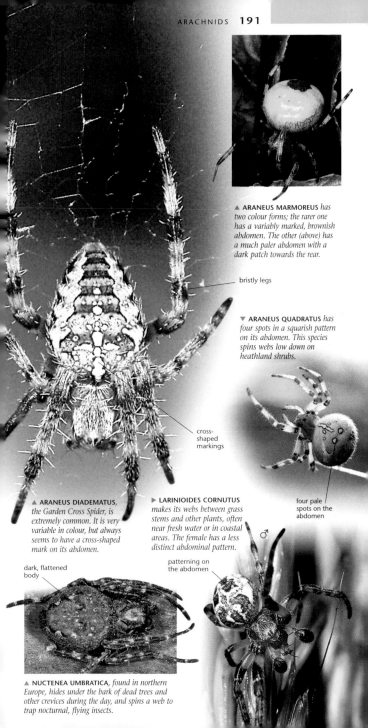

▲ **ARANEUS MARMOREUS** *has two colour forms; the rarer one has a variably marked, brownish abdomen. The other (above) has a much paler abdomen with a dark patch towards the rear.*

bristly legs

▼ **ARANEUS QUADRATUS** *has four spots in a squarish pattern on its abdomen. This species spins webs low down on heathland shrubs.*

cross-shaped markings

four pale spots on the abdomen

▲ **ARANEUS DIADEMATUS,** *the Garden Cross Spider, is extremely common. It is very variable in colour, but always seems to have a cross-shaped mark on its abdomen.*

▶ **LARINIOIDES CORNUTUS** *makes its webs between grass stems and other plants, often near fresh water or in coastal areas. The female has a less distinct abdominal pattern.*

♂

dark, flattened body

patterning on the abdomen

▲ **NUCTENEA UMBRATICA,** *found in northern Europe, hides under the bark of dead trees and other crevices during the day, and spins a web to trap nocturnal, flying insects.*

Nursery-web Spiders

Pisauridae

These large, long-legged hunting spiders are very similar in habit and appearance to wolf spiders (right), but differ in the size of their eyes. Viewed from the front, the two eyes forming the second row of eyes are quite small. The carapace is oval, with longitudinal markings. They do not make webs, but run and hunt on the ground, on the surface of still water, and on aquatic plants.

WIDESPREAD on grassland, heathland, woodland rides and margins, and also in marshy areas.

white stripe

pale lateral stripe

long, stout legs

▼ **DOLOMEDES FIMBRIATUS,** the Fishing Spider, lives in wet habitats and hunts for prey on the surface of water.

egg sac carried on fangs

▲ **PISAURA MIRABILIS** is seen here with an egg sac. Females make tent-like nursery webs just before the spiderlings emerge.

ORDER Araneae.
FAMILY Pisauridae.
NUMBER OF SPECIES 550.
SIZE 1–2.2cm.
FEEDING Immatures and adults: predators.
IMPACT Beneficial and harmless. Dolomedes fimbriatus is protected by law in the UK.

The Water Spider

Argyronetidae

This unique spider lives permanently underwater, and makes a dome-shaped, silk diving bell attached to submerged plants. Prey items are dragged back to the bell for eating. The water spider has a reddish brown cephalothorax and a dark brown abdomen with a distinctive dense pile of short hair. The third and fourth pairs of legs are much hairier than the first two pairs.

FOUND in very slow-flowing and still water with plenty of aquatic vegetation.

diving bell

◄ **ARGYRONETA AQUATICA** carries bubbles of air from the surface on the abdomen (left), and on the hind legs.

rear pair of legs are very hairy

ORDER Araneae.
FAMILY Argyronetidae.
NUMBER OF SPECIES 1
SIZE 0.8–1.8cm.
FEEDING Immatures and adults: predators, even including small fish and tadpoles.
IMPACT Can bite if handled.

Wolf Spiders

Lycosidae

Drably coloured, the bodies of wolf spiders are densely covered with light and dark hairs. These spiders have very good eyesight for hunting prey. The head has eight eyes: four small eyes in a row at the front, and above this a much larger pair of forward-facing eyes; another pair, further back, point sideways. Females often carry their egg sacs around with them, attached to their spinnerets. When the young spiderlings hatch, the mother may carry them on her back. Most live on the ground in leaf litter.

EVERYWHERE *from grassland to marshes and mudflats, on low vegetation.*

dark patches

pale chelicerae

▲ **LYCOSA NARBONENSIS** *lives in burrows from which it emerges to catch prey. It is a large spider that can give a painful bite.*

▼ **PARDOSA LUGUBRIS** *lives in wooded areas. Females are not as dark as the males, and have less distinct stripes.*

striped legs

light brown to black coloration

clear banding on legs

▲ **ARCTOSA PERITA** *lives in sandy soil on heaths and dune systems. Its colour depends on the habitat.*

distinct, light, central stripe

▼ **PIRATA PIRATICUS** *is common in north European wetlands. It moves quickly over water and plants and can even make small jumps.*

▶ **TROCHOSA RURICOLA** *hunts after dark. It lives under stones or among leaf litter in damp areas.*

light margins

light median stripe

dark brown

yellow mark

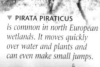

♂

ORDER *Araneae.*
FAMILY *Lycosidae.*
NUMBER OF SPECIES *3,000.*
SIZE *4–20mm.*
FEEDING *Immatures and adults: predators.*
IMPACT *Beneficial and harmless, but large species may bite.*

Jumping Spiders

Salticidae

Despite the fact that most of these short-legged, compact spiders are small, they are immediately recognizable. Four eyes form a row at the front of the square-fronted head, and the middle pair are very much larger than any of the others. Further back there are another two small eyes, and behind those, another pair of slightly larger eyes. These active hunters use their excellent eyesight to help stalk their prey, before leaping on top of victims at close range. Many species are attractively patterned and some have iridescent hair on the body.

FOUND *in a range of locations, including woods, hedgerows, heaths, grassland, and gardens.*

ant-like shape

flat face

◀ **MYRMARACHNE FORMICARIA** *occurs throughout northern Europe in sunny locations. It looks very ant-like and even walks and moves its legs in an ant-like manner.*

elongate abdomen

NOTE

Jumping spiders are mostly daytime hunters. A silk safety line ensures that they do not fall when stalking prey on vertical surfaces such as walls.

▶ **MARPISSA MUSCOSA** *is told by its striped legs and abdominal patterning. It lives on fence posts and lichen-covered tree bark and fences.*

stout first leg

black-and-white markings

aphid prey

▶ **SALTICUS SCENICUS,** *the Zebra Spider, is often seen on walls and other surfaces in sunny spots. It is pictured here feeding on an aphid.*

forward-facing eyes

◀ **EVARCHA FALCATA** *mainly hunts for prey on tree branches or on vegetation in woodland glades. It is dark brown with indistinct banding on the legs.*

mottled legs

large pedipalps

grasping front legs

ORDER *Araneae.*
FAMILY *Salticidae.*
NUMBER OF SPECIES *5,000.*
SIZE *2–12mm (body length).*
FEEDING *Immatures and adults: predators.*
IMPACT *Beneficial and harmless.*

Cobweb Spiders

Agelenidae

These spiders are also called funnel-weavers due to their web – a flat, tangled silk sheet with a funnel-shaped tube at one side. They are often long-legged and the front of the cephalothorax is narrowed, with eight smallish eyes grouped together. The abdomen is quite slender, oval, and may be patterned.

LIVE *in grassland, meadows, gardens, and similar habitats, often entering houses.*

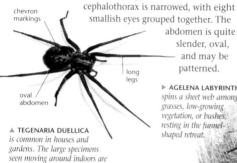

chevron markings

long legs

oval abdomen

▲ **TEGENARIA DUELLICA** *is common in houses and gardens. The large specimens seen moving around indoors are usually males looking for mates.*

funnel-shaped tube

▶ **AGELENA LABYRINTHICA** *spins a sheet web among grasses, low-growing vegetation, or bushes, resting in the funnel-shaped retreat.*

ORDER *Araneae.*
FAMILY *Agelenidae.*
NUMBER OF SPECIES *700.*
SIZE *4–16mm (body length).*
FEEDING *Immatures and adults: predators.*
IMPACT *Entirely harmless, but responsible for frightening arachnophobic householders.*

Spitting Spiders

Scytodidae

Spitting spiders do not spin webs but instead employ a unique hunting technique in which prey is pinned down with zigzag strands of sticky glue shot from the chelicerae. The large carapace of these spiders is very domed towards the rear and is cream or yellow-brown and black. The front of the carapace is narrowed and has only six eyes: a close-set pair pointing forwards and\a similar pair at each side.

MAINLY *found in buildings and among rocks, especially in warmer regions.*

domed cephalothorax

SCYTODES THORACICA *has a distinctively domed cephalothorax and unique colour pattern. It is a slow-moving, nocturnal, indoor species.*

six eyes

banded legs

ORDER *Araneae.*
FAMILY *Scytodidae*
NUMBER OF SPECIES *180.*
SIZE *3–7mm (body length).*
FEEDING *Immatures and adults: predators.*
IMPACT *Beneficial and harmless.*

Uloborids

Uloboridae

INHABIT *low vegetation such as heather, or the twigs of yew and box trees.*

These spiders make a horizontal orb web among low vegetation or a unique triangular snare among tree twigs. Unlike in any other spider family, there are no poison glands: the spiders use silk wrapping alone to subdue their prey. The head has eight dark eyes in two rows; those of the rear row are very widely spaced.

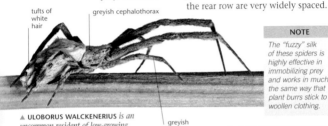

tufts of white hair

greyish cephalothorax

NOTE

The "fuzzy" silk of these spiders is highly effective in immobilizing prey and works in much the same way that plant burrs stick to woollen clothing.

▲ **ULOBORUS WALCKENERIUS** *is an uncommon resident of low-growing vegetation. Its body is covered with white hair, some forming distinctive tufts.*

greyish brown legs

ORDER	*Araneae.*
FAMILY	*Uloboridae.*
NUMBER OF SPECIES	*200.*
SIZE	*3–6mm.*
FEEDING	*Immatures and adults: predators.*
IMPACT	*Harmless.*

▶ **ULOBORUS PLUMIPES**, *the Feather-legged Spider, is quite variable in colour and lives in florists and commercial greenhouses.*

very long front legs

Oonopids

Oonopidae

FOUND *mainly in forested regions, often in leaf litter.*

These small spiders are pinkish, reddish, or sometimes yellowish, with a distinctive style of movement that alternates between a slow walk and a fast sprint. The head has six characteristically oval eyes, which are grouped very closely together. Oonopids do not spin webs but move about on the ground after dark to find prey.

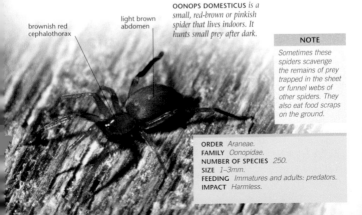

brownish red cephalothorax

light brown abdomen

OONOPS DOMESTICUS *is a small, red-brown or pinkish spider that lives indoors. It hunts small prey after dark.*

NOTE

Sometimes these spiders scavenge the remains of prey trapped in the sheet or funnel webs of other spiders. They also eat food scraps on the ground.

ORDER	*Araneae.*
FAMILY	*Oonopidae.*
NUMBER OF SPECIES	*250.*
SIZE	*1–3mm.*
FEEDING	*Immatures and adults: predators.*
IMPACT	*Harmless.*

Dysderids
Dysderidae

These nocturnal, ground-living spiders have six eyes arranged roughly in a circle on the head. The carapace is reddish brown or dark brown to black. The chelicerae can be large and the fangs are long and sharp to pierce the cuticle of their prey. The abdomen is pinkish grey or dark grey. *Dysdera* species are known as woodlice-eating spiders after their main prey.

FOUND in damp locations under stone, rotting wood, debris, or tree bark.

NOTE

The jaws of Dysdera crocata are wide and strong enough to penetrate human skin; a few people may have a serious allergic reaction to the venom.

◀ **HARPACTEA HOMBERGI** is a small, elongate species with a greyish brown abdomen and a dark, shiny cephalothorax.

▼ **DYSDERA CROCATA** lives wherever woodlice, its prey, occur. Its fangs open sideways to impale victims.

ORDER Araneae.
FAMILY Dysderidae.
NUMBER OF SPECIES 250.
SIZE 0.5–1.6cm.
FEEDING Immatures and adults: predators.
IMPACT Beneficial by controlling pests. Dysdera crocata can bite if handled roughly.

Six-eyed Spiders
Segestriidae

Despite their common name of six-eyed spiders, segestriids are not the only family of spiders with six eyes. The eyes are arranged in three groups of two – a close-set pair in the middle, facing forward, and one pair on each side. A good recognition feature for these spiders is that the first three pairs of legs are held forwards. They also lay threads like trip wires radiating from the nest entrance.

LIVE in tubular nests in holes in walls, and sometimes in bark.

silk tube

dark cephalothorax

SEGESTRIA SENOCULATA inhabits a funnel-shaped retreat in walls and bark, surrounded by radiating signal threads that alert it to suitable-sized prey.

ORDER Araneae.
FAMILY Segestriidae.
NUMBER OF SPECIES 100.
SIZE 0.7–2.1cm.
FEEDING Immatures and adults: predators.
IMPACT Harmless.

Daddy-Long-Legs Spiders

Pholcidae

FOUND *in caves and buildings, especially near ceilings and in dark corners.*

Also known as cellar spiders, these small spiders make irregular, tangled webs of criss-cross threads. They quickly wrap prey in silk before biting it. The carapace is rounded in outline and the legs are much longer than the body, giving a spindly appearance similar to crane flies (p.122). The head has a pair of small eyes flanked by two groups of three closely-set eyes.

NOTE

The males look very similar to females but have a slender abdomen and are slightly smaller. The mating of these spiders can last for hours.

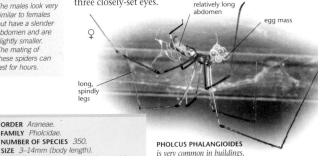

relatively long abdomen

egg mass

♀

long, spindly legs

ORDER *Araneae.*
FAMILY *Pholcidae.*
NUMBER OF SPECIES *350.*
SIZE *3–14mm (body length).*
FEEDING *Immatures and adults: predators.*
IMPACT *Beneficial and harmless, although sometimes regarded a nuisance in houses.*

PHOLCUS PHALANGIOIDES
is very common in buildings. When disturbed, it vibrates its body and web rapidly to blur its outline, confusing potential predators.

Ground Spiders

Gnaphosidae

Most ground spiders are greyish brown to black with no clear patterning on the abdomen, although some have patches or bands of white hairs. The head has eight eyes arranged in two rows. The two middle eyes of the second row have a distinctively oval or elongated shape. Most species hide in a silk nest under stones and logs during the day and hunt at night.

LIVE *in a variety of habitats from grassland, heathland, and wooded areas to parks and gardens.*

black cephalothorax

ZELOTES SP.
spend the day hiding under stones, where females attach their egg sacs.

sleek black abdomen

spinnerets

ORDER *Araneae.*
FAMILY *Gnaphosidae.*
NUMBER OF SPECIES *2,000.*
SIZE *0.3–1.8cm (body length).*
FEEDING *Immatures and adults: predators.*
IMPACT *Beneficial and harmless.*

Crab Spiders

Thomisidae

These spiders are named for their typically squat shape and characteristic sideways, scuttling movement. The carapace is nearly circular and the abdomen is short and often blunt-ended. The first two pairs of legs, which are used to seize prey, are larger and more spiny than the other two pairs and are turned to face forwards. The head has eight small, dark and beady, equally-sized eyes arranged in two rows.

OCCUR *on a variety of plants, especially the flowerheads, and on the bark of trees.*

▲ **TIBELLUS OBLONGUS** *conceals itself among grass and other low-growing foliage by holding its legs stretched out.*

camouflage posture

pale lower half of legs

▶ **XYSTICUS CRISTATUS** *has cryptic coloration to blend in with dried leaves on bushes and the ground, where it lies in wait for prey.*

NOTE

Crab spiders rely on superb camouflage to ambush their prey. Some species can change their body colour in the space of a day to blend in better.

reddish abdomen contrasts with greenish cephalothorax

◀ **DIAEA DORSATA** *drops on a thread when threatened, holding its first two pairs of legs straight out sideways.*

WHITE FORM

dark stripes on cephalothorax

♀

large abdomen

large front legs

chelicera

YELLOW FORM

palps

♀

▲ **MISUMENA VATIA** *has a white or yellow female, which changes colour to match its background. The male is far smaller, with dark markings.*

long legs

▼ **PHILODROMUS AUREOLUS** *lives on or near the ground. The male has dark markings, while the female is larger and light brown.*

♂

slightly iridescent

ORDER *Araneae.*
FAMILY *Thomisidae.*
NUMBER OF SPECIES *2,500.*
SIZE *3–12mm (body length).*
FEEDING *Immatures and adults: predators.*
IMPACT *Beneficial and harmless.*

Foliage Spiders

Clubionidae

FOUND *in a wide range of habitats, well vegetated with bushes or trees and places to hide; some in coastal areas or marshes.*

Similar in habits to ground spiders (p.198), these nocturnal hunters spend the day in a silken cell, in vegetation or under stones. Most species have relatively elongate bodies and are generally yellowish, reddish grey, or darkish brown in colour. The arrangment of the eight eyes is the same as in ground spiders, but the middle pair in the back row have a circular outline.

◀ **CHEIRACANTHIUM ERRATICUM** *is common on low-growing plants and grasses. It hunts at night, hiding during the day in a silk retreat.*

yellow band with dark central stripe

first pair of legs are longest

drab, reddish brown coloration

▶ **CLUBIONA TERRESTRIS** *is ant-like in its movements. It is found in leaf litter and under stones. Short, pale hairs cover the abdomen.*

ORDER *Araneae.*
FAMILY *Clubioniidae.*
NUMBER OF SPECIES *1,600.*
SIZE *3–15mm.*
FEEDING *Immature and adults: predators.*
IMPACT *Beneficial. Larger species can bite if handled.*

Pirate Spiders

Mimetidae

LIVE *in a variety of habitats on trees and bushes, as well as woodland, heathland, scrub, and gardens.*

Spider-eating spiders might be a better name as these small species invade the webs of other spiders and eat them. They pluck the threads of a web gently to attract the spider, and then bite it. This paralyzes the prey so they can suck the internal contents out through a small hole. They do not spin webs themselves. The abdomen is roughly spherical with one or two pairs of small, blunt conical bumps.

tubercle on abdomen

dark and light bands on legs

ERO ARPHANA *has clearly banded legs, and two pairs of small conical bumps (tubercle) on its abdomen. It lives among low heath vegetation.*

NOTE

Females do not carry their eggs around with them. Instead they hang the egg sac from a plant by a thin silk thread, and cover it with a tangle of silk.

ORDER *Araneae.*
FAMILY *Mimetidae.*
NUMBER OF SPECIES *150.*
SIZE *2–4mm.*
FEEDING *Immatures and adults: predators.*
IMPACT *Beneficial and harmless; attack other species.*

Comb-footed Spiders

Theridiidae

Also called cobweb spiders on account of their tangled, irregular webs, these nocturnal species can be greyish or brown to black. Many have intricate patterning on the rounded, almost spherical abdomen. The legs are typically banded. The hind pair have a comb-like row of stout bristles, but these are actually very difficult to see even under magnification. The head has eight eyes, arranged in two rows, with the outer eyes of each row set very close together.

SEEN *in a variety of habitats on shrubs, trees, gorse, heather, low vegetation; some in association with human habitation.*

pinkish red stripe

yellow central marks

black patches

▲ **ENOPLOGNATHA OVATA** *females are small with globular abdomens that have one or two pinkish red stripes. In both sexes there are two rows of black spots.*

row of black spots

▲ **THERIDION SISYPHIUM** *makes tangled webs on bushes, such as gorse. The abdomen has distinctive black and white markings. Females regurgitate fluid to feed spiderlings.*

pinkish white markings

pale bands

▼ **STEATODA BIPUNCTATA** *is associated with buildings and varies from light to dark brown. Females are large and may live for several years.*

▲ **STEATODA ALBOMACULATA** *is found on dry heaths, where it lives on ants and other insects. The spider is dark brown or black with a greyish, patterned abdomen.*

large globular abdomen

leg segments dark at tips

NOTE

These spiders have fast-acting venom. The prey is sucked out leaving a neat, entire shell, unlike araneids where the prey is mashed up by the chelicerae.

ORDER *Araneae.*
FAMILY *Theridiidae.*
NUMBER OF SPECIES *2,200.*
SIZE *2–10mm.*
FEEDING *Immatures and adults: predators.*
IMPACT *Beneficial; however, Steatoda nobilis can bite if handled.*

Long-jawed Orb Web Spiders

LIVE *in grassy places such as meadows, low vegetation, damp woodland, and dark places such as caves.*

Tetragnathidae

In common with orb web spiders (pp.190–91), most of these spiders spin an orb web; however, they differ in that the webs are not vertical but usually at an angle and the hub of the web is open with no silk spirals at the centre. Many species are elongated with long legs and very large diverging chelicerae; others are more oval-bodied with a rounded abdomen.

long abdomen

large jaws

long legs

▲ **TETRAGNATHA EXTENSA** *has an elongated abdomen and long, curved chelicerae and fangs. At rest, it holds its legs parallel to grass blades.*

pale triangular marks

pale brown, ringed legs

olive cephalothorax

▶ **META SEGMENTATA** *is a common and widespread species, which is sometimes placed in a separate family, the Metidae.*

ORDER *Araneae.*
FAMILY *Tetragnathidae.*
NUMBER OF SPECIES *800.*
SIZE *3–15mm.*
FEEDING *Immatures and adults: predators.*
IMPACT *Harmless; beneficial in controlling pest species.*

Ladybird Spiders

INHABIT *south-facing heathland and low vegetation.*

Eresidae

These are robust, fairly hairy spiders with a distinctively large, square-fronted head and eight small eyes, four of which are placed at each "corner" of the head. Females are long-lived, black, and velvety; they usually live inside silk-lined tubular burrows covered by a silk roof. The short-lived males resemble ladybirds due to their red abdomen with four black spots.

white bands on legs

black head

black spots on abdomen

♂

ERESUS CINNABERINUS *lives in silk-lined tubes in the ground and spins a small sheet of "fuzzy" silk above to catch prey.*

ORDER *Araneae.*
FAMILY *Eresidae.*
NUMBER OF SPECIES *120.*
SIZE *0.6–1.6cm.*
FEEDING *Immatures and adults: predators.*
IMPACT *May bite if handled; beneficial in controlling pest species.*

♀

NOTE

Eresus cinnaberinus is one of the most colourful European spiders and is protected due to its rarity. It has been recorded on heathland in Dorset.

Dwarf Spiders

Linyphiidae

As this family's common name implies, many of these
species are small. They vary widely in colour and pattern
and many have bristly legs. The head has eight eyes arranged
in two rows, but the heads of some males may have
strange extensions on top, sometimes bearing the eyes.
Dwarf spiders, also called money spiders,
are common and travel great distances
by "ballooning" on long silk threads.

FOUND *among lush vegetation; some species in leaf litter.*

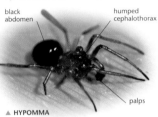

black abdomen

humped cephalothorax

palps

▲ **HYPOMMA BITUBERCULATUM** *has an orangish cephalothorax and black abdomen. It inhabits damp habitats such as streamsides.*

▲ **ERIGONE ATRA** *is a small, shiny black spider with yellowish brown legs in females and reddish brown legs in males. This and related species are often extremely common.*

NOTE

Some species spin horizontal sheet webs, which can be up to 30cm across and are supported by a random network of threads leading upwards.

◄ **LINYPHIA TRIANGULARIS** *is a very common species. It has a pale, speckled, quite elongated abdomen with a row of darkish marks.*

distinctive dark markings

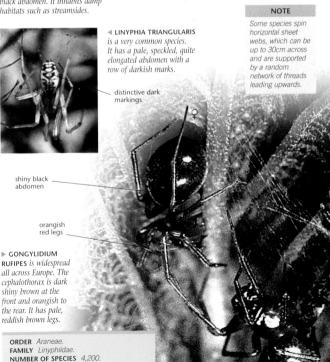

shiny black abdomen

orangish red legs

▶ **GONGYLIDIUM RUFIPES** *is widespread all across Europe. The cephalothorax is dark shiny brown at the front and orangish to the rear. It has pale, reddish brown legs.*

ORDER *Araneae.*
FAMILY *Linyphiidae.*
NUMBER OF SPECIES *4,200.*
SIZE *1–7mm.*
FEEDING *Immatures and adults: predators.*
IMPACT *Harmless; beneficial in controlling pest species.*

Other Arthropods

This chapter describes several remarkably diverse groups of arthropods that differ from insects and arachnids in various ways. Springtails occur in vast numbers in soil and leaf litter: hundreds of thousands may be found in one square metre. Both millipedes and centipedes have many pairs of legs, but whereas the former are largely scavengers, the latter are active predators that use poison claws to kill prey. Also included here are the woodlice (below), the only group of crustaceans widespread on land. They breathe with gills and so are confined to damp, dark locations.

SPRINGTAILS    MILLIPEDES    CENTIPEDES    DIPLURANS

Pauropods

Pauropodidae

These small myriapods have very pale, slender bodies and relatively long legs. Despite their size, they can move swiftly through crevices and inside gaps in the soil. The upper surface of the head and trunk carry long, pale, fine hairs that have a sensory function. The antennae have four segments, the last segment of which is divided into two small branches. Several species of pauropod are both abundant and widespread, in some cases being found throughout the Northern Hemisphere. The complete life cycle, from egg to adult, takes 3–4 months.

pale coloration

pair of legs on nine abdominal segments

FOUND in soil, leaf litter, and rotting logs in woodland and damp, sheltered places.

ALLOPAUROPUS DANICUS is present throughout Europe. Its long, fine body hairs are not visible on this slide-mounted specimen.

NOTE

In most pauropod species, females deposit their eggs in soil or among rotting plant matter. The eggs are laid singly or in small batches.

ORDER Pauropoda.
FAMILY Pauropodidae.
NUMBER OF SPECIES 450.
SIZE 0.5–2mm.
FEEDING Immatures and adults: scavengers, fungi-feeders.
IMPACT Harmless.

Scutigerellids

Scutigerellidae

These pale grey to straw-coloured or white myriapods are relatively short and stout. They are very flexible and run rapidly, twisting and turning through tiny crevices to escape predators. The trunk is made up of 14 segments, of which the first 12 have a pair of legs with six segments. The last segment of the trunk has a pair of silk-producing spinnerets.

OCCUR in soil and leaf litter in a variety of outdoor habitats, and in glasshouses.

relatively long antennae

white, flexible body

NOTE

Females pick up sperm droplets in their mouths, then smear an egg with sperm. They use their mouthparts to stick the egg onto a plant or into soil.

ORDER Pauropoda.
FAMILY Scutigerellidae.
NUMBER OF SPECIES 100.
SIZE 3–8mm.
FEEDING Immatures and adults: herbivores (mainly roots and tubers).
IMPACT Can damage seedlings and tubers.

SCUTIGERELLA IMMACULATA, often known as the Garden Symphylan, lives in gardens and may be a nuisance in greenhouses.

Geophilids

Geophilidae

The name of these rather slow-moving centipedes means "earth-loving" and is an apt description of their habitat preferences. The body is straw-coloured to brown and is very long, slender, and made up of at least 35 segments. The head is relatively small but usually wider than long and at least as big as the first segment of the trunk. The antennae are slender and the legs are short.

FOUND *in leaf litter, soil, rotting wood, and debris in a variety of habitats; sometimes inside buildings.*

small head

straw coloration

thread-like body

NOTE

Some geophilids produce a secretion that is luminescent. If one is held in the hand in complete darkness, a faint afterglow can often be seen behind it.

GEOPHILUS CARPOPHAGUS *is a slender centipede with a pale reddish brown body. It is nocturnal and creeps slowly through soil and damp leaf litter.*

very short legs

ORDER *Geophilida.*
FAMILY *Geophilidae.*
NUMBER OF SPECIES *200.*
SIZE *1–4.5cm.*
FEEDING *Immatures and adults: predators.*
IMPACT *Harmless.*

Himantariids

Himantariidae

These pale yellowish to brown, slender centipedes have a slightly flattened, ribbon-like appearance. The trunk segments are broadest in the middle of the body and become narrow towards either end, especially towards the head. The head is broader than long and always much narrower than the first trunk segment. The antennae are quite short and compressed.

INHABIT *soil, leaf litter, and debris in woods and grassland.*

short antennae

slim, flexible body

▶ **HAPLOPHILUS SUBTERRANEUS** *is a pale yellowish species with as many as 80 pairs of short legs. It feeds in soil and leaf mould.*

short legs

ORDER *Geophilida.*
FAMILY *Himantariidae.*
NUMBER OF SPECIES *100.*
SIZE *2.5–8cm.*
FEEDING *Immatures and adults: predators.*
IMPACT *Harmless.*

Lithobiids

Lithobiidae

Most lithobiids are reddish brown and the body is tough and quite flattened. The plates that cover the upper surface of the body segments are alternately large and small. There are 15 pairs of legs, with the last two pairs being longer than the others. The antennae are slender and tapering.

LIVE *in cracks and crevices, mainly in woodland but also in grassland, upland, and coastal areas.*

LITHOBIUS VARIEGATUS is common among the leaf litter of deciduous woods. It climbs trees in search of food.

poison claw

light and dark bands on legs (sometimes hard to see)

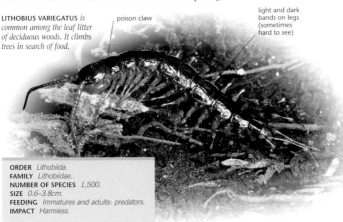

ORDER *Lithobiida.*
FAMILY *Lithobiidae.*
NUMBER OF SPECIES *1,500.*
SIZE *0.6–3.8cm.*
FEEDING *Immatures and adults: predators.*
IMPACT *Harmless.*

Scolopendrids

Scolopendridae

These robust centipedes are quite broad and flattened. They may be yellowish brown or greenish overall, with stripes or bands of other colours. The antennae are slender but have fewer than 35 segments; lithobiids (above) have 75–80 segments. As in all centipedes, the first pair of legs are modified as poison claws.

OCCUR *in scrub, olive groves, and rocky areas in warmer regions, hiding under stones or in leaf litter.*

darker at rear of each segment

poison claw

prey

tough plates along back

ORDER *Scolopendra.*
FAMILY *Scolopendridae.*
NUMBER OF SPECIES *400.*
SIZE *3–10cm.*
FEEDING *Immatures and adults: predators.*
IMPACT *Large species can deliver very painful bites.*

▲ **SCOLOPENDRA CINGULATA** *is a large centipede with strong legs that is capable of moving very fast over short distances. It lives in southern Europe.*

NOTE

Large species in this family prey mostly on large insects and can even kill small vertebrates. Their bites may cause severe swelling in humans.

Scutigerids

Scutigeridae

OCCUR in open habitats in southern Europe but in houses elsewhere, mainly on walls or indoors; also found in caves.

These shortish centipedes are brown with paler markings, but are immediately recognizable by their quick movement and their fifteen pairs of very long legs. The legs at the rear of the body are longer than those at the front. The body is kept straight by overlapping plates on the upper body surface, which may bear hairs, spines, or other projections.

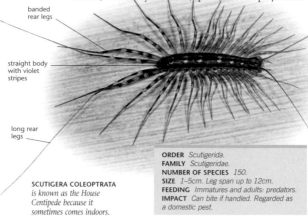

banded rear legs

straight body with violet stripes

long rear legs

SCUTIGERA COLEOPTRATA *is known as the House Centipede because it sometimes comes indoors.*

ORDER *Scutigerida.*
FAMILY *Scutigeridae.*
NUMBER OF SPECIES *150.*
SIZE *1–5cm. Leg span up to 12cm.*
FEEDING *Immatures and adults: predators.*
IMPACT *Can bite if handled. Regarded as a domestic pest.*

Pill Millipedes

Glomeridae

FOUND in many habitats, but especially in woodland, rough pasture, and farmland.

Pill millipedes are small. Their trunk has 13 segments, and the shape of the body plates allows them to roll into a tight ball with the head tucked in. These species should not be confused with pill woodlice (p.215), which can also roll up for protection. Millipedes have many more legs, and two pairs of legs for each body segment. The young have only three pairs of legs when they hatch. They reach the full complement of 15 pairs at adulthood.

tough, shiny body

saddle-shaped segment behind head

◄ **GLOMERIS MARGINATA** *is very widespread and common. It has a shinier body than the pill woodlouse.*

rolled-up position

ORDER *Glomerida.*
FAMILY *Glomeridae.*
NUMBER OF SPECIES *200.*
SIZE *0.2–2cm.*
FEEDING *Immatures and adults: scavengers, herbivores.*
IMPACT *Harmless.*

Blaniulids

Blaniulidae

These are small, slender-bodied species of less than 1mm in width. Blaniulids vary from creamy white to dark brown in colour and they often have red or very dark brown spots on most segments. Some species may have as many as 60 body segments. The legs and the antennae are short. Several species are common garden pests.

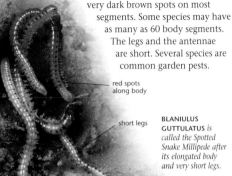

INHABIT *gardens, open land, and woodland, usually in fallen logs, tree stumps, leaf litter, and soil.*

red spots along body

short legs

BLANIULUS GUTTULATUS *is called the Spotted Snake Millipede after its elongated body and very short legs.*

ORDER *Julida.*
FAMILY *Blaniulidae.*
NUMBER OF SPECIES *120.*
SIZE *0.5–1.8cm.*
FEEDING *Immatures and adults: scavengers, herbivores.*
IMPACT *A few species damage seedlings.*

Cylinder Millipedes

Julidae

Cylinder millipedes vary from shortish, pale-coloured species to longer dark or black species with reddish stripes. The antennae are fairly long and slender. Most species are tough-bodied and relatively broad. As the common name implies, they have a circular cross-section. These are slow-moving species, which are good at pushing through soil and leaf litter.

LIVE *in grassland, heaths, and woodland, in soil and leaf litter and under stones and rotting wood.*

two yellow-brown stripes down body

▼ **TACHYPODOIULUS NIGER** *is quite large and shiny. It often grazes moss and algae on trees and shrubs.*

relatively long antennae

pale legs

▲ **OMMATOIULUS SABULOSUS** *is widespread in Europe. The dorsal stripes may become broken up into spots or patches.*

ORDER *Julida.*
FAMILY *Julidae.*
NUMBER OF SPECIES *450.*
SIZE *0.8–5cm.*
FEEDING *Immatures and adults: scavengers, herbivores.*
IMPACT *Harmless.*

Flat-backed Millipedes

Polydesmidae

The 20 or so body segments of these flattenend species have lateral expansions, which stick out sideways giving them an almost centipede-like appearance. However, each segment has two pairs of legs, and the upper surface has characteristic pitted sculpturing. Some species are reddish brown, while others are dark with pale lateral margins.

sculpturing on dorsal plate

two pairs of legs per segment

POLYDESMUS ANGUSTUS is a brownish, flat backed millipede. Males are generally slightly larger than females, and have stouter legs.

ORDER Polydesmida.
FAMILY Polydesmidae.
NUMBER OF SPECIES 200.
SIZE 0.5–3cm.
FEEDING Immatures and adults: scavengers, herbivores.
IMPACT May be pests of seedlings.

NOTE

These millipedes sometimes occur in large numbers. In most species, many body segments have glands that produce toxic chemicals to deter predators.

The Water Springtail

Poduridae

This common, squat species is greyish blue to dark bluish black in colour. The water springtail spends its life on the surface of water in ditches, ponds, canals, boggy areas, and even rain-filled rock pools. It can be so abundant that the water surface appears dark. The spring under the body is long and flattened to ensure that it can jump effectively.

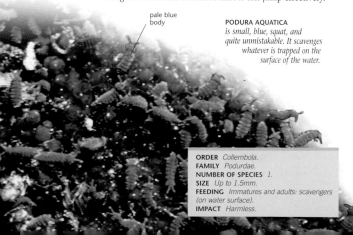

pale blue body

PODURA AQUATICA is small, blue, squat, and quite unmistakable. It scavenges whatever is trapped on the surface of the water.

ORDER Collembola.
FAMILY Poduridae.
NUMBER OF SPECIES 1.
SIZE Up to 1.5mm.
FEEDING Immatures and adults: scavengers (on water surface).
IMPACT Harmless.

Globular Springtails

Sminthuridae

Also known as garden springtails, these species are pale to
dark brown or green in colour with very rounded, almost
spherical bodies. The segmentation of the abdomen is very
indistinct, and the antennae are long and elbowed. Males
often look different to females, and their antennae are
often modfied for holding the
antennae of the female
during courtship.

COMMON *in a variety
of habitats, including
fields, pasture, leaf
litter in woodland,
and fresh water.*

SMINTHURUS AQUATICUS *is
widespread, but does not gather
in such large numbers as the
Water Springtail (below left).*

globular
abdomen

shortish,
bent
antennae

NOTE

Sminthurus viridis,
*known as the
Lucerne Flea, is a
widespread pest of
alfalfa, clover, and
some vegetables. It
nibbles holes in the
stems and leaves.*

ORDER Collembola.
FAMILY Sminthuridae.
NUMBER OF SPECIES 900.
SIZE 1–3mm.
FEEDING Immatures and adults: herbivores.
IMPACT Several species can be pests of
crop seedlings.

Tomocerid Springtails

Tomoceridae

This family includes some very widespread and common
species. Some species are darkly pigmented and smooth
with a slightly shiny appearance, while others may be
paler and rather hairy. The antennae are often longer
than the body and the third segment is typically
much longer than the fourth, allowing the
antenna to curl up in a spiral. Adults continue
to moult until they die.

OCCUR *in leaf litter,
woodland understorey,
and decaying wood.*

long, tapering
antennae

TOMOCERUS LONGICORNIS *is
quite a large springtail with
silvery-grey scales more or less
covering the body. The
antennae can curl
up at the ends.*

silvery-grey
scales

NOTE

Tomocerids jump
well, using a
furcula, or jumping
organ, that is folded
under the abdomen.
When released, the
furcula pushes the
animal into the air.

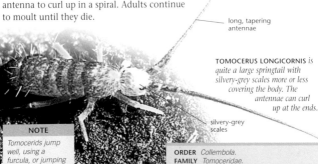

ORDER Collembola.
FAMILY Tomoceridae.
NUMBER OF SPECIES 125.
SIZE 2–6mm.
FEEDING Immatures and adults: fungi-
feeders, scavengers.
IMPACT Harmless.

Entomobryid Springtails

Entomobryidae

These pale yellowish springtails are elongate with a small pronotum and often have dark bands or other markings. In many species, the fourth abdominal segment is larger than the third segment. The antennae, which have between four and six segments, can be longer than the body length. All stages of the life cycle eat single-celled algae, fungal threads, or decaying plant matter.

FOUND *mainly in leaf litter, soil, fungi, and caves.*

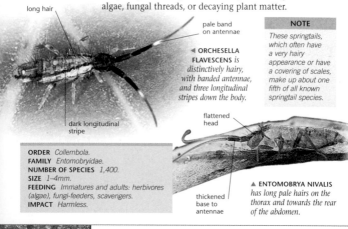

long hair

pale band on antennae

◀ **ORCHESELLA FLAVESCENS** *is distinctively hairy, with banded antennae, and three longitudinal stripes down the body.*

dark longitudinal stripe

flattened head

NOTE

These springtails, which often have a very hairy appearance or have a covering of scales, make up about one fifth of all known springtail species.

ORDER *Collembola.*
FAMILY *Entomobryidae.*
NUMBER OF SPECIES *1,400.*
SIZE *1–4mm.*
FEEDING *Immatures and adults: herbivores (algae), fungi-feeders, scavengers.*
IMPACT *Harmless.*

thickened base to antennae

▲ **ENTOMOBRYA NIVALIS** *has long pale hairs on the thorax and towards the rear of the abdomen.*

Isotomid Springtails

Isotomidae

Superficially very similar in general appearance to entomobryids (above), isotomids are generally brownish grey or green in colour and can be distinguished by the segments of the abdomen being of equal sizes. These springtails can be very abundant in suitable conditions, which are typically moist soils. Many species are well adapted to low temperatures.

ABUNDANT *in leaf litter and soil; also associated with habitats around ponds and streams.*

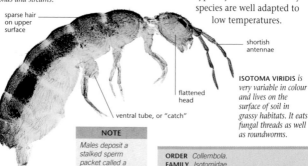

sparse hair on upper surface

shortish antennae

ISOTOMA VIRIDIS *is very variable in colour and lives on the surface of soil in grassy habitats. It eats fungal threads as well as roundworms.*

flattened head

ventral tube, or "catch"

spring, or "furcula"

NOTE

Males deposit a stalked sperm packet called a spermatophore on the ground, which is then picked up by the female's genital opening.

ORDER *Collembola.*
FAMILY *Isotomidae.*
NUMBER OF SPECIES *1,000.*
SIZE *1–4mm.*
FEEDING *Immatures and adults: scavengers, fungi-feeders.*
IMPACT *Harmless.*

Eosentomids

Eosentomidae

These blind hexapods are pale and soft-bodied with a conical head, no antennae, and an elongate body. The legs do not stick out very far from the body, enabling them to move easily through tiny cracks and crevices in soil, mosses, and leaf litter. The first pair of legs is larger than the middle and hind pairs of legs and has numerous sensory hairs. Spiracles are visible on the middle and hind segments of the thorax.

OCCUR *in leaf litter, mosses, decaying wood, and soil.*

pair of legs
on each of
three thoracic
segments

head

NOTE

As these creatures are very small and difficult to see they are collected by extraction or flotation techniques and examined microscopically.

legs have a
single spine-
like claw

fine body
hair

ORDER *Protura.*
FAMILY *Eosentomidae.*
NUMBER OF SPECIES *100.*
SIZE *0.5–2mm.*
FEEDING *Immatures and adults: scavengers, fungi-feeders.*
IMPACT *Harmless.*

EOSENTOMON DELICATUM
lives in soil, especially chalky soil, throughout much of Europe. The genus, as a whole, is found worldwide.

Campodeids

Campodeidae

These pale white or yellow-tinged diplurans are easily recognizable by their long, multi-segmented tails, known as cerci, at the end of the abdomen. The head has no eyes but does have a pair of slender antennae, which are usually shorter than the cerci. On the underside of the abdomen there are special projections that provide support for the body. The thorax has spiracles.

LIVE *in deep soil, leaf litter, decaying wood, compost heaps, and under tree bark.*

bead-like
antennal
segments

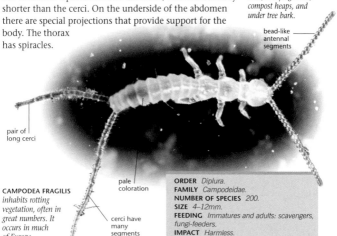

pair of
long cerci

pale
coloration

CAMPODEA FRAGILIS
inhabits rotting vegetation, often in great numbers. It occurs in much of Europe.

cerci have
many
segments

ORDER *Diplura.*
FAMILY *Campodeidae.*
NUMBER OF SPECIES *200.*
SIZE *4–12mm.*
FEEDING *Immatures and adults: scavengers, fungi-feeders.*
IMPACT *Harmless.*

Porcellionid Woodlice

Porcellionidae

WIDESPREAD *where there is a humid microhabitat provided by rotting plant matter.*

The body surface of these woodlice can be smooth and slightly glossy or warty, but is usually grey or greyish brown with other markings. The last section of the antennae, called the flagellum, is composed of two segments. The body of some species is narrow, and these species can run quickly. Woodlice excrete ammonia gas and this gives large colonies a characteristic smell.

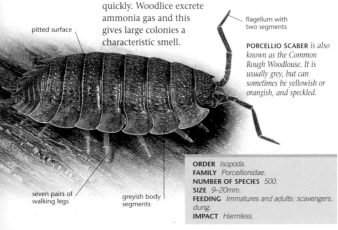

pitted surface

flagellum with two segments

PORCELLIO SCABER *is also known as the Common Rough Woodlouse. It is usually grey, but can sometimes be yellowish or orangish, and speckled.*

seven pairs of walking legs

greyish body segments

ORDER *Isopoda.*
FAMILY *Porcellionidae.*
NUMBER OF SPECIES 500.
SIZE 9–20mm.
FEEDING *Immatures and adults: scavengers, dung.*
IMPACT *Harmless.*

Oniscid Woodlice

Oniscidae

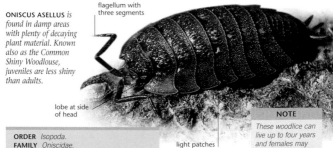

LIVE *in leaf litter, compost heaps, under stones and in rotting wood.*

The common, shiny woodlouse, *Oniscus asellus*, is the only member of this family you are likely to encounter very often. The last part of the antennae, after the longer fifth segment, is called the flagellum, and in this family, is made up of three segments. There are distinctive lobes on either side of the head. This species varies from greyish with paler markings to yellowish or orangish.

ONISCUS ASELLUS *is found in damp areas with plenty of decaying plant material. Known also as the Common Shiny Woodlouse, juveniles are less shiny than adults.*

flagellum with three segments

lobe at side of head

light patches

ORDER *Isopoda.*
FAMILY *Oniscidae.*
NUMBER OF SPECIES 1,100.
SIZE 1–1.8cm.
FEEDING *Immatures and adults: scavengers.*
IMPACT *Harmless but an important part of the nutrient recycling process.*

NOTE

These woodlice can live up to four years and females may carry as many as 80 eggs in their brood pouch which they keep moist, like a portable aquarium.

Pill Woodlice

Armadillidiidae

Light brown to black with yellow patches, these woodlice have a convex cross-section and a rounded hind margin. They are also known as pill bugs. When threatened, many can roll up into a ball to protect themselves. Some species, such as *Armadillidium vulgare* and *A. pictum*, make a more perfect ball than other species.

OCCUR *in many habitats from shoreline to mountains; in leaf litter and debris in woodland and gardens.*

convex body

flagellum with two segments

rolled up for defence

ORDER *Isopoda.*
FAMILY *Armadillidiidae.*
NUMBER OF SPECIES *250.*
SIZE *5–20mm.*
FEEDING *Immatures and adults: scavengers, herbivores, dung.*
IMPACT *Harmless.*

ARMADILLIDIUM VULGARE *is the Pill Woodlouse. It can tolerate drier conditions than other species, but is found in much the same places.*

NOTE

Pill woodlice have several narrow tail segments, whereas pill millipedes have a single, broad tail segment. They also roll into a looser ball than pill millipedes.

Sea Slaters

Ligiidae

Greyish green or light brown in colour, sea slaters have large, dark eyes at the sides of the head resembling the compound eyes of insects. The flagellum of the antennae has ten or more small segments. Most species run very fast when disturbed. *Ligia oceanica* is a large species, common on shores where it grazes on seaweed during the day, and hides in rock crevices at night. It can change colour to suit its background. *L. hypnorum* is smaller and is found in woodland litter.

FOUND *on seashores, among rocks and seaweeds up to the high tide mark and in the splash zone.*

flagellum with many segments

forked tail

ORDER *Isopoda.*
FAMILY *Ligiidae.*
NUMBER OF SPECIES *100.*
SIZE *8–30mm.*
FEEDING *Immatures and adults: scavengers, herbivores (algae).*
IMPACT *Harmless.*

greyish green mottled body

LIGIA OCEANICA *lives on rocky shores. It has a pair of forked tails at the rear, and specialized dermal cells that allow it to change colour.*

Glossary

Many of the terms defined here are illustrated in the general introduction (pp.8–13). Words in *italics* are defined elsewhere in the glossary.

ABDOMEN The rear main section of an arthropod's body. Except in myriapods, where there is only a head and a trunk.

APICAL SPUR A blunt, spine-like structure at the end of a leg segment, usually a *tibia*.

APTERYGOTA Primitively wingless insects. The smaller subclass of the class Insecta.

ASEXUAL Of reproduction without separate sexes. Reproduction occurring by *parthenogenesis*.

CARAPACE The shell-like *dorsal* surface of the *cephalothorax*.

CASTE Any group of individuals in a colony of social insects that are structurally or behaviourally different from individuals in other groups, as seen in Isoptera and some Hymenoptera.

CEPHALOTHORAX The front section of an arachnid made of the head and *thorax* fused together.

CERCI (sing. **CERCUS**) A pair of sensory appendages at the rear end of an insect's *abdomen*.

CHELICERAE The first, usually pincer-like, pair of appendages on the *cephalothorax* of an arachnid.

COCOON A silk case made by the fully grown *larvae* of many insects just before pupation.

COLONY An aggregation of social insects sharing a nest.

CORBICULUM The pollen basket of honey bees, being a concave, shiny area on the hind *tibiae*, fringed with stiff hairs.

CORNICLE One of a pair of spout-like structures on the back of an aphid's abdomen which carry defensive secretions.

COSMOPOLITAN Occurring throughout most of the world.

COXA (pl. **COXAE**) The first segment of an insect's leg, joining the rest of the leg to the *thorax*.

CUCKOO A species in which the *larvae* develop eating food stored by another species for its own larvae.

DIMORPHIC Occurring in two distinct forms. The sexes of some insects are differently coloured or shaped.

DORSAL Referring to the upper surface or back of a structure or animal.

DRONE A male honey bee.

ELYTRA (sing. **ELYTRON**) The rigid front wings of beetles, modified as covers for the hind wings and not used in flight.

EYESPOT A distinctive eye-like marking, typically on the wings of some insects.

FEMUR (pl. **FEMORA**) The part of an insect's leg corresponding to the mammalian thigh.

GALL An abnormal plant growth caused by a bacterium, virus, fungus, mite, or insect.

HALTERES The greatly modified hind wings of Diptera which serve as balancing organs.

HEMIMETABOLOUS Developing by incomplete or gradual metamorphosis, such as in Orthoptera and Hemiptera. Immature stages are called *nymphs*.

HOLOMETABOLOUS Developing by complete metamorphosis such as in Coleoptera and Diptera. Immature stages are called *larvae*.

LARVA (pl. larvae) The immature stage of an insect that undergoes complete metamorphosis.

MAXILLARY PALPS A pair of segmented sensory mouthpart structures used to taste food.

MESOTHORAX The middle section of an insect's *thorax*, carrying the middle pair of legs and, usually, the front pair of wings.

METATHORAX The rear section of an insect's *thorax*, carrying the hind pair of legs and, usually, the hind pair of wings.

MINE A variously shaped hollow space between the upper and lower surface of a leaf caused by a feeding insect *larva*.

NYMPH The immature stage of an insect showing incomplete metamorphosis, such as Hemiptera and Orthoptera (Exopterygota).

OCELLI Simple light-receptive organs on the head of many insects.

OVIPOSITOR An organ, often tube-like, for laying eggs.

PALPS A pair of segmented sensory appendages associated with an insect's mouthparts.

PARASITE A species living off the body or tissues of another species and giving nothing in return in many cases.

PARTHENOGENESIS Reproduction without the need for fertilization.

PEDIPALPS In arachnids, the second pair of appendages on the *cephalothorax*. They are tactile organs also variously used for handling and killing prey, and in male spiders, are organs of copulation.

POLYMORPHIC Having more than two forms.

PROLEG The unsegmented leg of an insect *larva* (different from the segmented thoracic legs).

PRONOTUM The *dorsal* cover of the first segment of the *thorax*.

PROTHORAX The first segment of an insect's *thorax*, carrying the front pair of legs.

PTEROSTIGMA A dark spot near the front edge of insect wings.

PTERYGOTA Winged insects. The larger subclass of the class Insecta.

QUADRILATERAL CELL A particular four-sided cell in the wings of certain insects.

ROSTRUM The tubular, slender sucking mouthparts of insects such as the Hemiptera. The prolonged part of the head of weevils and scorpionflies.

SCENT GLAND A gland inside the body of bugs and other insects that produces a secretion, often for defensive purposes.

SCUTELLUM The *dorsal* cover of the rear part of the middle or rear section of an insect's *thorax*.

SPIRACLE The breathing holes of insects, leading to the tracheal system.

STING The modified *ovipositor* of some Hymenoptera used for injecting venom.

STRIATION A longitudinal groove or mark, typically running down the wing cases, or *elytra*, of beetles.

STRIDULATION The act of producing sound, usually by rubbing two parts of the body together.

SYMBIOSIS Different species living in an association that brings mutual benefit.

TARSUS (pl. **TARSI**) The foot of an arthropod. It is attached to the end of the *tibia* and is made up of several tarsal segments.

THORAX (adj. **THORACIC**) The middle main section of an arthropod's body carrying the legs and (in most insects) the wings. In myriapods there is no thorax, only a head and a trunk.

TIBIA (pl. **TIBIAE**) The lower leg segment of insects; corresponds to the shin of mammals.

TRACHEAE (sing. **TRACHEA**) The internal airways of arthropods.

TUBERCLE A raised, wart-like structure on the surface of an arthropod.

VECTOR An intermediate host that carries and transmits a disease organism.

VENATION The pattern of veins in the wing of an insect.

VENTRAL The under or lower surface.

VESTIGIAL Of a structure that is greatly reduced in size and often non-functional.

Index

Acknowledgments

DORLING KINDERSLEY would like to thank John Dinsdale, jacket designer; Adam Powley, jacket copyeditor; Mariza O'Keeffe, jacket editor; and Kim Bryan and Erin Richards for editorial assistance. The author would like to thank Darren J Mann for sharing his extensive knowledge of insects; Dr Adrian Pont, Mike Ackland, and Dr David Goulson also provided invaluable help.

PICTURE CREDITS
Picture librarians: Richard Dabb, Claire Bowers

Abbreviations key: a = above, b = bottom, c = centre, f = far, l = left, r = right, t = top.

The publishers would like to thank the following for their kind permission to reproduce the photographs.

Alan Outen: 042 cl; 075 bl; 101 br; 105 br; 105 car; 127 cbr; 151 cb; 152 ca; 153 bl; 215 cb; 041 bl; 051 bl; 060 br; 073 br; 076 cra; 089 br; 113 cfl; 114 cl; 117 ca; 122 cra; 128 cbr; 157 cfr; 159 cl ; 160 cla; 169 cla. **Ardea.com:** Dennis Avon 085 cbr. **Beat Fecker:** 098 cbr; 101 cal; 102 cb; 103 car; 119 bcr; 149 cbl; 155 car; 155 cb; 160 car; 164 cbl; 055 car; 055 cbr; 135 clb; 188 cal. **Beat Wermelinger:** 054 bc; 154 ca; 158 cbr; 183 cb; 185 car; 212 cal; 039 bc; 155 cbr; 157 ca; 158 clb. **Bruce Coleman Ltd:** Kim Taylor 121 cb; 121 bl; Jeff Foott 210 bl. **Chris Gibson:** 036 bl; 072 bl; 076 cal; 169 cb; 187 tr; 188 cra; 033 tl; 034 bl; 034 cfl; 035 tr; 063 clb; 071 ca; 081 cfl; 141 cfl; 143 bc; 152 cra; 169 br; 178 cfr; 191 cfr. **Clive R.Turner:** 085 car. **David Bradford:** 192 cla; 201 car. **David Element:** 041 cfl; 048 cal; 049 br; 054 cfr; 130 cal; 142 cbl; 149 car; 154 bl; 167 cbr; 170 crb; 171 bc; 171 tr; 213 cb; 037 cbr; 052 car; 071 br; 078 clb; 102 cal; 105 clb; 107 tr; 157 cla; 172 cfr. **David Kitching:** 025 car; 025 cb; 028 br; 023 bl; 023 br; 023 cfr. **Diego Reggianti:** 020 cb; 021 car; 029 cbl; 037 ca; 068 bl; 079 cb; 125 cal; 134 cb; 170 bl; 180 bcr; 188 bl; 021 tc; 040 cla; 040 crb; 092 cl; 095 cla; 095 cr; 110cfl; 120 bl; 174 cla. **Dr. Alison Blackwell:** 125 cb. **Eddie Dunbar:** 041 car. **Entomology WSL:** 059 ca. **FLPA:** D.Jones 182 ca. **Forest Research Institution:** 074 cal. **Frank Koehler:** 084 car; 108 car; 085 clb; 087 cl ; 087 tl; 099 ca; 108 cl. **George McGavin:** 137 cfr; 215 cfr; 37 cfr; 48 tl; 72 tl; 74 tl. **György Csóka:** 024 crb; 040 car; 061bc; 069 car; 073 car; 074 bl; 074 car; 074 car; 114 bl; 117 bc; 118 car; 162 bc; 163 tr; 187 cfr; 187 cra; 001 ca; cl; 024 bcr; 040 cr; 067 car; 072 br; 072 cal; 072 cr; 073 clb; 073 tl; 091 car; 096 cbl; 096 cla; 096 cr; 097 cal; 097 cfl; 097 tl; 106 cfr; 107 cla; 116 cal; 116 cra; 117 cfr; 117 cra; 117 tl; 118cla; 128 br; 128 cal; 128 cl; 140 br; 140 clb; 141 br; 156 cla; 156 cra; 162 ca; 162 cla; 162 clb; 163 bc; 163 ca; 163 cb; 163 cfl; 163 cfr; 163 tl; 176 bl; 186 ca; 186 cal; 186 cfr; 187 cbr; 187 clb. **Holt Studios International:** 076 bl; 077 car; 140 car; 165 car; 185 br; 186 bl; 209 cla.; 077 cla; 042 car; 041 bl; 075 bl; 140cbr; Nigel Catlin 044 car. **Jarmo Holopainen:** 126 cal. **Jean Yves Raspulus:** 205 br. **Jens Schou:** 134 cr; 146 bcl; 183 cla; 061 tr; 147 cfr. **Josef Hlasek:** 026 cbr; 027 cbr; 038 cb; 070 cr; 080 cb; 093 cb; 098 cal; 100 bc; 112 cra; 026 cal ; 027 clb; 067 cl; 079 cal; 080 cal; 080 car; 083 car; 083 tr; 092 cal; 093 car; 093 cl; 093 cla; 093 cr; 103 clb; 110 cal; 111 cla; 112 cfl; 113 cr; 113 cra; 115 tr; 116 cfl; 117 tr; 197 car. **Keith Edkins:** 107 bc; 168 br; 169 tr; 048 cfr; 051 car; 054 cla; 058 cfr; 058 cl; 060 bl; 060 car; 060 cfr; 061 cla; 071 tl; 107 car; 107 cb; 107 cfr; 107 clb; 107 cfr; 115 cfr; 115 cfl. **Melvin Grey:** 020 ca; 022 bl; 022 ca; 030 ca; 150 ca; 150 ca; 150 clb; 152 cb; 153 ca; 020 bcl; 021cfl. **Michal Hoskovec:** 057 bc; 123 cal; 085 br; 087 tr; 104 bl; 113 cal; 157 cfl; 183 cfr. **Mike Amphlett:** 054 cal. **N.H.P.A.:** A. Bannister 062 ca; Dr. E. Elkan 121 cla; Daniel Heulin 047 ca.

Natural History Museum, London: 044 cla; 066 cra; 205 car; 212 cbl; 213 ca. **Neil Fletcher:** 002 ca; 091 cb; 018 ca; 021 cbl; 024 ca; 033 cb; 044 cb; 048 bl; 064 car; 078 car; 113 bc; 122 bl; 143 cb; 145 ca; 159 car; 190 cr; 191 cal; 192 bl; 204 ca; 206 br; 021 bl; 023 ca; 024 cb; 026 clb; 033 tr; 064 cla; 070 cr; 115 ca; 115 cla; 127 cfr; 141 tr; 164 cfl; 169 bc; 173 tr; 188 cfl; 189 cfr; 195 cal; 198 tl; 20 cfl; 20 tl; 200 cfl; 201 tr; 21 cfr; 213 cfr; 22 tl; 24 tl; 28 tl; 29 tr; 31 tr; 32 tl; 36 cfl; 38 cfl; 39 tr; 43 tr; 48 cfl; 49 cfr; 49 tr; 50 tl; 53 tr; 59 tr; 67 tr; 69 cfr; 69 tr; 75 cfr; 75 tr; 76 tl; 77 tr; 79 cfr; 79 tr; 88 cfl; 89 tr. **OSF/photo library.com:** 046 cb; 123 br; 212 cr; J.A.L. Cook 211 car; 185 cbr. **Paco Alarcon:** 196 cra; 196 cfr. **Paolo Mazzei:** 004 ca; 108 bl; 027 cla; 031 cb; 036 ca; 037 bl; 039 ca; 042 bc; 050 ca; 052 bl; 053 cbr; 060 car; 062 bcr; 063 cal; 065 cb; 066 cb; 067 bc; 082 bc; 086 bc; 088 bl; 090 br; 094 bc; 096 bc; 104 br; 104 cal; 106 bc; 110 cbr; 111 car; 120 br; 120 cbr; 131 bc; 133 clb; 138 cl; 147 cbl; 159 cb; 174 cra; 178 cb; 180 ca; 190 cal; 181 cbl; 184 cal; 192 car; 202 cbl; 206 ca; 207 cb; 208 ca; 028 cfr; 029 cla; 031 cla; 054 cl; 057 cfl; 057 cfr; 057 cla; 057 cr; 069 cla; 075 cbr; 079 car; 081 car; 081 cbr; 082 cr ; 083 cbr; 083 cla; 088 car; 091 cla; 092 car; 094 car; 094 cl; 095 tl; 096 car; 097 car; 099 cbr; 099 cr; 110 cr; 113 tl; 113 tr; 114 cra; 116 cb; 124 car; 124 car; 125 cra; 131 ca; 132 cbl; 139 cfl; 145 clb; 147 ca; 148 tr; 149 br; 158 cla; 169 cfr; 172 cla; 177 cla; 181 br; 193 car; 201 cla. **Patrick Roper:** 146 cra. **Peter Harvey:** 193 cl; 194 cb; 195 cbr; 198 car; 200 bl; 200 ca; 201 bc; 203 br; 060 cl; 069 cbr; 134 cl; 175 cb; 190 br; 194 car; 199 bcr; 199 cla; 200 cfr; 201 cfl; 202 cra; 203 car; 203 cfl; 203 cla. **Planet Earth:** Steven Hopkin 126 br. **Premaphotos Wildlife:** Ken Preston Mafham 077 bl; 144 ca: 161 br; Mark Preston Mafham 130 bl; Rod Preston Mafham 043 car; 196 bc; 197 br. **Professor Mike Claridge:** 165 bc. **Roger Key:** 043 cb; 045 ca; 049 car; 053 cla; 056 ca; 056 cb; 058 cb; 064 cbr; 069 bl; 078 br; 084 bl; 089 cb; 092 cb; 095 br; 097 tr; 099 bc; 103 bl; 109 cb; 111 br; 120 car; 124 cb; 127 cal; 132 cl; 135 ca; 136 bl; 136 ca; 137 br; 141 cb; 142 ca; 143 car; 144 cb; 156 cb; 157 cbl; 158 car; 161 car; 164 car; 166 cb; 167 cal; 172 cbl; 173 cb; 182 br; 189 bl; 189 car; 191 br; 195 car; 198 bl; 199 cbl; 207 ca; 208 cbl; 209 cbl; 210 ca; 211 bl; 214 cal; 214 cb; 215 car; 029 br; 031 cr; 032 crb; 041 cla; 049 cla; 050 bl; 051 cb; 051 tr; 052 cl; 053 car; 055 br; 055 tl; 055 tr; 057 cra; 058 cal; 059 clb; 061 car; 061 cr; 061 tl; 063 br; 063 cra; 070 cal; 071 tr; 082 cal; 082 cfl; 082 cr; 083 cbl; 083 cfl; 083 tl; 086 car; 087 br; 087 car; 087 cfr; 087 cla; 087 clb; 088 cla; 088 crb; 089 cal; 089 cr; 090 ca; 090 cbl; 090 cra; 091 cfr; 095 car; 095 cfl; 095 tr; 097 cbr; 100 ca; 100 cl; 100 cr; 102 bl; 104 cfr; 105 cla; 109 cla; 109 cr; 11 cla; 112 cb; 112 cr; 114 cfr; 115 bl; 115 cfr; 115 tl; 116 cfr; 117 cfl; 118 bl; 118 cbr; 122 cal; 129 br; 131 cra; 132 br; 132 cal; 133 ca; 133 cra; 133 cfr; 134 bcl; 134 ca; 135 br; 135 cb; 136 cfr; 137 car; 137 cla; 138 cfr; 139 br; 139 car; 139 cfr; 141 car; 151 br; 155 cfl; 156 ca; 157 cra; 159 cla; 159 cr; 161 cfl; 162 cra; 166 car; 166 cl; 168 cbl; 171 clb; 171 cr; 173 bl; 173 ca; 173 cla ; 174 crb; 176 cl; 176 cra; 177 cbr; 189 clb; 189 tc; 190 bl; 190 cbr; 191 bl; 191 tr; 193 bl; 193 cfr; 193 crb; 194 bl; 194 cal; 197 cla; 199 cfl; 199 cfr; 199 cra; 201 cal; 208 br; 209 br. **Science Photo Library:** Eye of Science 047 cb. Ted Benton: 023 cfl; 032 cbl; 035 bc; 040 bl; 081 cbr; 148 cra; 174 bl; 175 bl; 175 car; 176 cb; 177 cr; 179 cfl; 179 tr; 025 tl; 026 cra; 028 car; 031 cfl; 031cra; 032 br; 032 car; 032 cl; 033 ca; 033 cfl; 034 ca; 034 cb; 034 cr; 035 car; 035 cbl; 035 cfl; 035 cla; 035 cr; 068 cbr; 138 br; 139 cfb; 139 tl; 139 tr; 173 cfr; 176 cfr; 177 cbl; 177 cfb; 178 cal; 179 cb; 179 cr; 179 tl. **Wolfgang Wranik:** 038 ca. **Yannich Fourie:** 065 car.

All other images © Dorling Kindersley